DEMOCRACY & RHETORIC

Studies in Rhetoric/Communication
Thomas W. Benson, Series Editor

DEMOCRACY & RHETORIC

John Dewey on the Arts of Becoming

NATHAN CRICK

THE UNIVERSITY OF SOUTH CAROLINA PRESS

© 2010 University of South Carolina

Published by the University of South Carolina Press
Columbia, South Carolina 29208

www.sc.edu/uscpress

Manufactured in the United States of America

19 18 17 16 15 14 13 12 11 10   10 9 8 7 6 5 4 3 2 1

Crick, Nathan.
   Democracy and rhetoric : John Dewey on the arts of becoming / Nathan Crick.
     p. cm. — (Studies in rhetoric/communication)
   Includes bibliographical references and (p.   ) and index.
   ISBN 978-1-57003-876-1 (cloth : alk. paper)
   1. Dewey, John, 1859–1952. 2. Rhetoric—Philosophy. 3. Democracy—Philosophy.
I. Title.
   B945.D44C67 2010
   191—dc22
                         2009043342

This book was printed on Glatfelter Natures, a recycled paper with 30 percent postconsumer waste content.

For my father, for whom
excellence was a habit
and precision was beauty

CONTENTS

Series Editor's Preface *ix*
Acknowledgments *xi*

Introduction *1*

CHAPTER 1: Rhetoric and the Ethics of Democracy *16*
  Protagoras and the Ontology of Becoming 22
  Finding the Rhetorical Situation 26
  Experience and Nature 30
  Continuity and Transaction 33
  Events and Objects 36
  The Rhetorical Situation as Event 41
  Mind, Consciousness, and Free Will 44
  The Habitual Self 47
  Propaganda and the Mass Society 53
  Rhetoric and Character 56
  Locating the Public 59
  Public Opinion and the Public Sphere 62
  Constitutive Rhetoric 65
  Assembling Social Democracy 68
  Intelligence and Freedom 73
  Summary 75

CHAPTER 2: The Rhetoric of Inquiry *80*
  Logos, Logic, and Rhetoric 85
  The Colonization of the Lifeworld 89
  The Rhetoric of Science 93
  Naturalism in Logic 96
  Science and Common Sense 99
  Contextualism and Warranted Assertions 102
  Recoupling Science and Common Sense 107
  The Stages of Inquiry 111

Science, Art, and Democracy   123
Summary   126

CHAPTER 3: **Rhetoric and Aesthetics**   130
The Rhetorical and the Poetical   135
Enjoyment and Interest   140
Subject and Substance   142
Perception and Recognition   144
The Fine and the Useful   147
Form   151
Rhythm   154
Imagination and Morality   157
The Universality of Art   160
Solidarity and Self-creation   162
Categories of Rhetorical Experience   164
The Experience of Eloquence   168
Remaking the Self   171
Room, Volume, Spacing, Position   174
The Art of the Possible   175
Criticism and Construction   178
Kairos and Decorum   180
Summary   185

Conclusion   187

Notes   195
Bibliography   211
Index   221
About the Author   225

SERIES EDITOR'S PREFACE

In *Democracy and Rhetoric: John Dewey on the Arts of Becoming,* Nathan Crick explores what it would mean for rhetoric to act as a means of radical democracy. He claims that the American philosopher John Dewey (1859–1952) points us to an understanding that rhetoric must reassert its status as an art that engages ethics, intellectual inquiry, and aesthetics. In developing a model of rhetorical action based on Dewey's approach, Professor Crick goes beyond Dewey's own statements on rhetoric and persuasion to reflect on the implications for rhetorical thought and action of the broad range of Dewey's philosophical writings on democracy, intellectual inquiry, and aesthetics. Crick's reflections thus explore what a rhetorical way of thinking can do with the thought of John Dewey and what John Dewey's views can do for rhetorical theory.

Professor Crick argues that, for Dewey, democracy implies faith that men and women can act together to improve their lives. Dewey was suspicious of the claim that democracy was merely a collection of individuals acting separately in their own interests. At the same time, he saw the need not only for conversation and cooperation but also for leadership and persuasion, and for the advocacy of minority views. Rhetoric in this view is a mode of advocacy called for in situations of "moral conflict, cognitive uncertainty, and practical urgency." Dewey's philosophy leads to a rhetoric that can be transformative and radical, and it is for this reason, argues Professor Crick, that rhetorical theorists needs to go beyond Dewey's writings on communication to understand more fully his writings on human character and experience as ever in a process of becoming. In Dewey's writings on nature, knowing, and aesthetics as human experiences, Professor Crick discovers the radically democratic rhetorical theory that Dewey's philosophy makes possible.

ACKNOWLEDGMENTS

This book is a product of the environment of which I am but a part. Its origins are not found in scholarly debates about the meanings of concepts; it grows out of the soil of experience in which the seeds of ideas were fortunate to take root. A few people who formed that environment are thus worth recognizing. I would like to thank my sister for the gift of humility and my brother for proving that life is an adventure, Joe Gabriel for showing me that much that is worthwhile is kept hidden, Ernest DeNapoli for giving music to life, John "May I call you John?" Miller for the challenge of literature, Elizabeth Cohen for applying dialectical method to the imagination, Nathan Swanson for the joy of emancipation, Norman Sims for the art of the pointed question, David DuBois for opening up more than one world, Thom Randall for welcoming me to the wilderness and John Manson for visiting me there, Matthew Arnold for the experience of an artistic community, Sandra Baril and Richard Jarvis for the opportunity to engage with science and Greg Dardis for showing me how it is done, Pam for joining me on the adventure of life, and William, Dean, Sofia, and Leo for continuing to make it one.

The trajectory of this book also would not have been possible without the fortune to be at the University of Pittsburgh during a time of great energy and ideas. And this is, indeed, a "fortune," for I am in debt to John Lyne for stealing my application from the History and Philosophy of Science Department and introducing me to rhetoric. Perhaps I may regret this path on the day that rhetoric breathes its last, but I hope that I will contribute to its health and not its decline. I would like to thank Gordon Mitchell for his unabashed commitment to democratic action, Peter Simonson for introducing me to the pragmatic tradition, Ted McGuire for asking, "What about 'time'?," and my dear friend John Poulakos for always striving to make the modern university a Greek symposium. If I learned anything from John, it is that one finds the greatest gleams of gold in a darkening office as the sun is going down and the conversation is too intense to get up and turn on the light. I am forever grateful to have crossed passed with a true philosopher—a lover of the wisdom found in the act of dialogue. Lastly, my presence at Pitt coincided with a "class" of students of exceptional character and talent—Eli Brennan, Alessandra Beasley, Zachary Furness, Jessica Mudry, Marcus Paroske, and David Cram-Helwich. Not untypical of graduate student life, I much of my education occurred with my peers at the bar or over the pool table than in the formal seminars.

The final draft of this manuscript, however, was produced in my Louisiana State University office, which looks out on the beautiful quad lined by live oaks that were planted here in 1928, the year the Communication Department was founded. It is an honor to be a part of a long tradition of rhetoric at LSU, a tradition represented at its best by the same Andy King who still "walks the land" here in Baton Rouge and on campus. In large part through his example and leadership, a sense of community that remains rare in the modern university exists here. Finally, then, I would like to recognize my colleagues and Andy King for their incredible support of my research since I arrived here in 2006. As any professional scholar quickly realizes, the myth of the heroic scholar is wholly a fantasy; the only people who still believe that are those who work in a lonely world. Genuine scholarship arises out of an interaction between a scholar and his or her professional, cultural, and natural environment. Thus I am fortunate to have landed once again on fertile soil.

Introduction

The end of democracy is a radical end. For it is an end that has not been adequately realized in any country at any time. It is radical because it requires great change in existing social institutions, economic, legal and cultural.... There is, moreover, nothing more radical than insistence upon democratic methods as the means by which radical social changes be effected.... It is easy to understand why those who are in close contact with the inequities and tragedies of life that mark the present system, and who are aware that we now have the resources for initiating a social system of security and opportunity for all, should be impatient and long for the overthrow of the existing system by any means whatever. But democratic means and the attainment of democratic ends are one and inseparable. The revival of democratic faith as a buoyant, crusading and militant faith is a consummation to be devoutly wished for. But the crusade can win at the best but partial victory unless it springs from a living faith in our common human nature and in the power of voluntary action based on collective intelligence.[1]

RHETORIC IS THE RADICAL EXPRESSION of a radical faith. Dewey calls this faith "democratic," but democracy is merely its political manifestation. The faith that makes both rhetoric and democracy radical is the faith in the constitutive and communicative power of art unfettered.[2] A truly radical art thus eschews both the elitism of aristocratic metaphysics and the easy radicalisms of mass culture, which wallow in the shallow sensationalism of cheap dogma in order to inoculate a population against the subtleties of life. Such radicalisms at their best promise much but deliver little and at their worst destroy that which long effort has struggled to create and preserve. Radical art, like a radical society, is radical not because it seeks extremes but because it dares to place the burden of hope for the future on the shoulders of an art which is sweeping, visionary, rapturous, disciplined, intelligent, and open. Democracy is radical when it commits itself to the possibility that life can achieve the status of art. Rhetoric is radical when it harnesses the power of the arts to shatter that which shuns and constrains and to liberate that which desires to build and grow.

Driving both projects is the always fragile faith in the intrinsic worth and potential of shared human experience. Sightless dogmatism, cynical irony, and apathetic ennui come easy in this and any age, for they offer escape from the demands of ethics, judgment, and beauty. Nothing in the history of philosophy has revealed philosophers, as a class, to be any less susceptible to these manifestations of the will to nothingness. Of Dewey's considerable contributions to the intellectual traditional of humanism, his greatest achievement is to leave behind a corpus of writing that embodies the virtue of intelligent imaginative vision. It is and always has been the task of the greatest rhetoric to translate idealistic hope into social praxis, to turn visionary word into practical deed and thus bring forth a better world over time. Dewey points us toward such an art. It falls to those now living, the inheritors of the legacies of the past, to struggle in a world still wrought by strife, insecurity, and fear in search of discourses that dare to lift us toward unknown possibilities in the working faith that human beings have within themselves the capacities to—as William Faulker eloquently put it—not just endure but prevail.

However, given the problems of the modern public, such a hope in the progressive powers of rhetoric may seem hopelessly naïve, the natural consequence of employing nineteenth-century terminology to address a twenty-first-century problem. After all, the local community of the Athenian polis is long gone. What we have now is what Jacques Ellul categorizes as a "technological society" in which propaganda, not rhetoric, becomes the primary means by which an atomized group of individuals forms a mass society. For Ellul it is in the "midst of increasing mechanization and technological organization" brought about by the modern industrial state that "propaganda is simply the means used to prevent these things from being felt as too oppressive and to persuade man to submit with good grace."[3] Ellul's thesis, of course, is further advanced in work by critical theorists such as Michel Foucault, for whom it is no longer sufficient to adopt a Platonic model of emancipation by which one might unmask the base while promulgating the good. For Foucault truth is no longer to be associated with true ideology but with a "circular relation with systems of power that produce and sustain it, and to effects of power which it induces and which extend it—a 'regime' of truth."[4] In a technological society one has transcended even the traditional binary between rhetoric and propaganda. One now has only coordinated systems of action that arise out of a network of power relations and discourses that are difficult to identify and even more recalcitrant to change.

From this contemporary critical perspective, the justification for rhetorical studies initially penned by Herbert A. Wichelns in 1925—just two years prior to Dewey's work *The Public and Its Problems*—sounds quaint. In "The Literary Criticism of Oratory," Wichelns attempted to establish speech communication as a discipline distinct from English literature. Although often categorized as the father of neo-Aristotelianism, Wichelns actually had a strong moral and political motivation behind his advocacy of oratory as a distinct field of study—the taming of the "Leviathan, the public mind . . . to the end that he shall not threaten civilization." What clearly troubled Wichelns was the rise of "propaganda and publicity," in the guise of public education, that now had the potential to rouse and move the Leviathan toward nefarious ends. Rather than advocate for a kind of Platonic censorship, however, Wichelns sought to fight fire with fire, employing the knowledge of rhetoric not to condemn but to improve the level of public discourse. His hope was to improve the art of "popularization by the instructed element of the state"—meaning the enlightened scholars, poets, and scientists—who might then function as potent factors in the "progress of the race." The duty of the rhetorician, for him, is to study the "interactions of the inventive genius, the popularizing talent, and the public mind" in order to bring about a rhetorical enlightenment.[5]

Backing Wilchens's project is the Greek ideal of *paideia,* a term used to "denote the sum-total of all ideal perfections of mind and body" as well as the constitutions of "a genuine intellectual and spiritual culture."[6] As Werner Jaeger puts it, the project of *paideia* necessitates the production of a "true" rhetoric, for "true rhetoric, which is true philosophy and culture, leads to a higher kind of self-enrichment than that achieved by greed, theft, and violence—namely, to the culture of the personality."[7] In a democracy this culture of personality speaks to not only the character of the individual but also the spirit of the community. According to Thomas Farrell, for instance, "Great rhetoric" is that which "finds an imaginative way to individuate breadth of vision within the recognizable particularities of appearance" and results in revelatory experiences in which that "larger vision is wedded clearly to both the critical judgment and the ordinary convictions of others, all at the same time."[8] In "Great rhetoric" the centrifugal forces of society are harnessed and turned toward the particular, creating a sense of judgment that attends the uniqueness of our experiences while pointing us toward grander horizons.

There is an undeniable attractiveness and nobility to this tradition. As Ronald Greene points out, however, it tends to posit a heroic notion of the humanistic self capable of using an aesthetically formed moral discourse to emancipate others from their social binds. In short it ignores the more pervasive technological and economic influences and constraints that form the self within concrete sets of power relations. As a result this view of the heroic rhetor actually makes it complicit with the systemic forces it presumes to confront. Greene thus argues that the "tendency to translate communication into an aesthetic-moral theory of eloquent citizenship puts argumentation studies to work for, rather than against, new forms of bio-political control." Worse still, Greene lays part of the blame for this complicity at the feet of Dewey's social theory. For Greene, Dewey's privileging of aesthetic-moral ideals over aesthetic-economic realities means that "Dewey provides a modern solution to democratic crisis that may no longer be relevant for a postmodern understanding of capitalism."[9] The humanistic tradition originating in Greece and running through Dewey, Wichelns, and Farrell is thus challenged by the rise of the new world order.

With the waning of the humanistic faith in the emancipatory potential of aesthetic-moral discourses guided by Enlightenment virtues, contemporary rhetoricians have naturally shifted from advocacy to criticism. Instead of seeking, with Wichelns, to better "educate" the Leviathan, contemporary rhetoricians often adopt the critical project of calling the whole idea of the Leviathan into question, deconstructing the discourses that would impose a totalizing character upon it and championing those discourses that give voice to marginalized perspectives and identities without imposing new constraints. Rhetoric as a performance becomes a target, and rhetoric as a theory becomes a hermeneutic. But rhetoric as a productive art is placed under suspicion as an instrument of power and domination. In other words the emancipation of human freedom comes not through the means of rhetorical advocacy but by route of humble suggestion, which follows on the heels of sweeping criticism.

As Foucault explores in his later work, however, Greek history offers the possibility of a third alternative to the projects of "liberation" and "criticism." What came to fascinate Foucault was the way in which "the subject constitutes itself in an active fashion through practices of the self." This question arose through his study of works such as the Platonic-dialogue *Alcibiades,* in which the dominant question is whether or not Alcibiades is properly caring for himself through self-discipline. What interested Foucault about the Greek notion of ethos, or "character," was the way in which it emphasizes pedagogical methods of self-mastery by which an individual can achieve freedom, both in one's household and in public. The manner in which ethos is constructed thus bridges the dualism between subject and culture. Although the models and methods for good character are obviously "proposed, suggested, imposed upon him by his culture, his society, and his social group," the self has the potential to provide the form in which they are expressed—that is, if one can rigorously follow a certain discipline. What Foucault calls "practices of freedom" are thus not emancipatory exercises based solely on criticism of oppressive discourses; rather, they are dedicated artistic acts of consolidating power relations into a new concrete form that may achieve a degree of autonomy through self-mastery.[10] Drawing from Foucault, Robert Danisch concludes, "Systemic power can be resisted by an individual's will to live his or her life aesthetically, as an artistic phenomenon. The display of such an artistic phenomenon has the ability to do more than just resist systemic power—it can produce new relations of power. The self can be an artistic project, and it is as local as any resistance can get."[11]

The emphasis on "art" should not be confused with popular notions of "fine" or "popular" art. We are not talking here about mere surface or appearance. For the classical Greeks, art means neither domination nor decoration but *technē*, a term that refers to "every branch of human or divine skill, or applied intelligence, as opposed to the unaided work of nature."[12] For them civilization itself is the product of art, because art allows human beings to bring nature into an ordered whole. In Aeschylus's *Prometheus Bound*, for example, Prometheus tells the Chorus of his generous gifts to mortals:

> Mindless was all they did until I showed
> The dubious rise and setting of the stars.
> That triumph next of scientific mind,
> The count numerical for man I find
> And history's instrument, skill of the bard,
> That great compositor, the written word.[13]

In this single passage Prometheus attributes human survival to the arts of astronomy and other sciences, mathematics, poetry, and writing, all *technai* to be used in the service of improving the state of humanity. The Sophist Isocrates follows in this tradition when he places the accomplishments of civilization squarely on the shoulders of the spoken word. Claiming that the power of persuasion has helped humankind escape the "life of wild beasts," Isocrates credits speech with the creation of institutions, the writing of laws, the establishment of virtues, and the cultivation of intelligence.[14] As later explored by Foucault, the Greeks perceive both self and civilization as a product of art, and as such they require attention to matters of method and self-discipline.

If rhetoric is to function as a means to radical democracy, it must find a way to reassert its status as an art. It is in this spirit that the work of John Dewey requires renewed attention. Greene's challenge that Dewey's work is no longer relevant to a postmodern capitalistic age is based less on Dewey's own writing than on the manner in which it has been appropriated over time.[15] Undoubtedly Dewey put great faith in the emancipatory potential of aesthetic experience, but his attitude toward art—as a mode of production—was wholly continuous with the Greek tradition that linked it not just to sculpture and painting but also to industry, knowledge, and economy. Indeed this attitude is explicit in Dewey's reading of the Sophists. The Sophists, according to Dewey, were not even primarily rhetoricians; they were an entrepreneurial professional class of artists who cultivated the modern spirit of experimental method:

> The Sophists taught that man could largely control the fortunes of life by mastery of the arts.... [For them] arts based on knowledge cooperate with nature and render it amenable to human happiness. The gods recede into twilight. Divination has a powerful competitor. Worship becomes

moral. Medicine, war, and the crafts desert the temple and the altar of
the patron-god of the guild, as inventions, tools, techniques of action and
works multiply.... Through instrumental arts, arts of control based on
study of nature, objects which are fulfilling and good, may be multiplied
and rendered secure. This road after almost two millennia of obscuration
and desertion was refound and retaken; its rediscovery marks what we call
the modern era.[16]

This reading of the Sophists reveals Dewey's consistent habit of situating all discourses and arts within the complex network of social forces. For him democracy cannot simply represent the impossible ideal of a community of eloquent citizens. As he writes in one of his earliest works, "Democracy is not in reality what it is in name until it is industrial, as well as civil and political."[17] In this sense the Sophists were not democrats because they taught eloquent speech; they were democrats because they provided citizens the means of artistic self-mastery that enabled the flourishing of the practices of freedom at least for a slightly wider group of male Athenian citizens.

It is widely accepted that Dewey praised communication, in all its forms, as a vital means for widening and enriching the practices of freedom that Greek civilization cultivated in embryo. Yet this belief easily drifts into a view of Dewey as just another Enlightenment liberal blind to the evils of humanity. For example, even in defending himself against his critics, he sounds much like John Stewart Mill:

I have been accused more than once and from opposed quarters of an
undue, a utopian, faith in the possibilities of intelligence and in education
as a correlate of intelligence. At all events, I did not invent this faith. I
acquired it from my surroundings as far as those surroundings were ani-
mated by the democratic spirit. For what is the faith of democracy in the
role of consultation, of conference, of persuasion, of discussion, in formation of public opinion, which in the long run is self-corrective, except
faith in the capacity of the intelligence of the common man to respond
with commonsense to the free play of facts and ideas which are secured
by effective guarantees of free inquiry, free assembly and free communication?[18]

If this were all there was to Dewey, then it would be better to turn to Jürgen Habermas for a more contemporary analysis of the structure of the public sphere. Moreover, if Dewey had anything to do with fathering the "cult of conversation" as defined by Michael Schudson, then his books would better be left unopened.[19] Given the popular version of Dewey as a good-natured uncle who advises us to "keep giving it the old college try" in the face of apocalypse, it is a wonder anyone reads him at all.

However, these caricatures of Dewey ignore the radical nature of a philosophy developed through decades that saw two world wars and the Great Depression. If Dewey toyed with notions of a utopian Christian democracy in his youth, by the time of World War II he readily confronted the recalcitrant forces rallied against the possibility of freedom, particularly at home. In his 1940 address "The Basic Loyalties and Values of Democracy," Dewey lays out a bleak picture for his American audience:

> Our anti-democratic heritage of Negro slavery has left us with habits of intolerance toward the colored race—habits which belie profession of democratic loyalty. The very tenets of religion have been employed to foster anti-semitism. There are still many, too many, persons who feel free to cultivate and express racial prejudices as if they were within their personal rights, not recognizing how the attitude of intolerance infects, perhaps fatally as the example of Germany so surely proves, the basic humanities without which democracy is but a name. For it is humanity and the human spirit that are at stake, and not just what is sometimes called the "individual," since the latter is a value in potential humanity and not as something separate and atomic. The attempt to identify democracy with economic individualism as the essence of free action has done harm to the reality of democracy and is capable of doing even greater injury than it has already done.[20]

This paragraph singles out a litany of threats to democratic social life—the persistence of racial and religious intolerance, the way in which personal prejudices spread through communities, the mistaken belief in the autonomous individual, and the pervasive mythology that links laissez-faire capitalism with freedom. Dewey's point thus resonates with that of Foucault—if we are to achieve a genuine democracy, we need to focus less on defeating an external enemy and more at caring for ourselves. For the longer we ignore the centrality of actually forming individuals capable of autonomy, the more economic and political networks of power will do the work for us.

Dewey reminds us that expressing faith in democracy does not commit one to the naïve hope of an archaic social philosophy. Faith in democracy, at least as defined by Dewey, is simply another word for faith in the power of human beings to improve their lives through shared endeavor. That does not mean that this power is always actualized. Indeed the counterpart of this faith is the knowledge that often, if not most of the time, it will give way to more instrumental forms of domination. Thus John Peters only accounts for one side of this faith when he says of Dewey that his "energy against the darkness is admirable; his failure to measure its domination is fatal."[21] Indeed, if the latter accusation is true, the former compliment is meaningless. For genuine courage is neither the smug satisfaction of the intellectual nihilistically resigned to evil nor the enthusiasm of a child who smiles ignorantly in the face of death; courage comes from measuring domination and yet rallying energy against it. If Dewey remained hopeful even after witnessing the worst of humanity, it is not because he possessed a childlike blindness to the darkness but because he refused to acquiesce to it. That courage is not naïve; it is genuinely radical.

Another way of describing this radical faith is through what I call the "ontology of becoming."[22] In contrast with both the ontology of nonbeing, which views existence as an illusion, and the ontology of being, which views change as but the appearance of flux that either masks or is guided by an underlying unity, the ontology of becoming is fundamentally historical, continuous, and naturalistic. One sees this ontology reflected in the later work of Foucault. For him "history is the concrete body of becoming; with its moments of intensity, its lapses, its extended periods of feverish agitation, its fainting spells; and only a metaphysician would seek its soul in the distant ideality of the origin." It is thus from this historical sense that Foucault's interest in "discontinuity" should be understood; as he confesses, "No one is more of a continuist than I am: to recognize a discontinuity is never anything more than to register a problem that needs to be solved."[23] He seeks not to deny the existence of continuity but to reveal its turbulent and ruptured trajectory. Indeed, without the continuity of becoming, philosophy itself, including the kind done by Foucault, would be impossible. As he writes, "The movement by which, not without effort and uncertainty, dreams and illusions, one detaches oneself from what is accepted as true and seeks other rules—that is philosophy. The displacement and transformation of frameworks of thinking, the changing of received values and all the work that has been done to think otherwise, to do something else, to become other than what one is—that, too, is philosophy." No wonder, then, that Foucault, like Dewey, views the work of philosophy as itself a productive art, as a *technē*. For in the ontology of becoming, the worth of a discourse is not its epistemological relationship to a static being but its functional relationship to a world and a self in the making.[24] In this sense poetry, philosophy, science, logic, and rhetoric are all categorized equally as arts of becoming.

The challenge for rhetoricians, then, is to determine what specific role the art of rhetoric performs within a democratic social life guided by the ontology of becoming. Given this challenge, however, it may seem odd to ask John Dewey for advice. For if one abides by the letter of Dewey's work, then rhetoric plays virtually no role in democracy. Dewey offers lavish praise of conversations, poems, newspapers, and novels, but he almost never speaks of the constitutive function of rhetoric. It was not that Dewey was unfamiliar with the rhetorical tradition, having had a thorough education in rhetoric at the University of Vermont and a subsequent training classical Greek thought at Johns

Hopkins as a doctoral student.[25] Nonetheless Dewey habitually preferred the language of logic over that of rhetoric, more often than not using "rhetoric" as a synonym for "grammar" or "style."[26] Consequently Dewey may have sung that of "all affairs, communication is the most wonderful" and is "a wonder by the side of which transubstantiation pales," but he rarely lavished such praise upon rhetoric.[27] Although never denigrating the art, it also almost never appeared on his radar.

Yet if one follows the spirit of Dewey's work, one finds oneself within a rhetorical universe. As Don Burks recognized in 1968, "Dewey's many-sided philosophy has numerous applications for rhetorical theory. Perhaps no philosopher since Aristotle has more to offer the rhetorician than does John Dewey."[28] Moreover, if one looks deeper into the history of Dewey's development, one finds that this relationship is not simply a product of contemporary interpretation. Dewey experienced rhetoric during its formative stages at a modern university discipline through the figure of Fred Newton Scott. In 1890 Scott was a former graduate student of Dewey's as well a "newly appointed brilliant young instructor of English and Rhetoric" at the University of Michigan, where Dewey was chair of the Department of Philosophy.[29] The year Scott arrived Dewey arranged for the two of them to teach a course in aesthetics, and later they acted as faculty advisers to the *Inlander,* the student literary monthly in which they each published a biographical essay on the other.[30] Dewey's piece is notable for its praise of Scott's perspective on rhetoric, which amounted to the most explicit and thoughtful reference to rhetoric in all of Dewey's writings. This brief reference, in fact, provides suitable evidence that Dewey did have a sense that rhetoric is, or at least could be, an art worthy of serious academic study:

> One of the characteristic features of Mr. Scott's work in theoretical as well as practical rhetoric, has been his sense—a sense which he has imparted to his classes—that writing is not a pyrotechnic exhibition of fine phrases, or an ornamental addition to the bare truth of things, but the direct, natural reporting of what one has one's self seen and thought. On the side of the theory of style and literature this original germ of practice is now evolving into a comprehensive theory of the social character of literary expression that livens up the dry bones of formal theories. A theory which sees in the style and matter of literature phases of the movement of intelligence toward complete social expression is significant as theory and inspiring and effective on the practical side.[31]

That Dewey would find Scott's rhetorical theory "inspiring and effective" is not surprising. Scott had, after all, included Dewey's *Psychology* on his list of references in his 1890 *Principles of Style,*[32] and in most cases Scott's rhetorical theory grew out of similar idealistic principles. Although from a modern perspective this idealism might seem overly simplistic, in his own time, Scott's theories were controversial. As Stewart and Stewart observe, Scott was not only "active in seeking to make of rhetoric a legitimate field" but employed an "empirical approach to language issues was certainly unique in his time" for its use of conclusions from "anthropology, biology, linguistics, physiology, and anatomy to support his theory."[33] Thus "Scott was ahead of his time. The new psychology, which offered so many opportunities for enriching rhetorical theory, was not widely enough understood for its bearing on rhetoric to be appreciated."[34] Consequently, in more conservative environments like Harvard, "Scott's ideas were smothered by the demands for correctness."[35] But in Michigan he thrived, creating the first college course in newspaper writing in the country and actually establishing a separate Department of Rhetoric in 1903.[36] It was thus at Michigan, while working with Dewey, that Scott first began his quest to recover rhetoric as a genuine *technē*.

It is an unanswered part of history why Dewey did not retain his interest in rhetoric as a "movement of intelligence toward complete social expression."[37] Yet his brief exposure to rhetoric licenses the search for further rhetorical insight within Dewey's works. For instance, Robert Danisch argues that, given the scope of his interests in all forms of human discourse, "Dewey provides the theoretical grounds for a reconstruction of rhetoric in greater variety than oratory."[38] At the same time we should not limit ourselves to a one-way conversation. Rhetorical theory might benefit from some more Dewey, but Dewey might also benefit from a little more rhetoric. In fact one of the core arguments of this book it that it is only by bringing rhetoric to Dewey, and by creating something new through the transaction, that we can produce a novel perspective on the arts of rhetoric and of democracy.

If Dewey's philosophy gives greater social breadth and historical scope to the art of rhetoric, the rhetorical tradition brings forth in Dewey's philosophy its latent Sophistical attitude, which values radical individuality, aesthetic experience, creative intelligence, and persuasive advocacy as productive means to the formation of communities of judgment. This perspective complements the more explicit communicative requirements of radical democracy promoted by Dewey, including the rational deliberation within an egalitarian public sphere and the artistic presentation of the results of social inquiry by a system of organized intelligence and dissemination. These latter features are clearly necessary conditions for democratic social life, but their overemphasis often comes at a cost. Peters, for instance, rightly notes that Dewey often does not sufficiently revel in "frivolity or folly, cackling at the moon, what Malinowski called the coefficient of weirdness."[39] Always the sober professor, the spirit of Dewey's writing seems carried over into the impenetrable dryness of other political theorists. Yet Dewey had his Sophistical side too. We find this part of his personality expressed in a poem on language found in his wastebasket after he left Columbia University in 1930:

> Language, fourth dimension of the mind,
> Wherein to round square things are curled;
> Or turn unbroken inside out;
> Firm certitudes melt to doubt,
> And doubtful things, a fertile seed
> Tho' not existent, pregnant breed
> Falsities of those who say sooth,
> Lush growing i' the crops of truth—
> Simples to turn Men's minds about
> Peasant to prophet, philosopher to lout,
> Making wise the humble, and sage a fool,
> Stone to gods, and heaven t'earth's footstool.[40]

Although no Gorgias, this rare aesthetic expression of his thoughts reveals a distinctly Sophistical attitude toward language and art that one can find running as an undercurrent throughout Dewey's writing. For what propels both Sophistry and pragmatism is the spirit of creative intelligence, which approaches ideas as experiments in a world of practice. Ideas, according to Dewey, "are worthless except as they pass into actions which rearrange and reconstruct in some way, be it little or large, the world in which we live."[41] Language does not transform stones to gods, peasants to prophets, philosophers to louts, and heavens to footstools because it is miraculous; it does so because it alters our attitudes toward the events and objects of experience. Rhetoric harnesses the intrinsic transformational capacity of language within particular situations that call for the disruption of convention, the inspiration of feeling, and the charting of paths to new possibilities of shared experience. Rhetoric is the transformative power of language compressed and channeled toward the unknown future which speaks to us when we feel ourselves thrown by the turbulent waters of the present. Democracy is the ship we build while sailing, steer while reflecting, and command while consulting.

A rhetorical reading of Dewey thus discloses features of his social theory that resonate with the Sophistical tradition, a tradition that, as John Poulakos argues, represents the distinctly rhetorical qualities of "opportunity, playfulness, and possibility." In fact I believe Dewey's democratic theory gives to rhetoric the burden of performing what was the most controversial function of rhetoric in classical Greece—the burden of making the weaker argument appear the stronger. As John Poulakos points out, a literal interpretation from the Greek makes it seem that the Sophists were attempting to replace that which is *to kreitton*, "superior" or "greater," with that which is *to hetton*, "inferior" or "lesser" than something else. However, a rhetorical perspective denies these fixed attributions and assumes that "the status or position of an argument is always situationally determined" and thus capable of change. It takes *to hetton* to refer "to that argument or position which commands less power because the majority shuns it or is not persuaded by it" and *to kreitton* to refer "to that argument or position which is dominant because the majority has found it more persuasive than other alternatives." From such a perspective, the function of Sophistical rhetoric is to "reverse in some measure the established hierarchy of things" by employing "the resources of language and its surrounding circumstances to move what is regarded as weaker to a position of strength."[42] In other words to make a minority view into one accepted by the majority, one must seize the opportunity to envision new possibilities by making full use of the playfulness of language to break the ingrained habits of thought of one's audience through aesthetic performance that simultaneously critiques, advocates, and creates. What I wish to argue is that Dewey's view leads us to the conclusion that in addition to the more general functions of persuasion it fulfills, the unique function of rhetoric in a democracy is to express and advance minority viewpoints in exigent circumstances such that they have the opportunity to transform public opinion through persuasion in an egalitarian public sphere.

The alignment of a Deweyan theory of rhetoric with a Sophistical orientation serves to highlight an important and often neglected aspect of his concept of democracy. All too frequently Dewey is aligned with a communitarian democratic ethos in which conversation and discussion are the paradigm forms of communication, with rhetoric being merely a stylized form of rational argument. However, this interpretation neglects the individualistic spirit of Dewey's democratic theory. As he writes, "It is true that all valuable as well as new ideas begin with minorities, perhaps a minority of one. The important consideration is that opportunity be given that idea to spread and to become the possession of the multitude." Consequently Dewey recognizes that this opportunity cannot be fulfilled simply by the existence of an egalitarian public sphere that guarantees free and open communication. It also requires training in the arts of rhetoric. As Dewey famously declared, "The essential need, in other words, is the improvement of the methods and conditions of debate, discussion and persuasion. That is *the* problem of the public."[43] While communitarians wish to interpret this statement as a call for conversation, it actually calls for exactly what is says—persuasion. For only by persuasion can a "minority of one" spread a new idea to the multitude.

Consistent with his view of the public as a plurality of publics interacting within a shared environment, Dewey recognizes that democracy thrives not because of it brutishly enforces the will of the majority but because it cultivates and gives voice to the ideas of the minority. Consequently not majority rule but "the means by which a majority comes to be a majority is the more important thing." Democratic means included "antecedent debates, modification of views to meet the opinions of minorities, the relative satisfaction given by the [minority] by the fact that it has had a chance and that next time it may be successful in becoming a majority."[44] In this way Dewey reinforces the basic principles of rhetorical democracy. For him "a genuine democracy will always secure to every individual a maximum of liberty of expression and will establish the conditions which will enable the minority by use of communication and persuasion to become a majority."[45] By contrast undemocratic persuasion allows a powerful, economically entrenched minority to "suppress and misrepresent another minority which is at an economic disadvantage" and "use methods of suppressive force or of perversion and degradation of opinion by means of propaganda." In such a situation "the responsibility of the actual majority is not for originating the suppression but for standing passively by and permitting it to occur."[46] Thus, in undemocratic persuasion, the egalitarian character of the public sphere itself is compromised by overwhelming it by a single persuasive message promulgated by propaganda that simultaneously shuts out opposing views and threatens force to maintain its control.

In many ways the relationship between persuasion and the public sphere articulated by Dewey mirrors that of Farrell's in the latter's *Norms of Rhetorical Culture*. Like Dewey, Farrell emphasizes the importance of creating and maintaining rhetorical forums environments "within which issues, interests, positions, constituencies, and messages are advanced, shaped, and provisionally judged." Similarly Farrell rejects the Kantian notion that rhetoric is merely "a crude subset of perlocutionary speech" relegated to "the nonreflective domain of strategy." To the contrary, Farrell insists that "rhetoric is the collaborative art of addressing and guiding decision and judgment." As such it has both a critical and constructive function. Critically "rhetoric is the primary practical instrumentality for generating and sustaining the critical publicity which keeps the promise of a public sphere alive." Thus rhetoric undermines the power of propaganda and keeps the public sphere free of suppressive influence. Constructively, rhetoric promotes invention by "expanding the boundaries of the commonplace to admit and transform new information and ideas." The result is a vision of public life in which training in the art of rhetoric allows us "to recognize and hear eloquence while seeing through and beyond its vision at the same time."[47]

What distinguishes Dewey's position from Farrell's Aristotelian framework is the Sophistical spirit in which Dewey approaches the arts of language. As Charland observes, Farrell's work embodies a somewhat "pious" tone in which "the Sophistic love of paradox and linguistic play that is at the origin of inquiry into the art of persuasion is notably absent."[48] Dewey, by contrast, balances the considerable piety of his attitude toward subjects such as science, logic, education, and ethics with a distinctly playful approach to art and aesthetics. For him art is the performance of imaginative vision. Artists give expressive form to ideas or emotions that for the rest of us might be vague notions or raw impulses. In doing so they enable an audience not only to embrace the meaning of the work but also to make new meanings of their own that transcend traditional boundaries. For Dewey democracy requires a Sophistical sensibility in which play and aesthetics stand alongside judgment and reason as necessary means of persuasion and action, for it is art that gives gods feet of clay, just as it provides the raw material for the construction of new idols that inspire not obedience but possibility and imagination.

What is "radical" about this orientation both to rhetoric and to democracy boils down to a single fundamental faith—faith in the civilizing power of art unfettered. The radical nature of this faith only becomes apparent, however, when contrasted with the extreme positions that have long denied, and continue to deny, its legitimacy. On the one hand the agents of idealism praise art only when it directs our gaze toward the absolute; thus anything that falls outside of sanctified bounds becomes an enemy of the spirit, even when that spirit is the God of Reason. On the other hand critical skeptics reject the presence of spirit see all art as a mask, whether that mask hides domination, ignorance, weakness, or sheer emptiness; thus faith of any kind makes one a dupe and an unsuspecting tool of a faceless power. The first attitude charts a path to tyranny in its many forms while the second attitude throws barriers in the road. In neither, however, do the arts of rhetoric flourish within a democratic social life.

Against these two perspectives, which today represent the vacillations between fundamentalism and nihilism, stands the Promethean faith that art is the benefactor of civilization. For to believe in art, defined as *technē*, is to also believe in the human capacity to create and appreciate art as semiautonomous beings with the power of imagination, intelligence, passion, and will. This attitude incorporates elements from three extremes and combines them into a new experimental attitude. Like idealism, it adopts a forward-looking vision of the future and its belief in ideas and ideals as real, motivational, and practical. Like skepticism, it approaches all such ideals as fallible hypothesis, thus encouraging critical judgment and analysis. And like materialism, it accepts that we are always bound by the constraints of our environment. The resulting pragmatism, which is another word for faith in *technē*, encourages a critical but productive practice that freely advocates new courses of action even while welcoming the possibility of refutation and change. Rhetoric, then, is the art of public advocacy that functions in a timely relationship to shared problematic situations of moral conflict, cognitive uncertainty, and practical urgency. Radical democracy is the commitment to act upon the judgments of collective intelligence as constituted by the arts of free, full, and moving communication. And rhetoric is radical when eloquence unites aesthetic form with intelligent judgment in such a way that transforms the experiences of a community to better orient themselves to the contingencies of the future.

An enriched art of rhetoric must dedicate itself to the productive transformation of experience, not only of the individual but also of the community as understood as a reservoir of potential freedom as well as a network of constraining powers. As a philosophy of experience, Dewey's work assists in that project. By taking experience seriously, Dewey provides a framework to give "substance" to rhetoric—that substance being the experiences of the people who transact with rhetorical works of art. Rhetoric is unique among the arts not for its transformational potential, which is shared by all human symbolic creations touched by language, but for its method of transformation. Rhetoric fuses the instrumental and aesthetic spectrums of experiences in a way that is only possible within *kairotic* moments that generate the energy necessary for dramatic shifts in orientation to one's environment. Consequently it is Dewey's naturalistic, logical, and aesthetic theories, not his thoughts on communication as such, which provide the richest resources for constructing a productive rhetorical theory. Like Aristotle before him, Dewey envisions a discourse which can simultaneously facilitate judgment while constituting feelings of ecstasy. The democratic significance of rhetoric lies in the ability of a single discourse to disrupt the present even as it borrows from the past to propel us into new futures. Commitment to the ontology of becoming corresponds with the faith that such a future might be better and that its creation is our own responsibility—and that faith in self-determination has always been radical.

1 Rhetoric and the Ethics of Democracy

What does it mean to say that rhetoric and democracy have an "ethics"? Traditionally the answers fall into one of two categories. On the one hand Kantian rationalism dictates that persuasive and political acts must follow from universal moral principles. In rhetoric one finds this ethics expressed most fully by Richard Weaver, for whom an "ethics of rhetoric requires that ultimate terms be ultimate in some rational sense" such that they achieve "an ordering of our own minds and our own passions."[1] For Weaver the worst sin of rhetoric is to exploit circumstances through use of charismatic terms, and the worst sin of democracy is to slip into thoughtful demagoguery based on desire for short-term gratification. On the other hand Benthamite utilitarianism recommends that we judge the worth of any public behavior on the basis of its cumulative results, regardless of the motive. In rhetoric this attitude finds a home in the neo-Aristotelian tradition that grew out of Herbert Wichelns, in which rhetoric is "not concerned with permanence, nor yet with beauty. It is concerned with effect."[2] From the effects perspective, universal principles are elusive and motives are hard to determine; better that we bracket such "idealistic" categories and get to work on the hedonistic calculus that measures the total sum of pleasures and pains.

Not surprisingly, these competing ethical standards are but further manifestation of the classical binaries between idealism and materialism, rationalism and empiricism, and realism and nominalism. Whereas one side denies the reality of flux and puts faith in the eternal, the other side dives headlong into the river in the belief that even the stability of the banks is but an illusion. The problem with such extremes is that they produce deafness and blindness respectively. To always act from principle, regardless of the circumstance, is to march steadfastly ahead despite cries of pain and appeals for sympathy. Yet to plunge into circumstances is to risk losing oneself in the swirl of motion and emotion such that the horizon never comes into focus. Ironically, then, both ethical perspectives are equally unethical insofar as they remain incapable of placing means and ends into a meaningful relation. By valorizing ends, the former keeps saying the same thing, but by denying ends, the latter has nothing to say. Meanwhile the operation of technological means continues its domination of society unabated.

If neither side provides a sufficient interpretation of ethics, they both grasp some aspect of necessity. For Dewey a more functional ethics requires the application of charitable continuity. "The theoretical value of the utilitarian position consists in the fact that it warns us against overlooking the essential place of the intellectual factor, namely, foresight of consequences," he writes. "The practical value of the theory which lays stress on motive is that it calls attention of the part played by character, by personal disposition and attitude, in determining the direction which the intellectual factor takes." Successfully combining these insights requires more than simply saying "both/and." One must set them within a methodological whole. For Dewey that requires viewing ethics from the perspective of the entire act as it occurs as a process of judgment in which aspects of character, both individual and social, interact with environmental conditions over time. These acts must "involve awareness of what one is about; a fact which in the concrete signifies that there must be a purpose, an aim, and end in view, something for the sake of which the particular act is done."[3] For Dewey, then, ethical acts occur as a voluntary and purposive choices made in situations of doubt and crisis by agents who possess a relatively formed and stable character.

This definition incorporates but significantly alters the principles of the rationalistic and utilitarian positions. One the one hand, like the rationalist tradition, Dewey's pragmatic ethics recognizes the importance of defining and seeking an ideal of the good. However, the good is defined not in terms of transcendent goals or fixed principles, but flexible ends and guidelines that grow out of situational conditions and are reflective of personal attitudes. On the other hand, like the utilitarian position, it measures the virtue of an act by its cumulative consequences. Yet it neither assumes a fixed "measure" of those consequences on an objective scale of pleasure or happiness, nor does it limit consequences to immediate gratifications. A genuine good is thus one that produces long-term beneficial consequences as measured by the needs and desires of a shared historical community. To possess a moral will is thus to possess "an active tendency to foresee consequences, to form resolute purposes, and to use all the efforts at command to produce the intended consequences in fact."[4] In other words a moral will is the ability to define a fitting end and determine the means that contribute to its consummation without undermining its long-term stability.

Only from a means/ends analysis can one distinguish the ethics of democracy from any other form of social organization. This is the emphasis of Dewey's earliest writing on the subject, his 1888 "Ethics of Democracy." In that work Dewey compared democracy with "aristocracy," a term he used to characterize any society that "limits the range of men who are regarded as participating in the state." The clear reference point for Dewey, at the time, was Plato's *Republic*, but today it can equally stand for any regime that would profess noble ends but employ restrictive or oppresive means.[5] His intent was to point out that both aristocracy and democracy in practice seek to achieve a form of social life in which individuals achieve self-realization within the context of a social whole. What makes them different, therefore, is the relationship between means and ends. "Personal responsibility, individual initiation, these are the notes of democracy," Dewey explains. "Aristocracy and democracy both imply that the actual state of society exists for the sake of realizing an end which is ethical, but aristocracy implies that this is to be done primarily by means of special institutions or organizations within society, while democracy holds that the ideal is already at work in every personality, and must be trusted to care for itself."[6]

It is vital not to misinterpret Dewey on this point; he is not simply repeating the ethical stance of classical liberalism in which the best society is one free from negative constraints. As he would later make clear, find "a man who believes that all men need is freedom *from* oppressive legal and political measures, and you have found a man who, unless he is merely obstinately maintaining his own private privileges, carries at the back of his head some heritage of the metaphysical doctrine of free-will, plus an optimistic confidence in natural harmony."[7] But even in 1888, when writing as a Christian idealist, Dewey still recognized the importance of creating individuals capable of personal responsibility and individual initiation. Democracy thus meant for him that "personality is the first and final reality" at the same time that it "admits that the full significance of personality can be learned by the individual only as it is already presented to him in objective form in society" and that the "chief stimuli and encouragements to the realization of personality come from society."[8] Dewey would later abandon the idealistic term "personality," which was linked to a Hegelian teleology, but his basic point remained the same. By making the individual both the means and the end of democracy, it committed itself to investing its energies into creating individuals capable of possessing a moral will that achieves enough autonomy from dominant social forces that it is capable of reacting back upon those forces with intelligence and power.

By 1932, when his final treatise on ethics was published, Dewey had decided that four dominant virtues characterized democratic social life: wisdom, faithfulness, thoughtfulness, and conscientiousness. By wisdom, Dewey means the ability to subordinate the "satisfaction of an immediately urgent single appetite" to a more "inclusive satisfaction" such that, for instance, one does not win the battle and lose the war. By faithfulness, he means the willingness of a self to acknowledge "the claims involved in its relations with others," thereby recognizing the possibility of indirect public consequences for others in any act done primarily to satisfy a private interest. By thoughtfulness, he means being solicitous "in the award of praise and blame" in order that one not snap to quick judgment of another based on isolated acts and limited evaluations. Lastly, by conscientiousness, Dewey means possessing the "active will to discover new values and to revise former notions."[9] This last virtue is the most challenging and the most democratic. For individuals can be wise, faithful, and thoughtful in most of their everyday dealings with others in any society that has achieved a degree of stability. Yet to discover new values or revise old ones—to enact, in other words, a transvaluation of values—is intrinsically to situate oneself within the realm of moral conflict that is anathema to all forms of aristocracy.

The implications of Dewey's moral theory go further still; for wherever there is moral conflict, there is rhetoric. Rhetoric and democracy are thus bound together through the fundamental ethical imperative of the ontology of becoming—that the nature of our future selves, as individuals, cultures, and civilizations, is a product of the present choices we make and the future goals toward which we aspire as they have been inherited and altered from the past. Dewey observes:

> Except as the outcome of arrested development, there is no such thing as a fixed, ready-made, finished self. Every living self causes acts and is itself caused in return by what it does. All voluntary action is a remaking of self, since it creates new desires, instigates to new modes of endeavor, brings to light new conditions which institute new ends. Our personal identity is found in the thread of continuous development which binds together these changes. In the strictest sense, it is impossible for the self to stand still; it is becoming, and becoming for the better or the worse. It is in the quality of becoming that virtue resides. We set up this and that end to be reached, but the end is growth itself.

What is true for the self is also true for society. The character of democratic society stands for the thread of continuous development that binds together the growth of individuals toward a common endeavor. What makes this growth democratic is its fundamental rhetorical tolerance for views that may seem, judged by the standards of the present, to be immoral. Dewey notes, for instance, that "history shows how much of moral progress has been due to those who in their own time were regarded as rebels and treated as criminals." Given this fact, a democracy cannot view toleration as "just an attitude of good-humored indifference. It is positive willingness to permit reflection and inquiry to go on in the faith that the truly right will be rendered more secure through questioning and discussion, while things which have endured merely from custom will be amended or done away with."[10] With this process of bringing forth, amending, and doing away being a fundamental rhetorical activity, the tolerance of which Dewey speaks can only be a tolerance for rhetoric in all its glory and misery.

We are spiraling toward the basic principle of the ontology of becoming that will structure our understanding of rhetoric and democracy—that we understand the possibility of growth through continuity only by focusing on the moments of discontinuity within a shared environment that both force and allow for the moral choices that determine our future selves. Once again we find a similar emphasis operating in the work of Foucault. For him the history of thought is the history of problematizations—those moments that allow one "to step back from this way of acting or reacting, to present it to oneself as an object of thought and to question it as to its meaning, its conditions, and its goals." And it is crucial for Foucault, as for Dewey, that these moments of problematization do not simply occur in the mind or come about solely because of language itself. According to Foucault, "For a domain of action, a behavior, to enter the field of thought, it is necessary for a certain number of factors [largely resulting from social, economic, or political processes] to have made it uncertain, to have made it lose its familiarity, or to have provoked a certain number of difficulties around it."[11] The function of philosophy, for Foucault, is thus to bring about and reflect upon these moments of transformation to posit what might be and what might have been.

Clearly, however, this role has traditionally been reserved not for philosophy but for rhetoric. It was its infatuation with moments of crisis and transformation that made it so closely aligned in the Sophistical era of classical Greece with the spirit of *kairos*. Variously interpreted practically as "opportune moment," "due measure," or "right occasion,"[12] *kairos*, according to Carolyn Miller, "encourages us to be creative in responding to the unforeseen, to the lack of order in human life. The challenge is to invent, within a set of unfolding and unprecedented circumstances, an action (rhetorical or otherwise) that will be understood as uniquely meaningful within those circumstances."[13] As a god Kairos was originally portrayed as a young man with wings on his shoulder and heels balanced on the edge of a knife while holding a pair of scales. For Greeks living in an age in which triumph and disaster equally seemed probable in the next moment and in which their literal fate as victors or slaves might depend on a single decision, their worship of *kairos* was understandable. The rise of democracy simply made this principle applicable to the rhetorical discourse, as timely judgment and action became contingent upon timely advocacy and speech. As teachers of rhetoric, the Sophists understandably became the masters of *kairos*. According to John Poulakos, *kairos* was a "radical principle of occasionality"[14] which emphasized that "speech exists in time and is uttered both as a spontaneous formulation of and a barely constituted response to a new situation unfolding in the immediate present."[15] Being masters of improvisation, the Sophists saw rhetoric a way of reacting almost instinctively to the slightest flux within a situation in order to best set the course of future events.

Attention to *kairos* makes rhetoric something different than other, more systematic forms of persuasion such as propaganda and discursive forms of power/knowledge, just as the social consequences of *kairotic* discourse make it incompatible with undemocratic forms of social life. Take, for instance, the following passage created by the Sophist Thrasymachus during the Peloponnesian War: "I wish I had been alive in the old days, when the younger generation could happily remain silent, since matters did not force them to make speeches and their elders were looking after the city. But since it is our fate to found ourselves alive now, at a time when we submit to others ruling the city, but endure its disasters ourselves, and since the greater of these disasters are due not to the gods or to fortune, but to those who are in charge, I have no choice but to speak."[16] The simple line "I have no choice but to speak" represents an ethical stance that recognizes both circumstantial conditions and moral responsibilities. Presumably one must speak because no one else has spoken appropriately to overcome the shared problem that faces them in the present. To speak in this situation thus mandates that one not only speak for but speak against—and, most important, that one must speak for oneself. This form of expression stands in tension not only with forms of propaganda, in which the individual only speaks on behalf of a organization and within the limits of a narrowly defined method and goal, but also with more dominant forms of social discourse, in which the individual merely reinscribes conventional power relations by conforming to the patterns of expression that constitute them.

That is to say, rhetoric attends to the particular situation as it relates to a more universal social context always in the process of transition and change. Wichelns is thus correct in observing that rhetoric is "the art of influencing men in some concrete situation,"[17] but so too is Philip Wander correct in emphasizing how rhetoric always occurs within "an historical context" involving "the efforts of real people to create a better world."[18] Such perspectives are only seen to conflict when viewed through the many-headed dualisms of theory and practice that have ever forced upon us a decision to either stare at our feet or gaze up at the heavens. When viewed pragmatically, however, they each simply highlight differing facets of an action performed in historical time that emerges from the past, speaks to the present, and alters the future. Rhetoric, in sum, always exists in temporal relationship to crisis. It is thus a creature of drama, and as such it makes, dominates, rouses, and molds the personalities, movements, climaxes, spectacles, and actions that constitute the narratives of historical change. Rhetoric's role in that drama is to harness the energies that accumulate within moments of tension and then channel a new path for their expression.

The ethics of any rhetorical act is determined neither by conformity to ideals nor crass utilitarianism but by how any rhetorical act directs experience within problematic situations in which long-term happiness is contingent a complete interpenetration of means and ends fitting to environmental conditions. There are thus four major components to any rhetorical action that determine its ethical significance: self, other, situation, and message. This chapter will outline the relationship among the first three terms, while the remaining chapters will explore different facets of last. The overall purpose is understand how rhetoric functions within a democratic context in which citizen and public interact within a shared natural and social environment that encompasses both the particularities of a situated moment and the more universal traits of historical time.

Protagoras and the Ontology of Becoming

Rhetoric is a form of symbolic action that induces movement in the face of recalcitrance. To understand this kinetic function of rhetoric necessitates an interpretation of the human environment in which individuals feel impelled to act, are constrained from movement, and have the power to overcome those constraints. Put another way, the art of rhetoric can only exist as an art in a world of becoming that stands between the block universe of determinism and the vacuum of free will. Any other perspective renders rhetoric not an art of facilitating action but a vehicle of expression that lacks the capacity to affect real change. On the one hand, absent forces with the capacity to both limit and privilege ways of thinking and acting, rhetoric would have no resources upon which to draw to analyze or alter a situation; it could only give voice to the contents of one's solipsistic consciousness. On the other hand, absent the possibility of genuine choice, rhetors would have no reason to adapt to an audience; they would simply represent the state of things to whoever wished to listen. An art of rhetoric thus can exist only when knowledge is possible but contingent, when we can tentatively make judgments about our environment even as we attempt to change the nature of that environment. The world of becoming, which includes both permanence and change, is thus the world of the creative artist, for only as things are capable of change is creation possible, but only as our creations have lasting value and impact are we inspired to invest our energies in bringing them into being.

The connection between rhetorical practice and the ontology of becoming is not a product of contemporary philosophy; it is present at the very origins of rhetoric. Dewey notes that in the original Greek, *phusis,* the word translated as "nature," is "etymologically connected with a root meaning 'to grow.' Now growth is change; it is coming into Being and passing out of Being, altering between the two extremes of birth and death."[19] The split between philosophy and rhetoric was born out of the reaction to this experience of change. The Presocratic philosopher Parmenides viewed the fact of change as a limitation to be transcended. Consequently he sought to see through and beyond the experience of change to the fixed qualities of being. In contradistinction the Sophist Protagoras accepted change as a real part of the world. For Protagoras it was so obvious that "all things are in motion" that he believed that "the verb 'to be' must be totally abolished." What concerned Protagoras was how to manage change: "To the sick man the things he eats both appear and are bitter, while to the healthy man they both appear and are the opposite. Now what we have to do is not to make the one of these two wiser than the other. . . . What we have to do is to make a change from the one to the other, because the other state is better."[20] For a dualist metaphysician such as Parmenides, the sick man could heal himself by partaking in philosophy, which would help him ignore his body and find oneness in the eternal. For a rhetorician such as Protagoras, the sick man required a dose of rhetoric—if only to get him to take his medicine—to alter his experience for the better so he might get back to dealing more effectively with the affairs of practice.

The inescapable problem with the Protagorean perspective has always been the absence of evaluative standards. In one of Dewey's early logical essay written in this Protagorean vein, he writes that "the question of truth is not as to whether Being or Non-Being, Reality or mere Appearance, is experienced, but as to the *worth* of a certain correctly experienced thing."[21] Yet a Socrates would immediately ask, On what grounds does the ontology of becoming allow one to make a distinction between a merely "experienced" thing and a "correctly experienced thing"? If, as Protagoras states, all that "one is immediately experiencing is always true,"[22] then is not the "thing" experienced by the sick man on equal ontological footing with that of the healthy man? Moreover, by what criteria do we judge what is "better"? Without absolute standards of good, are not all experiences equally better and worse? Pressed in these ways, what initially appears to be a progressive and pragmatic orientation toward language and truth dissolves into an irresponsible relativism that licenses any sort of behavior as long as it brings about some momentary experience of pleasure. Rhetoric becomes not the means of advancing civilization but the tool for its manipulation and exploitation.

It does not require a great leap of the imagination to see how one might read this attitude as culminating in dystopian visions such as Plato's Callicean tyranny. As Hauser explains, this dystopic vision results from spinning out the negative consequences of opening "the Pandora's box of persuasion, which may lead to manipulation for personal gain under the guise of the common good."[23]

The traditional solution to this problem, of course, has always been to make persuasion subordinate to some a priori rationalistic ideal that makes it a vehicle for transmitting only the good, the beautiful, and the true. In other words persuasion becomes the partisan of being in a world of appearances. In Plato's *Statesman,* for example, an effective state based on knowledge is achieved when "that part of rhetoric which in partnership with kingship persuades people of what is just and so helps in steering through the business of cities."[24] The ideal *politikos* is portrayed as a ruler who weaves the social fabric from numerous strands of expertise and employs the art of rhetoric to huddle the masses under its protective cover. The rationalistic view of society admits the practical nature of rhetoric and the possibility of growth, but it interprets rhetorical practice as applied philosophy and interprets progressive growth only as it exists in relation to a predetermined end. Becoming is thus not seen as "real" but as transitory. The only reality exists in being, and once rhetoric helps actualize being, it is as a ladder than can then be thrown away.

Despite the clear philosophical problems with this proposal, it was directed toward resolving a very real problem. After all, the threat posed by a contemporary "democracies" is that the breakdown of tradition combined with the new freedom of movement in act, idea, and expression will produce two related tendencies. In the first case it might rapidly descend into a Hobbesian war of all against all. In the words of James Madison, "Hence it is that such democracies have ever been spectacles of turbulence and contention; have ever been found incompatible with personal security or the rights of property; and have in general been as short in their lives as they have been violent in their deaths."[25] In the second case it might lead to a mere mechanical uniformity in which genuine individuality is suffocated. The result is the production of the "lonely crowd" characterized by "isolation in the mass" and guided by the cool and systematic hand of mass propaganda.[26] Of course, these two tendencies are mirror images of each other.

What remains prescient in Plato's discourse, then, is not his appeal to absolutes but his insight into the dangers of democracy and willingness to take the long view on matters of social practice. What he had witnessed was the end of the age of the Older Sophists and the beginning of the age of demagoguery. In the three decades of the Peloponnesian War, the population of Athens had been reduced to something of a mob, with decisions being made based on immediate fears and desires as they were exploited by rapacious orators. The age of Thucydides, writes Edith Hamilton, was an age in which vices "were esteemed as virtues," when "deceit was praised as shrewdness, recklessness held to be courage, loyalty, moderation, generosity, scorned as proofs of weakness."[27] It was precisely Plato's willingness and ability to directly confront these social challenges that led to Dewey to advocate a "Back to Plato" movement in philosophy; only for him, "it would have to be back to the dramatic, restless, cooperatively inquiring Plato of the *Dialogues,* trying one mode of attack after another to see what it might yield; back to the Plato whose highest flight of metaphysics always terminated with a social and practical turn."[28] The task for the rhetoric of becoming, in other words, is to incorporate this long view without slipping back into the arms of the idea.

Perhaps, however, Dewey might have equally recommended a "Back to Protagoras" movement. Of all the Older Sophists, after all, it was Protagoras who came closest to developing a framework that would accomplish the ends of Plato but through rhetorical and democratic means. The key insight of Protagoras was that truth, beauty, and goodness were not only relative to experience and to practice but also were products of time and community. For Protagoras truth claims are not simply expressions of personal whim; they also exist as shared constitutive components of *nomos,* the norms, conventions, laws, and beliefs of a larger cultural system. Hence we find Protagoras arguing in Plato's *Theaetetus,* "Whatever in any city is regarded as just and admirable is just and admirable, in that city and for so long as that convention maintains itself."[29] Yet conventions change as the environment changes. Unexpected challenges make old conventions obsolete and new conventions necessary. It is in that moment of change, then, that rhetoric demonstrates its progressive value. Hence, for Protagoras, "wise and efficient politician is the man who makes wholesome things seem just to a city instead of pernicious ones."[30] What we find in Protagoras, then, is an attempt to moderate and control the pace of social change through a rhetorical sensibility that considers both the appropriate and the possible simultaneously. As Poulakos describes it, a Sophistic rhetor must first address an audience "as they are and where they are" but subsequently must "lift them from the vicissitudes of custom and habit and take them into a new place where new discoveries and new conquests can be made."[31] Protagoras recognizes the importance of reaffirming the truths present in a culture before then attempting to transcend them toward better and more "wholesome" states of being in which the nature of "wholesome" is determined not by a fixed ideal but by the qualities of experience itself. Protagoras expresses a diachronic view of truth that perceives it as a process of growth and experimental development over time and within a shared community, and it is in this way that his thought can be said to embody the spirit of rhetorical democracy.

Even if we accept the basic premises of Protagoras, however, the Platonic questions remain before us: What kind of art is possible in a world of becoming? And what kind of future does it promise? These are the very questions that Dewey dedicated his life's work to answering. Like Protagoras, Dewey believed that arts which embrace the ontology of becoming have always been the driving force behind the growth of civilization. For only in a world in which human agency can productively interact with and influence the forces of permanence and change can we genuinely find meaning and value in our relationship to our environment. As Dewey explains, the "the significance of morals and politics, of the arts both technical and fine, of religion and of science itself as inquiry and discovery, all have their source and meaning in the union in Nature of the settled and the unsettled, the stable and the hazardous. Apart from this union, there are no such things as 'ends,' either as consummations or as those ends-in-view we call purposes."[32] In other words only insofar as the world presents actual problems to be solved and the possibility for their creative reconstruction and resolution in experience is art as a form of productive transformation genuinely possible. Attending to the conditions that improve the state of the art is the primary function of theory in a democracy.

Finding the Rhetorical Situation

Considering Dewey's emphasis on the relationship between art and the environment, particularly within problematic contexts, it is hardly surprising that his work was highly influential in the development of the contemporary notion of the "rhetorical situation." Proposed by Lloyd Bitzer in his 1969 article of the same title, the concept of the rhetorical situation was developed in large part to defend a definition of rhetoric as a discursive solution that comes into existence in response to an objective problem, an "exigence," that makes rhetoric more than mere "persuasion" that can happen at any time. Although unacknowledged in his original essay, it was Dewey's pragmatism that had informed much of Bitzer's approach.[33] In a later essay he corrects this absence by explicitly citing Dewey's *Theory of Valuation,* quoting the passage "Valuation takes place only when there is something the matter; when there is some trouble to be done away with, some need, lack, or privation to be made good, some conflict of tendencies to be resolved by means of changing conditions."[34] The idea of the rhetorical situation emerges once we identify those situations in which resolutions require rhetorical persuasion to produce a collective valuation that facilitates practical judgment. Thus, for Bitzer, the "practical justification of rhetoric is analogous to that of scientific inquiry: the world presents objects to be known, puzzles to be resolved, complexities to be understood.... Hence the practical need for rhetorical intervention and discourse."[35] Consistent with Dewey, Bitzer ultimately justifies rhetorical practice by placing it within a democratic framework. Rhetoric is not simply a way of persuading people to think what we want them to think, it is a practical art that helps us solve problems in a changing and contingent social world.

Yet Bitzer's tendency to speak of rhetoric "scientifically," as a means by which independent agents respond to observable, objective, and "real" exigencies, opened him up to the criticism that his approach relies on the metaphysics of epistemological realism and the values of Enlightenment rationalism—or, as Richard Vatz pithily characterized it, a "Platonist *Weltanschauung.*"[36] The concept of the rhetorical situation has come to represent a philosophical battle ground on which arguments over the metaphysics and ontology of rhetoric are fought.[37] Bitzer emerges not as a pragmatist who embraces the ontology of becoming but as a realist locked within the rationalistic metaphysics of being. Vatz, for instance, mocks Bitzer's account of rhetoric as an "academic exercise of determining whether the rhetor understood the 'situation' correctly." Such an approach, for Vatz, begs the question. The issue is not whether one understands a situation correctly but whether a "situation" actually exists at all before rhetoric gives it definition. Vatz bases this criticism on the principle that any observation is merely "a fitting of a scene into a category or categories found in the head of the observer. No situation can have a nature independent of the perception of its interpreter or independent of the rhetoric with which he chooses to characterize it." Consequently, rhetoric does not respond to situations; rather, "situations obtain their character from the rhetoric which surrounds them or creates them." For Vatz, rhetoric creates the world in which we live and to which we react.[38]

Furthermore, as other critics argue, not only does it create the world, but it creates the selves who live and act within that world. Thus Bitzer assumes both an objective reality and an autonomous ego. For instance, Barbara Biesecker, drawing on Derrida's theory of difference, then suggests that we should view rhetoric as constitutive of subjects implicated in the creation, reception, and application of discourse. According to Biescker, "Derrida underscores the radically historical character of the subject" by showing how (here quoting Derrida) that "an element functions and signifies, takes on or conveys meaning, only by referring to another past or future element in an economy of traces." She concludes that if "the subject is shifting and unstable (constituted in and by the play of *différence*), then the rhetorical event may be seen as an incident that produces and reproduces the identities of subjects and constructs and reconstructs linkages between them."[39] Biesecker thus defines an individual as a constructed subject that is a product of identities whose meaning is, in turn, produced and reconstructed by rhetoric.

Put in more general terms, one sees in the reaction to Bitzer's original definition the rejection of the neo-Aristotelian desire for objective grounding in favor of the neo-Sophistical embrace of the fluid and ineffable nature of discourse. Yet both perspectives are equally insufficient to stand on their own. Bitzer's important accomplishment was to apply to Dewey's pragmatic interpretation of *technē* in defining rhetoric as an art—as "a mode of altering reality, not by direct application of energy to objects, but by the creation of discourse which changes reality through the mediation of thought and action."[40] Regretfully, Bitzer did not fully embrace the implications of this perspective. Instead of exploring all the ways in which rhetoric alters reality, he eventually retreated into a dualist language that distinguished between "genuine rhetorical situations" and "sophistical and spurious ones" whose determination appeared to be the responsibility of the empirical sciences.[41] Despite the valuable focus on rhetoric's practical and situational character, Bitzer's conception ultimately made rhetoric the handmaiden of knowledge. The possible lines of inquiry opened by his original essay were thus shut down by a neo-Aristotelian ideal that insisted that we must know before we act.

The various neo-Sophistical responses to Bitzer rightly challenge his hierarchical structure by emphasizing the genealogical and relativistic character of knowledge that makes rhetoric a constitutive component of what we believe to be the case in any particular context. Yet this effort often results in the evaporation of the situation itself. Ironically many critics challenge epistemological dualism with dualism of their own—a mind/body dualism that turns the mind into a cognitive machine whose purpose is primarily to perceive or observe stimuli that come from the bodily senses. Instead of a shared problem to which people collectively respond, one has a disconnected assortment of "perceptions" that exist only in the "mind." The prominent use of the term "perception" is often indicative of these types of interpretations, used as a term of opposition to "reality." Thus one commentary on Bitzer's essay argues that "the exigence *generates perceptions* within the mind of each potential auditor *and* rhetor"[42] while another states that "the goal of rhetorical discourse is *consensus,* the transformation of issue perceptions, bringing about a realignment and reconciliation between perceptual disparities."[43] Both of these essays define language in terms of cognitive "perception" that can do no more than seek perceptual consensus among a group of solipsistic minds, a consensus that may have little or no connection with "real" situations. The best one can achieve is consensus about perception. The "situation"—including the selves participating within it—is just another meaning in the mind.

However, to say that the goal of rhetoric is to create uniformity in perception is to confuse the functions of rhetoric and logic. Rhetoric does not seek perceptual consensus; it seeks coordination of action in a situation fraught with conflict and burdened by the essentially moral question "Why should I act thus and not otherwise?"[44] In other words the defining characteristic of a rhetorical situation is not in the "mind" but in our total experience, which demands of us to make a real choice, here and now, that requires some deep commitment. But what is the nature of "choice?" Dewey answers: "Simply hitting in imagination upon an object which furnishes an adequate stimulus to the recovery of overt action. Choice is made as soon as some habit, or some combination of elements of habits and impulse, finds a way fully open. Then energy is released. The mind is made up, composed, unified. As long as deliberation pictures shoals or rocks or troublesome gales as marking the route of a contemplated voyage. Deliberation goes on. But when the various factors in action fit harmoniously together, when imagination finds no annoying hindrance, when there is a picture of open seas, filled sails and favoring winds, the voyage is definitely entered upon."[45] It is in this interpretation of choice as imaginative deliberation intended to aid in the recovery of overt action in the face of constraint and obstacle in which we find the meaning of the rhetorical situation. The function of rhetoric with respect to choice is thus twofold; not only must it paint a picture of open seas, but at times it must also stir the waters of habit and belief that make us desire to journey into strange waters.

To take a paradigmatic rhetorical example, Joseph McCarthy could not prosecute Communists until he created a situation in which Communist infiltration was an immediate crisis. But as Darsey has shown, McCarthy's rhetoric stopped at the point where he had to fill the sails; he derived his power only within the rhetorical moment of crisis, and hence his rhetoric was a never-ending sequence of shoals and rocks and troublesome gales. For Darsey, McCarthy's rhetoric thrived within the "fantastic" moment, by which he meant a "celebration of ambiguity, something indefinite, a moment of hesitation and indecision."[46] Consequently McCarthy never proposed any solutions or advocated any ideas. His sole purpose was sustaining the sense of fear and mystification that lent credence to a politics of suspicion and paralysis. Thus whereas the "traditional response of great leader in times of crisis is to judge . . . Joe McCarthy's response to chaos was not certitude, but incredulity."[47] McCarthy thus demonstrates a rhetoric that only goes halfway—that creates a real sense of moral crisis and epistemological uncertainty only to let those energies fester and turn back on themselves. Great rhetoric, by contrast, not only generates the tension of the rhetorical situation, but then uses that tension for productive ends by the means of directing choice.

Given the inherited wisdom that McCarthy was a huckster, attempts to treat his discourse as something other than a spectacular illusion, and his loyal followers as something other than dupes, requires great exertion of the counterfactual imagination. Usually McCarthy is pointed to as an example of how rhetoric creates perceptions that lack empirical validity, such as when Smith and Lybarger argue that "Joseph McCarthy's 'list' of subversives in the State Department created the perception of an exigence that required action, even though the exigence was exaggerated at best and completely contrived at worst." Their conclusion, once again, seeks to contradict Bitzer's notion of exigence, disproving the idea that "there is uniformity of perception within the observers of a rhetorical situation due to the nature of the situation itself" while revealing how rhetoric contributes to the "social construction of reality." For Smith and Lybarger, to put oneself in the shoes of the participants, and to consider the possibility that Communists *were* infiltrating the State Department, is a priori to explore what it means to be a victim of "deliberate deception."[48] From their enlightened position writing in 1996, they are thus licensed to draw conclusions about what the rhetorical situation really was, regardless of how people experienced the situation at the time.

The simple fact is that rhetoric will always remain under the cloak of epistemology so long as it is understood primarily from the perspective of an "outsider" with the benefit of critical distance and reflective analysis. As an art that inhabits a particular moment within the flow of becoming, rhetoric lives only within the situated experience of those it touches. As people's experience shifts, so does the meaning of any particular rhetorical artifact as well as the meaning of the situation in which it is implicated. What *never* happens is that rhetoric "distorts" the "perceptions" of "observers" to a rhetorical situation. Indeed nothing is more telling in Smith and Lybarger's account than the transformation of rhetorical actors into "observers." The American citizens who were frightened by McCarthy's assertions, inspired by his courage, pulled before his committee, intimidated into silence, or ruined by his ambition were not "observing" a situation, they were participating in one. And McCarthy's rhetoric itself did not create the situation ex nihilo. His discourse came about in the context of a long historical development and within a situated moment of political uncertainty that gave the discourses of suspicion, threat, and crisis particular power. To say that McCarthy's exigence was "contrived" may help us feel superior to the poor souls caught up in the Red scare, but it does little to facilitate the understanding of how the rhetoric of that historical moment functioned. To understand that we must attend not just to language and the "mind" but also to experience.

Experience and Nature

The great merit of Dewey's naturalism is that it encourages us speak in the language of experience that accepts the *reality* of becoming. To accept the reality of becoming does not mean to be a realist; it means to accept the fact that change is real insofar as it is experienced as real. Dewey's "naturalistic humanism" transcends the binaries between the subject and the object, the self and the world, the mind and the body, the individual and the social, not by metaphysical gymnastics but simply by treating experience as the only way in which we establish any sort of relationships within an environment. Experience and nature thus interpenetrate one another; as Dewey writes, "Experience is *of* as well as *in* nature."[49] The switch of the preposition from "of" to "in" effectively embodies the whole of Dewey's naturalism. To be "in" nature means that we are no longer "observers" of something external; we are ourselves parts of nature.

Our experience is itself a natural event produced through interaction of things within some contextual and organic whole. By association, social institutions and cultural forms are components of our natural environment. Experience is thus of as well as in both culture and history; it is "a matter of the interaction of organism with its environment, an environment that is human as well as physical, that includes the materials of tradition and institutions as well as local surroundings."[50] Experience represents the product of our total interaction with our environment within a situated qualitative moment. Its ability to refer equally to the object and the subject of experience thus makes it a "double-barreled word" in that

> experiencing has no existence apart from subject-matter experienced; we perceive objects, veridical or illusory, not percepts; we remember events and not memories; we think topics and subjects, not thoughts; we love persons, not loves; and so on, although the person loved may by metonymy be called a "love." Experiencing is not itself an immediate subject-matter; it is not experienced as a complete and self-sufficient event. But everything experienced is in part made what it is because there enters into it a way of experiencing something; not a *way* of experiencing it, which would be self-contradictory, but a way of experiencing something *other than itself.* No complete account of what is experienced, then, can be given until we know how it is experienced or the mode of experiencing that enters into its formation.[51]

From many contemporary philosophers, Dewey's insistence that experience must involve something other than itself, and that experience at its best functions as "a growing progressive self-disclosure of nature itself," sounds suspiciously like a return to either realism or idealism.[52] Richard Rorty, for example, argues that Dewey's work retained a "shadow of Kant's notion that something called a 'metaphysics of experience' is needed to provide the 'philosophical basis' for the criticism of culture." Consequently Rorty downplays the importance of Dewey's "metaphysics of experience" and focuses our attention on Dewey's writing as a cultural critic, which appeared "in much of his older (and best) work."[53] What troubles Rorty is Dewey's insistence that experience exists within a world that has boundaries that extend beyond the limits of bodily stimulus and linguistic meaning and thus embody actual relations between things. For Rorty defining "experience" as anything more than the functioning of the nervous system is simply another manifestation of the desire to connect with some nonhuman reality. Better, he suggests, to abandon this hope and to concentrate on the construction, critique, and reinvention of the vocabularies that constitute the meaning of our selves and our world. It is language, not experience, toward which we should turn our attention.

Unfortunately Rorty simply tips the metaphysical seesaw from being to nonbeing without altering the common pivot which joins both perspectives. That common pivot is the fundamental principle of all metaphysical dualism—that experience has no meaningful substance. Regardless of whether experience is defined as a veil through which we struggle to get beyond, a mask in which we hide behind, or a route by which our senses are stimulated, experience remains a means only. In traditional epistemology the problem was always how knowledge of nature is possible when perception of nature is so clearly unstable and unreliable. For them nature is something "complete apart from experience" while experience is something "casual and sporadic" that "forms a veil or screen which shuts us off from nature, unless in some way it can be 'transcended.'"[54] Thus Dewey's naturalistic perspective on experience is viewed by realists as too subjective and relativistic because it relies on no clear foundations outside of experience itself. Yet his very assumption that experience—even when it intrinsically involves the emotions, cognitions, values, goals, and attitudes of the individual—is still *in* something other than itself makes it anathema to those who reject the whole idea of a nature as something "real." For these critics, overcoming the dualism means collapsing the object into the subject; "objects" are not Kantian *nuomena* that lurk behind an impenetrable wall but products of the fusion of subjective perception and discourse. Experience is thus a vessel not for "reality" but for "language" through which we receive through the gates of perception. But experience is a vessel still.

Addressing this longstanding philosophical debate over the nature of experience is important insofar as the attitude we take toward experience directly determines our attitudes toward both rhetoric and democracy. On the one hand, as long as experience is viewed as a prison through whose bars we occasionally catch a glimpse of the sun, as it is in the metaphysics of being, rhetoric will always be judged by the degree to which it embodies the light. Democracy, from this perspective, can only be justified when it promotes discourses of light and suppresses all those that turn our attention to shadow. On the other hand, as long as experience is viewed as a puppet that language makes dance and sing, as it is in the metaphysics of nonbeing, rhetoric will always be seen as a tool of manipulation to be judged by its capacity for power. When the puppet fails to move an audience to tears or applause, it thus condemns itself to be dominated by the hands of others. Democracy, from this perspective, is neither a government nor a form of social life but a collective fantasy, as are the "people" who believe themselves to be citizens.[55] In sum rhetoric in the metaphysics of nonbeing is the fabrication of simulacrum, while in the metaphysics of being that veil of illusion might be occasionally pierced by the light of the real that shines in eloquence.

If rhetoric is to function as an art, then experience itself must be substantial and capable of taking on the qualities of form. It must involve, in Dewey's words, "an operation of doing and making" with respect to experience—"a *poiesis* expressed in the very word poetry."[56] Following the ontological tradition stemming from Protagoras, experience must be both a resource for and a product of artistic transformation. The habitation of rhetoric is thus always at the moment of concentration between the old and the new, when the human organism feels is must reorient itself to its environment. Consistent with neo-Aristotelianism, rhetoric is thrown into a situation with a history that constrains the possibilities of action through the forces of recalcitrance. Yet consistent with neo-Sophism, rhetoric has the capacity to transform experience such that one emerges as a new self in a new world. The ontology of becoming denies neither the being of things nor their capacity to be not; it chooses instead to narrate the life of being as a drama over time as relations among its parts shift to create a new whole. Most important for rhetoric, however, the drama of becoming plays out on the stage of experience. Hence the only access we have to the world, which is also the only reality it possesses, comes to us within the qualitative immediacy of its disclosure in time.

Continuity and Transaction

The two principles that mark the ontology of becoming within a naturalistic humanism are continuity and transaction. Continuity "demands that statements be made as descriptions of events in terms of durations in time and areas of space."[57] Continuity in time means that experience is not limited to the atomic moment that only produces meaning after many such experiences are strung together like a movie reel. Rather, experience always absorbs the processes of growth and decline, rise and fall, ebb and flow that accompany any natural activity. Similarly continuity in space means that experience includes the things of our experience as well as the means by which we experience them. Our traditional desire to "know" what a thing is before "having" it thus inverts the natural order of experience. In actual fact we feel ourselves involved with the things of our environment before we ever step back and try to cognize them. As Dewey notes, "Things are objects to be treated, used, acted upon and with, enjoyed and endured, even more than things to be known. They are things *had* before they are things *cognized*."[58] And to "have" a thing means to possess it in time and in space; it means to "experience" it.

The principle of continuity leads naturally to the principle of transaction. The term "transaction" derives from its commonsense definition as "a 'deal' that has been 'put across' by two or more actors,"[59] in this case the actors being the "organism, on one side, and environment, on the other."[60] Transaction shifts the meaning of being from exist*ence* to exist*ing*, from the noun to the verb. "Existence" implies the presence of a static entity in which certain qualities inhere; "existing" conveys a sense of movement in which that entity functions in association with other things within some shared environment. Transaction refers to the process of mutual change that occurs as two or more things interact through the continuity of time and space. Using an example from nature, Dewey explains that "no one would be able successfully to speak of the hunt*er* and the hunt*ed* as isolated with respect to hunt*ing*." This analogy, simple on its face, becomes something more radical when applied to human cognition, communication, and action. For Dewey the transactional point of view leads to the conclusion that "knowing is cooperative and as such is integral with communication," and that "systems of description and naming are employed to deal with aspects and phases of action."[61] A system of calls and signals between hunting organisms is one form of such knowledge, but so is the system of logical marks and symbols that form the basis of physics or the system of metaphors and images that might embody some concept of God. All of these are transactional forms of knowledge that effect transformations in ourselves and the world around us and only have meaning with a total continuous environment. This, then, is the full meaning of Dewey's "metaphysics," or what I believe is more appropriately described as the naturalistic ontology of becoming:

> The main features of human life (culture, experience, history—or whatever name may be preferred) are indicative of outstanding features of nature itself—of centres and perspectives, contingencies and fulfillments, crises and intervals, histories, uniformities, and particularizations. This is the extent and method of my "metaphysics":—the large and constant features of human sufferings, enjoyments, trials, failures and successes together with the institutions of art, science, technology, politics, and religion which mark them, communicate genuine features of the world within which man lives. The method differs no whit from that of any investigator who, by making certain observations and experiments, and by utilizing the existing body of ideas available for calculation and interpretation, concludes that he really succeeds in finding out something about some limited aspect of nature. If there is any novelty in Experience and Nature, it is not, I should say, this "metaphysics" which is that of the common man, but lies in the use made of the method to understand a group of special problems which have troubled philosophy.[62]

The most telling aspect of this passage in Dewey's comment is that his metaphysics is that of the "common man." By this term Dewey means to align himself with the attitude of the practical citizen who approaches the world as a series of problems that require methodical and experimental interaction with her surroundings to affect a resolution. For the common man and woman, experience exists as the most reliable route by which to understand and adapt to a constantly changing world. The fact that experience may equally lead to misinterpretations, misjudgments, and transgressions as to knowledge, virtues, and enjoyments simply makes experience a contingent affair that seeks guidance from the arts of becoming such as rhetoric, science, poetry, literature, philosophy, history, logic, and religion. But these arts are not something apart from experience. Rather, they are the "outcome of a skilled and intelligent art of dealing with natural things for the sake of intensifying, purifying, prolonging and deepening the satisfactions which they spontaneously afford."[63] We do not escape experience in order to control it; quite the opposite, we delve into experience in order to perceive its depths, chart its connections, and imagine its possibilities.

Against both idealism and nihilism, the metaphysics of common sense accepts the experiences of change and stability, comedy and tragedy, growth and decay as being all real and actual parts of a world that is continuous and yet constantly in motion. The goal is not to set one side against the other but to understand them as a continuous transaction. As Dewey explains:

> We live in a world which is an impressive and irresistible mixture of sufficiencies, tight completenesses, order recurrences which make possible prediction and control, and singularities, ambiguities, uncertain possibilities, processes going on to consequences as yet indeterminate. They are mixed not mechanically but vitally like the wheat and tares of the parables. We may recognize them separately but we cannot divide them, for unlike wheat and tares they grow from the same root. Qualities have defects as necessary conditions of their excellencies; the instrumentalities of truth are the causes of error; change gives meaning to permanence and recurrence makes novelty possible. A world that was wholly risky would be a world in which adventure is impossible, and only a living world can include death.[64]

In other words the flux of experience participates within the flux of the natural world; both elude fixed descriptions even as they exist within a productive and mutually constitutive relationship with the other. The point is that our engagement with the world is also a transformation of that world, whether that transformation is in the direction of novelty or recurrence. But this is simply the metaphysics of the productive artist who has always been the driving force behind the growth of civilization.

The challenge for theory has always been to contribute to the advancement of arts of becoming by providing a reflecting account of its processes that resists slipping back into what Dewey called the "philosophic fallacy."[65] At it most basic level, the philosophic fallacy represents "the habit of philosophers of neglecting the indispensability of context, both in particular and in general."[66] This neglect of context is not merely the result of absentmindedness. It is the consequence of the metaphysical belief that one can interpret the events of becoming through the language of being, meaning that interpretations of experiences of contingency, change, and choice are made as if they were but merely subjective perceptions of deeper and more permanent realities. Context is neglected here because context is assumed to only have meaning with respect to an individual's experience, and as long as experience is a mere vessel for subjective perception, then it is irrelevant for philosophical analysis. Consequently, dualist theories of art—including the arts of science and of philosophy—tend to focus on the forces that are *really* at work behind the veil of appearances and then attribute the experience of artistic production and reception to those forces (including what Dewey calls "mathematical subsistences, esthetic essences, the purely physical order of nature, or God").[67] As Bruno Latour points out, the more recent addition of "discourse" or the "social" to that list makes them no less fallacious and no less a neglect of context than those who would attribute all the triumphs of human civilization to spirit or truth.[68]

It is the pervasive neglect of the continuity of time that makes the commonsense ontology of becoming so difficult to employ in the language of theory. The philosophic fallacy is so pervasive because we use the same language to describe a thing as it is immediately experienced as we do for the same thing after it has been reflectively analyzed and categorically defined. When discrepancies occur between those two descriptions, then, we are trapped within an either/or situation in which we are forced to choose between which account is more "true." Consequently we take the former to be a "subjective appearance" in contrast to the "objective reality" as it has come to be known. Thus we have critics such as Smith and Lybarger trying to explain how it is that people actually could have believed that there existed Communists in the State Department; clearly, since we now "know" that this fact was largely manufactured, then people's conceptions must have been a result of errors in perception brought about through rhetorical manipulation of appearances. The counterassertion that we can reasonably hold conflicting propositions in our mind simultaneously and thereby conclude that McCarthy was probably lying while also asserting that the experience of crisis he produced was real, would expose oneself to all manners of epistemological refutations. For the logic of being, either something is or is not. For the logic of becoming, a thing can simultaneously be and be not, depending on the experience in which it is disclosed.

Events and Objects

The first public declaration that Dewey had embarked upon the controversial path of Protagoras came in his 1905 essay,"The Postulate of Immediate Empiricism," which stated, quite brazenly, that "things—anything, everything, in the ordinary or nontechnical use of the term 'thing'—are what they are experienced as. Hence, if one wishes to describe anything truly, his task is to tell what it is experienced as being." This postulate got Dewey into a lot of trouble, not the least of which was the accusation that he appeared to do away with knowledge entirely and reduce it to the content of our immediate impressions. But irrational solipsism was never a good fit for Dewey. Written in the period of his middle work that focused on the question of practical judgment, Dewey's primary goal was to show how logical inquiry was an experimental process by which all propositions were tested in subsequent experience which, like the original experience, was equally real. His postulate shifted discussion from what something "is" to what it "becomes" as a result of changed conditions, actions, or understandings. Dewey gives the following quotidian example to make his point:

> I start and am flustered by a noise heard. Empirically, that noise *is* fearsome; it *really* is, not merely phenomenally or subjectively so. That is what it is experienced as being. But, when I experience the noise as a *known* thing, I find it to be innocent of harm. It is the tapping of a shade against the window, owing to the movements of the wind. The experience has changed; that is, the thing experienced has changed. . . . This is a change of experienced existence effected through the medium of cognition. The content of the latter experience cognitively regarded is doubtless *truer* than the content of the earlier, but it is in no sense more real. . . . It is only in regard to contrasted content in a subsequent experience that the determination "truer" has force.[69]

In Dewey's original formulation, the words "true" and "real" carry the burden of time. Truth in this passage refers to the pragmatic efficiency of a descriptive representation produced after a period of abstract reflection and experimentation; it stands for the worth of an idea for future practice. In contradistinction "real" refers to qualities of experience that are felt to be really there in the moment of experiencing. "Truth" is cognitive and instrumental, while "real" is an affective and aesthetic. Based on this distinction, any evaluative statements later considered true about a particular experience have no bearing on the reality of that experience in its immediacy. Thus a child who awakes to a noise and believes it to be a monster often remains frightened even after the worried parents turns on the lights and reveals that monster to be a window shade. For the child the cognitive truth that the noise was a window shade does not dispel the very real memory of being threatened by imminent destruction. The parent who attempts to convince the child that she is mistaken is met with an indignant denial on the part of the child, who insists that the monster *really* was there. Dewey's point is simply that we cannot ever go back and "correct" past realities. The only thing we can do is, through the production of new truths, alter what is experienced to be real in the future.

What Dewey discovered is that people find it difficult to separate the true from the real. Consistent with the logic of being, truth is seen as something which aspires to approximate reality, not alter it through transaction over time.

Consequently Dewey eventually incorporated a new set of terms that made more explicit temporal connotations. For Dewey reality refers to qualities of *events,* or those qualitative wholes that represents some part of continuous experience "had" in the moment of experiencing, while truth refers primarily to properties of *objects,* or aspects of one or more experiences transformed through communication into reflective conceptual form. In the language of Dewey's example, the waking with fear and uncertainty upon hearing a loud noise represents an event which was real—and always will be real—as it occurred in that moment. However, when some aspect of that event is isolated and subjected to inquiry and reflection, it ceases to be an event in subsequent experience and becomes an object that can be represented in a proposition: "That was just the tapping of the window shade." This object then can be challenged, modified, expanded, or diminished as inquiry proceeds and new problems arise. The tapping might then be seen as the result of a broken seal on the window and a loose fixture that needs repair. The practical outcome of those truths is the modification of the situation such that the wind no longer blows and the shade no longer taps; one then experiences the event of a good night's sleep.

When the event that gives rise to inquiry expands from a household annoyance to a social crisis, such that a broken window shade becomes an impending war, intolerable poverty, civil strife, environmental disaster, or moral anarchy, the rhetorical relevance of Dewey's example becomes clear. Speaking philosophically Dewey notes that the "business of reflection is to take events which brutely occur and brutely affect us, to convert them into objects by means of inference as to their probable consequences." In other words reflection gives meaning to events such that we might better control them in the future, in which meaning is understood to be "a method of action, a way of using things as means to a shared consummation."[70] Rhetoric here functions as a means of social reflection upon matters of public controversy that call for prudent judgment. Rhetoric gives meaning to the brute realities of past events and thereby produces objects with tentative claims to truth, at least in practical contexts if not always philosophical ones. The result is a constitution of a new event, a total qualitative "situation" in which reality discloses itself to an audience with a feeling of brute occurrence. It is this ability to transform events into objects which then react back upon events which makes "communication" so wonderful for Dewey. Hence this distinction between events and objects warrants a closer look at one of the most frequently quoted passages from Dewey about communication:

> Of all affairs, communication is the most wonderful. That things should be able to pass from the plane of external pushing and pulling to that of revealing themselves to man, and thereby to themselves; and that the fruit

of communication should be participation, sharing, is a wonder by the side of which transubstantiation pales. When communication occurs, all natural events are subject to reconsideration and revision. . . . Events turn into objects, things with a meaning. . . . Events when once they are named lead an independent and double life. In addition to their original existence, they are subject to ideal experimentation: their meanings may be infinitely combined end re-arranged in imagination, and the outcome of this inner experimentation—which is thought—may issue forth in interaction with crude or raw events.[71]

Within this short passage is the kernel of Dewey's entire philosophy of communication. Communication is wonderful because it functions as a transformational medium between events and objects and in the process creates new forms of character and social identity. Through communication, the natural world of pushing and pulling that exists at any moment as a network of infinite relations becomes meaningful through the shared use of symbols. "Wants and impulses" are then attached to these common meaning and "are thereby transformed into desires and purposes, which, since they implicate a common or mutually understood meaning, present new ties, converting a conjoint activity into a community of interest and endeavor." Whatever "truth" resides within these meaning are thus not found in reference to any original event to which it can be compared. As Dewey makes clear, "events cannot be passed from one to another, but [only] meanings [which] may be shared by means of signs."[72] The truth of these meaningful signs, which represent objects, are thus found in the richness and quality of experience which that meaning produces in future events. Democracy thus stands for a shared commitment to conjoint communication dedicated to experimenting with new meaningful objects that may prove themselves true by generating the events we desire.

A sympathetic comparison between events and objects with the traditional conceptions of percept and concept might lead one to assume that Dewey is simply putting a new spin on old ideas. Following this line of thought, one might be tempted to understand events as affairs of the perceptual body and objects as affairs of the mental concepts, with the distinction of time being between momentary sensations and universal ideas. After all, Dewey clearly associates objects with the products of rational and symbolic thought that can only be produced by organisms with the mental capacity for communication and reflection, while his definition of events links us to our biological history by making us one with other mammals in our capacity to experience an environment in its qualitative immediacy. Yet as soon as the distinction between percept and concept is made on the basis of a mind/body dualism, communication ceases to be a wonderful affair and becomes embroiled into the metaphysical problem of how percept and concepts relate not only to one another but also to the "outside" world, even when that latter relation is purely fabricated. The inevitable result of this problem is the familiar division between realism and skepticism that comes to rhetoric in the form of the tension between the neo-Aristotelian and the neo-Sophistical perspectives.

However, rhetoric interpreted from such a naturalistic reading of communication is constitutive in a way neo-Aristotelian or neo-Sophistical readings are not. Dewey's comparison of communication with transubstantiation is telling in this regard. For Dewey the phenomenon of one substance turning into another is not a "miracle," it is a quotidian affair that occurs whenever communication alters our relationship to something and thereby brings about a new event. In this way, turning a monster into window shade is as literal a transformation as turning bread into the body of Christ. For the neo-Aristotelian and the neo-Sophist alike, transubstantiation is a matter of distorted perception; they only disagree as to whether there exists a "real" object to which we owe our allegiance. For Dewey the experience of transubstantiation is an irreducible event in which mind and body, subject and object, are completely unified and indistinguishable. Whatever rhetorical discourse prepared the ground for this experience has no bearing on the reality of the event once it is had; the only concern for rhetoric—indeed, for any art—is what meaning we attribute to that event in reflection so as to improve the quality of our future events. The priest who makes someone feel they are eating the body of Christ has thus brought about as real of transubstantiation as the atheist who turns it back to bread.

The distinction between events and objects is thus not found in the difference between perception and cognition; it is found in terms of time and coherence. An event is always temporally continuous and qualitatively whole; it involves a total field of relations that comes to us in experience. An object is lasting, refined, and molded; it involves a selection and accumulation of qualities that cohere within a symbolic form and can be analyzed as having a distinct "meaning" or "definition." Objects can thus endure unchanged through events; events, however, lose their eventfulness as soon as they pass out of existence and enter into reflection. Dewey's list of objects, then, is a diverse collection, including "tables, the milky way, chairs, stars, cats, dogs, electrons, ghosts, centaurs, historic epochs and all the infinitely multifarious subject-matter of discourse designable by common nouns, verbs and their qualifiers."[73] Whereas we experience events—such as a startling noise, a joyous holiday, a bad year, or a tragic age—as a total qualitative drama, an object only exists insofar as there is present a relationship between an event and a symbol that implicates certain patterns of thought, feeling, and action that are consistent across a variety of contexts. The habitual interpretation of a noise as the tapping of a window shade thus stands for an object; the unique way this interpretation transacts within any situated moment stands for an event. Communication forms the medium through which these phases of experience interact, such that we can simultaneously experience the world both as an event and as an object. Put another way, communication enables us to act cooperatively within a shared eventful environment populated by objects.

The Rhetorical Situation as Event

The entire controversy over the rhetorical situation thus stems from the ingrained habit of interpreting past events as if they were actually objects—which is to say, the habit of employing the logic of the philosophic fallacy either to determine or to deny the reality lurking behind appearances. Both sides of this debate thus fail to acknowledge the eventful status of the rhetorical situation as something that only exists within shared experiences characterized by the realities of conflict, urgency, and uncertainty. The term "situation" rather than "event" is used only to symbolize a broader field of relations between events and objects that form a "contextual whole."[74] A rhetorical situation is simply a variant on what Dewey calls a "problematic" situation in which there is experienced to exist "something questionable, and hence provocative of investigation, examination, discussion."[75] A problematic situation is characterized "by such adjectives as confusing, perplexing, disturbed, unsettled, indecisive; and by such nouns as jars, hitches, breaks, blocks."[76] Most important, these characterizations are not descriptions of "subjective" or "distorted" perception; they describe actual parts of a situation that must be experienced before they are known. As Dewey observes, a "problem must be felt before it can be stated."[77] Only after a problematic situation is described in propositional form does it take on the properties of an object that then obtains truth value in reflection. Situations in their immediate form are like any other experienced event—they are things had before they are things cognized.

All this is to say that the nature of the rhetorical situation exists only in experience, not in some objective reality or persuasive discourse in isolation. A rhetorical situation is the product of the total relationship between an organism and its environment that lends force and effectiveness to rhetorical discourse. Absent the qualities that mark a situation as problematic, rhetoric lacks the motivation force to make audiences to action. In this respect it shares the same fate as any activity of reflective and critical thought. Dewey observes that "as long as our activity glides smoothly along from one thing to another, or as long as we permit our imagination to entertain fancies at pleasure, there is no call for reflection." Without a problem that confronts some habit or obstructs some desire, thought becomes mere fancy or busy-work. Genuine thinking begins in what Dewey calls a "forked-road situation, a situation which is ambiguous, which presents a dilemma, which proposes alternatives." Then, in the "suspense of uncertainty, we metaphorically climb a tree; we try to find some standpoint from which we may survey additional facts and, getting a more commanding view of the situation, may decide how the facts stand related to one another."[78] Rhetoric enters into this situation when people look for guidance from conflicting voices emanating from different trees, each voice charting a different horizon and projecting a different path.[79]

A rhetorical situation is thus the opposite of a technical one. In a technical situation only proper application of the tools of instrumental rationality is needed for resolution, much as a "How To" book provides an index of how to repair common household problems. In contradistinction, a rhetorical situation features the presence of a moral conflict that cannot be resolved by logical reasoning alone. Distinguishing between moral and nonmoral situations is thus vital for any understanding of the rhetorical situation. Nonmoral situations are those which only involve questions of means. In Dewey's terminology, this situation is "then a technical rather than a moral affair. It is a question of taste and of skill—of personal preference and of practical wisdom, or of economy, expediency."[80] A moral situation intrinsically confronts one with a clash of ends. The essence of the moral situation is an "internal and intrinsic conflict" in which one is "ignorant of the end and of good consequences."[81] In a moral situation "the practical meaning of the situation—that is to say the action needed to satisfy it—is not self-evident. It has to be searched for. There are conflicting desires and alternative apparent goods. What is needed is to find the right course of action, the right good."[82] Problematic situations with moral character thus require more than turning on the light to check a broken window shade; they require one to compare value systems, project consequences, and determine the proper relations of means and ends. Dewey offers the following prescient example:

> Take . . . the case of a citizen of a nation which has just declared war on another country. He is deeply attached to his own State. He has formed habits of loyalty and of abiding by its laws, and now one of its decrees is that he shall support war. . . . But he believes that this war is unjust, or perhaps he has a conviction that all war is a form of murder and hence wrong. One side of his nature, one set of convictions and habits, leads him to acquiesce in war; another deep part of his being protests. He is torn between two duties: he experiences a conflict between the incompatible values presented to him by his habits of citizenship and by his religious beliefs respectively. Up to this time, he has never experienced a struggle between the two; they have coincided and reenforced one another. Now he has to make a choice between competing moral loyalties and convictions.[83]

Being a problematic situation, a moral situation is not marked by the mere question of whether or not to obey some "table of commandments in a catechism." Such situations do not involve a clash of opposing goods but the violation of an acknowledged good for the sake of a recognized evil. This latter kind is a "conflict which takes place when an individual is tempted to do something which he is convinced is wrong" and is "merely permitting his desire to govern his beliefs." When the issue is simply the classification of an act as praiseworthy or blameworthy, one can usually draw on the resources of what Dewey calls "customary" morality. In customary morality, one "places the standard and rules of conduct in ancestral habit" and therefore emphasizes "conforming to prevailing modes of action." In Dewey's example of the pacifist torn between his allegiance to his ideals and to the state, something other than the conformity to established modes of action is at stake. We have instead what Dewey refers to as a "reflective" moral situation which forces us to rely on "conscience, reason, or to some principle which includes thought."[84] In a reflective moral situation, the problem is not getting oneself to do the good one already knows one should do; the problem is in determining the "good" one does not know and finding a means of pursing it.

Moral situations enter the field of the rhetorical when the debate over the good enters the public sphere and has public consequences. The man who questions his support for a war remains in the field of the dialectical insofar as he converses only with his friends and family and experiences his problem only to be his own. Yet his decision clearly has larger public significance when its consequences are placed in a larger social context. When these consequences begin to be felt by others, and when others begin to share his predicament, a public moral controversy arises concerning the obligation of a citizen and the duties of conscience. Dewey observes, for instance, that "there are periods in history when a whole community or a group in a community finds itself in the presence of new issues which its old customs do not adequately meet," such as "the age in Greece following the time of Pericles." In such times there arises "the necessity of criticizing existing customs and institutions from a new point of view"[85] and hence the necessity of rhetorical discourse to break with the past and forge a new future. Shared problems of reflective morality are thus at the heart of any rhetorical situation. More than just a feeling of uncertainty, rhetorical situations demand the tension of conflict that arises when two competing value systems clash within the context of judgment. During these times individuals require more than the familiar run-down of moral platitudes that mark most of what we conventionally label as "rhetoric"; they require suggestions of new avenues of thought and of action that might help them resolve their conflict in a novel way and thereby fill in the gaps left by habit and tradition.

A rhetorical situation thus represents a shared experience of crisis and conflict in public moral judgment that lends force and effectiveness to rhetorical discourse. Within those situations, rhetoric functions as the art of public advocacy that functions in a timely relationship to shared problematic situations of moral conflict, cognitive uncertainty, and practical urgency—regardless of whether that "timely relationship" is one of the prior constitution of those situations or subsequent reaction and framing of them. In the ontology of becoming, notions of cause and consequence are hypothetical projections—possible "truths"—used to guide action within any contextual moment. The only reality in the ontology of becoming is the reality as we experience at the moment of transformation and continuity. The question for rhetorical theory is not whether rhetorical situations "really" exist or not; indeed, if a rhetorical situation is not experienced as such, then it de facto does not exist. The question is how the shared experience of a rhetorical situation comes to be constituted and what realities are produced as a result of rhetorical intervention.

Mind, Consciousness, and Free Will

What makes this determination all the more problematic is that the "selves" immersed within a changing situation are themselves in a state of flux. To assume that becoming is only a condition of external nature, while the human individual stands above it as a god, is simply to revert back to the logic of being. Not even Plato dared assume stability in our mortal life. As he writes in the *Symposium*, "Even while each living thing is said to be alive and to be the same . . . he never consist of the same things, though he is called the same, but he is always being renewed and in other respects passing away, in his hair and flesh and bones and blood and his entire body. And it's not just in his body, but in his soul, too, for none of his manners, customs, opinions, desires, pleasures, pains or fears ever remains the same, but some are coming to be in him while other are passing away."[86] Given such a state of affairs, what makes rhetoric problematic as a theoretical object is that those who create and perform rhetorical discourse are as significantly altered by its activity as those who receive and interpret its message. Consequently one cannot ever assume a "stable" object in a rhetorical act. Self, audience, and situation are all objects that are coming to be in time, including the time spent on the razor's edge. A rhetorical theory must account for this quality of becoming while providing enough stability on which to practice both criticism and art. The key, once again, is in applying the naturalistic principles of continuity and transaction as they occur over time and in relationship to a contextual environment.

Dealing as it does with the nature of advocacy and choice, rhetoric intrinsically raises knotty issues of free will and determinism that have long plagued ethical philosophy. And rhetoric has always been schizophrenic about this issue. For instance, in the *Encomium of Helen* written by the Sophist Gorgias, logos emerges a mighty lord that makes people its slaves, such that the frail Helen should not be blamed for running off with Paris as a result of the suitor's irresistible eloquence. Yet if persuasion stripped Helen of her free will, what allowed Paris the autonomy to manipulate discourse as he saw fit? Gorgias thus appears to divide the world into gods and dupes, into those who stand apart from the domination of discourse and those caught completely within its web. For a Sophistical entrepreneur like Gorgias, this argument made his teaching all the more attractive for ambitious young men like Callicles who aspire to the role of god. But for a rhetorical theorist like Aristotle, attempting to develop a coherent system of thought, it was little more than showmanship that had scant connection with the study of human nature. There is more to rhetoric than overwhelming power.

What Aristotle recognized was that rhetoric can exist as an art only in a world of constrained choice. On the one hand, in a world marked by complete free will, of unconstrained choice, persuasion as such would be impossible because nobody could force or impel another to make a decision. The closest approximation could only be suggestion, or the laying before another of a possibility that they might embrace or reject. In this case, however, artistry becomes impotent to affect change insofar as its influence is a function of force. In a world of free will, one only requires the ability to transmit ideas from one mind to the other. On the other hand, in a world marked by complete determinism, of the denial of choice, persuasion can function as a force but at the expense of invention. For if a rhetor is also part of a deterministic system, then what they produce is simply a point of articulation of forces beyond themselves. Any art as a creative pursuit of doing and making thereby becomes an impossibility insofar as creativity is an illusion. If rhetorical theory is to account for both the inventive and persuasive components of rhetoric as an art, then, it must admit the possibility of choice both in creativity and in judgment while admitting that choices are always made within limits and are constrained by forces within one's social and natural environment. We possess, as it were, free will within limits such that our actions are determined but they may still be our own.

Dewey provides the starting point for a vocabulary of "choice" by distinguishing between "mind" and "consciousness." For him "mind" is a background, something "structural, substantial" that represents a system of meanings accumulated through time.[87] These "meanings" are not simply cognitive propositions that exist within a purely linguistic realm; these meanings are fundamentally practical. Thus "mind denotes the whole system of meanings *as they are embodied in the workings of organic life.*"[88] From this naturalistic premise it follows that the purpose of "mind" is not to represent "reality" but to create a system of meanings and practically guide us through our lived environment. Instead of being a kind of substance that inheres within the body, "mind is primarily a verb" and "denotes all the ways in which we deal consciously and expressly with the situation in which we find ourselves."[89] We do not articulate what is "on our minds"; we mind the aspects of situations that require "volitional, practical, acting in a purposive way."⁹⁰ Dewey emphasizes this practical nature of the mind by using the term "body-mind," which "simply designates what actually takes place when a living body is implicated in situations of discourse, communication, and participation."⁹¹ In other words Dewey uses "mind" as one might refer to a person as having an "artistic mind" or a "scientific mind," meaning that his or her acts are consistent with a certain coherent body of attitudes that mark a person's behavior as possessing a general quality.

Consciousness represents the moments in which components of mind are brought to bear in some practical situation. Consciousness is a *foreground,* and is a "process, a series of heres and nows."⁹² As such, one should not consider consciousness as an *entity* but an *activity.* Consciousness "is a name of the purposeful quality of an activity, for the fact that it is directed by a human aim."⁹³ These aims and methods clearly draw from the resources of mind, but they differ because they are developed and employed within some contextual event that has a unique character of its own. Consciousness is not simply a deductive application of mind; it is "that phase of a system of meanings which at a given time is undergoing re-direction, transitive transformation."⁹⁴ One thus has a distinct experience of consciousness only when these redirections and transformations occur. As with thinking, consciousness is not a pervasive and ongoing part of our experience. It happens at some times and not at others. What determines whether or not we fully engage the tools of consciousness is thus the context. Conscious choices occur only within total qualitative moments in which forces interact to produce a unique experience of contingency that denies easy categorization into one or another pigeonhole.

In this way it is to miss the point to argue against the possibility of conscious choice—or what is commonly termed "agency"—by observing that our thoughts are socially constructed by the discourses of culture. Dewey freely admits that "communication is a condition of consciousness" insofar as one must develop a socialized "mind" before being able to engage in conscious thinking at all. As Dewey notes, "Soliloquy is the product and reflect of converse with others, social communication not an effect of soliloquy. If we had not talked with others and they with us, we should never talk to and with ourselves."⁹⁵ Clearly our most private soliloquies thus draw from and refer back to the universes of discourse in which we live. Dewey continues: "Even the composition conceived in the head and, therefore, physically private, is public in its significant content, since it is conceived with reference to execution in a product that is perceptible and hence belongs to the common world."⁹⁶ Yet our soliloquies and private compositions, while drawing from the resources of mind, are still artistic productions with the potential to bring something new into that common world.

From the perspective of consciousness, the meaning of the rhetorical situation is not found in an objective problem that exists outside of human experience;

it is found within those experiential contexts in which the activities of consciousness become manifest. In other words, although "mind" provides rhetoric background resources from which to draw within the context of invention and judgment, it is "consciousness" which acts as the foreground in which those resources transact with environmental conditions in order to bring about some transformation of meaning which then re-acts upon mind. The important thing to consider is that while consciousness always exists within some immediate eventful moment, all events do not require the activity of consciousness. So long as we can succeed by "minding" a situation by drawing from existing meanings, consciousness lies largely dormant. Action follows a script that has already been written, with one event leading naturally to the next and each accompanied by some habitual action. The *telos* of rhetoric can thus be described as the provocation of the activity of consciousness by setting forth and then narrowing the available choices for subsequent action. The rhetorical situation represents a type of experience that pushes consciousness to the foreground such that genuine transformation is possible.[97]

A modern parallel of Dewey's distinction between mind and consciousness is Foucault's distinction between discourse and thought. Foucault associates discourse with a broader network of meanings and power relations tied up in forms of coordinated action, while thought is connected with more individual and particular moments of critical reflection which tend to break free—even if for a moment—from the limits of discourse. Thus despite tendencies in his early work that imply that we are locked within disciplinary systems of micropower, he never abandoned hope that we might achieve genuine transformation through thought. "Thought does exist, both beyond and before systems and edifices of discourse," he writes. "It is something that is often hidden but always drives everyday behaviors. There is always a little thought occurring even in the most stupid institutions; there is always thought even in silent habits. Criticism consists in uncovering that thought and trying to change it; showing that things are not as obvious as people believe, making it so that what is taken for granted is no longer taken for granted. To do criticism is to make harder those acts which are now too easy."[98] Both Dewey and Foucault emphasize the importance of using language to bring about a sense of public moral crisis that stimulates conscious thought and prepares the ground for the kind of genuine transformation often made possible through rhetorical intervention.

The Habitual Self

Rhetorical theory must explain how these types of transformative situations come into being over time. This explanation, however, cannot be determined only through a synchronic interpretation of experience as a set of discrete data points; experience must be viewed diachronically in the context of the total eventful relationship between the organism and its environment. The most lasting product of this relationship is the formation of habits. For Dewey, habits are "interactions of elements contributed by the make-up of an individual with elements supplied by the out-door world."[99] Habits are reservoirs of experience that come to represent the life history of an individual in the form of sets of behaviors which aid navigation through a familiar world. In the sense that they involve the forming of material for practical, then, habits are themselves a kind of *technē*. As Dewey explains, "Habits are arts. They involve skill of sensory and motor organs, cunning or craft, and objective materials. They assimilate objective energies, and eventuate in command of environment."[100] In this way Dewey's use of "habit" is synonymous with what Kenneth Burke calls a "pattern of experience." Burke explains: "Experience arising out of a relationship between an organism and its environment, the adjustments of the organism will depend upon the nature of the environment. By 'adjustments of the organism' we refer to any kind of adaptation; thus: firm musculature as the concomitant of life under pioneer conditions; obesity as the concomitant of plenty and confinement; vindictiveness as the concomitant of oppression; timidity as the concomitant of protection; trustfulness as the concomitant of fair dealing—a distinction in the environment calling forth a distinction in the organism."[101]

A habit, then, is a pattern of experience that comes into existence as a way of adjusting to persistent environmental conditions. Habits are neither mere repetitions nor thoughtless actions; they are methodical ways of acting in response to certain problems or tasks that involve physical as well as mental processes. Thus "habit does not preclude the use of thought, but it determines the channels within which it operates. Thinking is secreted in the interstices of habits."[102] Foucault makes a similar point with respect to another synonym of habit—attitude—when he calls it a "mode of relating to contemporary reality . . . a way of thinking and feeling; a way, too, of acting and behaving that at one and the same time marks a relation of belonging and presents itself as a task."[103] Foucault's notion of attitude is consistent with Dewey's conception of habit. For instance, Dewey notes that "the sailor, miner, fisherman and farmer think, but their thoughts fall within the framework of accustomed occupations and relationships."[104] The existence of habits/attitudes/patterns of experience reveal the erroneousness of assuming that acts of cognition, of "mind," are somehow detached from situational context. For Dewey, thought and action are inextricably bound together, for "thought which does not exist within ordinary habits of action lacks means of execution."[105] Based on this principle, even "mind" is itself a kind of habit, for it represents the power to understand meanings "in terms of the use to which they are turned in joined or shared situations."[106] Without habits of mind developed through social communication, we would be unable to develop a shared sense of experience that characterizes human culture.

It is the very habitual nature of human culture that provides the contextual backdrop to rhetorical practice. Habit, in other words, tends to coalesce within a community and formalize into custom, or those traditional habits that any social group instills in its members through ritual and education. These customs function as a form of recalcitrance to any attempt at rhetorical transformation. According to Dewey, "Habit is energy organized in certain channels. When interfered with, it swells as resentment and as an avenging force. To say that it will be obeyed, that custom makes law, that *nomos* is lord of all, is after all only to say that habit is habit."[107] The recognition of the power of *nomos* is another way of recognizing the power of habit. Following Aristotle, Dewey observes that habits eventually become a kind of "second nature."[108] Consequently "habit is even more solidly entrenched in beliefs, in modes of thinking and understanding, than in outer actions."[109] One of the reasons for this fact is that stability of habits of belief gives us a sense of peace and security by assuring us that the world not only makes sense but also makes sense in such a way as to justify our familiar practices: "Habits bind us to orderly and established ways of action because they generate ease, skill and interest in things to which we have grown used and because they instigate fear to walk in different ways, and because they leave us incapacitated for the trial of them."[110] Habits of thought and habits of action thus positively reinforce one another; habits of thought envision the world in such a way as to enable habits of action that actualize or sustain that vision of the world. In this sense habits penetrate to the very core of what we call the self. "All habits are demands for certain kinds of activity; and they constitute the self," Dewey explains. "In any intelligible sense of the word will, they are will. They form our effective desires and they furnish us with our working capacities. They rule our thoughts, determining which shall appear and be strong and which shall pass from light into obscurity."[111]

The notion that the habits we acquire from our social environment rule our thoughts and guide our actions puts the lie to any lingering notion of the antonymous self that can create or interpret rhetorical discourse at will. For Dewey habit *is* will in much the same way that, for Burke, motive is attitude. Consequently selfhood is not something that springs forth from the romantic inner self, for "selfhood is not something which exists apart from association and intercourse. The relationships which are produced by the fact that interests are formed in this social environment are far more important than are the adjustments of isolated selves." The family, for instance, is more than just an aggregate of egos, "it is an enduring form of association . . . in which each member gets direction for his conduct by thinking of the whole group and his place in it." The same goes for associations of community and nation. Their codes articulate conceptions of virtue and vice that function to channel behaviors within certain grooves and thereby create a sense of common origin and destiny. The natural result, of course, is that "customary morals naturally 'make it hot' for those who transgress its code, and make it comfortable for those who conform." At their best, then, these collective identifications create a sense of well-being and sympathetic community; at their worst, they culminate in factionalism and strife in which "the standards of valuation are based on the class, race, color, with which one identifies oneself" and "national life is organized on the basis of exclusiveness and tends to generate suspicion, fear, often hatred, of other peoples."[112] Regardless of whether rhetoric reinforces, exploits, or confronts these habitual valuations, it must take account of them.

Here, then, is one challenge to the possibility of a democratic rhetoric. If habit is so resilient, how is genuine transformation possible? How can choice and creativity exist in an environment dominated by habit, custom, and convention, particularly as they are formed as systems of micropower organized by discourse and propaganda? The answer to this question lies in the relationship of habit to what Dewey called "impulse." For Dewey "the word impulse suggests something primitive, yet loose, undirected, initial." As an example Dewey points to the case of a newborn baby whose experience has not yet been socialized and exists largely as a flux of "inchoate and scattered impulses." The baby does not know what it wants or how to get it but only feels a mix of biological urges and unformed emotions that usually find their outlet in the baby's one dominant form of expression—crying. Impulse, as something instinctual, loose, and expressive, acts as a dialectical partner to habit, which suggests something cultured, formal, and purposeful. Whereas habit is a well-worn path, impulse is a point of deviation and initiation: "Impulses are the pivots upon which the re-organization of activities turn, they are agencies of deviation, for giving new directions to old habits and changing their quality."[113] The presence of impulse provides the freedom to move or be moved in any direction, and thus it provides the potential energy necessary to chart new paths of thought and action.

Impulses, however, neither have "agency" of their own nor are always present. They occur only with certain situational contexts and even then have no particular end or purpose. They are simply moments of tension that build up energy that seeks release. Without such a translation into some form of "linear" behavior that contains some purpose, either constitutive or expressive, impulse festers or dissolves. Dewey has us imagine, for instance, a person who feels the impulse of anger brought about by some interpersonal exchange. Without some outlet, anger is merely "a physical spasm, a blind dispersive burst of wasteful energy." However, if this person is a poet who sits down to try to make sense of this feeling, anger then "gets quality, significance, when it becomes a smouldering sullenness, an annoying interruption, a peevish irritation, a murderous revenge, a blazing indignation." In other words the bare impulse of "anger" is given purpose and significance by being translated into language and placed within the realm of socially accepted meanings that can be understood and acted upon in a controlled manner. Another rhetorically rich example Dewey offers us comes in the form of fear: "Any impulse may become organized into almost any disposition according to the way it interacts with surroundings. Fear may become abject cowardice, prudent caution, reverence for superiors or respect for equals; an agency for credulous swallowing of absurd superstitions or for wary skepticism. A man may be chiefly afraid of the spirits of his ancestors, of officials, of arousing the disapproval of his associates, of being deceived, of fresh air, or of Bolshevism. The actual outcome depends upon how the impulse of fear is interwoven with other impulses."[114]

The idea that the same bare impulse may be formed into different kinds of fear speaks to the neo-Sophistical rhetorical spirit. That rhetoric might turn a bump into the night into a ghost, an open window, or a Bolshevik simply signals the malleability of impulse once it becomes incorporated into a larger system of habitual meanings. Yet this observation on its own tells us nothing about how such habitual interpretations of impulse can be changed. Dewey notes that "impulse is a source, an indispensable source, of liberation; but only as it is employed in giving habits pertinence and freshness does it liberate power."[115] The function of radical rhetoric is precisely to give habits new pertinence, freshness, and power to liberate experience beyond the constraints of convention. The problem with neo-Sophistical interpretations is that they understand the relationship between rhetoric and impulse only in the immediate moment, but impulse, like consciousness, only arises within a background of habits that already have worn interpretive pathways into the self. It is one thing to convince a young child that the thumps on the roof are Santa Claus; it is something much more difficult to convince that child after a few years have passed that Santa Claus does not exist. Once habits are in place, they greedily absorb impulses into a preexisting interpretive frame that resists modification by linguistic appeal alone.

The answer to the rhetorical question of change must do more than acknowledge the constitutive power of language; it must situate that power within the relationship between the organism and its environment. The most important aspect of Dewey's naturalism for rhetorical theory is his insistence on tying the rise of impulse and the activity of consciousness with the disruption of habits. No matter how "real" is an objective problem or how potentially "persuasive" is a rhetorical discourse, transformation is largely impossible as long as preexisting habits can continue without constraint. However, when habits "operate in a situation to which they are not accustomed, in an unusual situation, a new adjustment is required. Hence there is shock, and an accompanying perception of dissolving and reforming meaning . . . together with suspense as to what it will be."[116] This sense of shock and suspense gives rhetoric its force and effectiveness. When situations arise that obstruct the habits of a community, rhetoric steps in to redirect impulses into new channels created in part by modifying or recombining already established habits. The result is change with continuity, or a new form of practice that nonetheless draws from the traditions of the past situations by transforming the meaning of one's environment such that old habits no longer seem up to the task of fulfilling new demands—when, in Burke's terms, we have pushed the neo-Malthusian "proliferation of *habits* to their physical limits" and have, as it were, come to the end of the road and must forge a new path.[117]

Of course, when shared events have not already brought about sense of shock and disruption, a rhetor must somehow create a sense of urgency. This cannot happen simply by acting the role of Chicken Little, however. Simply stating that a problem exists, even when a reasonable conclusion, does little to alter habits so long as they work unhindered. Change must come instead by attempting to exploit tensions between habits that exist simultaneously within a culture. This strategy of change is only possible because, being a creature of habit, the human "self is capable of including within itself a number of inconsistent selves, of unharmonized dispositions." The same principle then applies to a community or a culture of selves. According to Dewey, "No adult environment is all of one piece. The more complex a culture is, the more certain it is to include habits formed on differing, even conflicting patterns. Each custom may be rigid, unintelligent in itself, and yet this rigidity may cause it to wear upon others. The resulting attrition may release impulse for new adventures."[118] In the absence of dramatic disruptive events, patient rhetors thus work to exaggerate this tension between cultural habits, exploiting the discomfort of dissonance until the situation arises when something must give and impulses break free of their moorings. This the kind of situation Burke says is marked by "perspective by incongruity," a stage of "rending and tearing" by which swift and shrewd eloquence arises from the "merging of categories once felt to be mutually exclusive."[119]

This sense of being set loose on a new adventure, of standing on unfamiliar ground, is the reason why rhetorical discourse has always derived its power from emotion. From a rationalistic standpoint, emotions have always been seen as "internal" states that cloud reason and perception with subjective feeling. In contradistinction, Dewey externalizes emotions while making it a means by which we come to "know" our surroundings. Emotion, for him, is primarily a form of adaptive behavior that makes us aware of and concerned about the relationship of ourselves to our natural and social environment. An emotion is "an attitude or disposition which is a function of objective things,"[120] and the "more anything, whether an object, scene, idea, fact, or study, cuts into and across our experience, the more it stirs and arouses. An emotion is the register of the extent and way in which we are personally implicated, involved, in anything, no matter how external it is to us physically."[121] We do not simply love, fear, envy, or hope in a void; we love some body, we fear some thing, we envy some situation, we hope for some end. Emotions function as ties that bind us to our environment.

Rhetorical situations are naturally emotional because they are populated by events and objects that disrupt our habits. Like impulse, emotion arises when there is a break in habits which causes us a disturbance and leads us to search for some way of returning to a state of balance: "Emotion is a perturbation from clash or failure of habit, and reflection, roughly speaking, is the painful effort of disturbed habits to readjust themselves."[122] However, an emotion differs from a bare impulse in being "to or from or about something objective, whether in fact or in idea."[123] Emotion makes us aware of and relate to our environment in ways in which impulse does not. In the moments when habits fail to guide our behavior, emotion tells us what is threatening, what is discordant, and what is troubling, just as much as it tells us what is desirable, what it helpful, and what is trustworthy. To use Dewey's earlier example, when one feels the *impulse* of anger, one cannot identify its cause or channel where its energy should be directed. The result is a lashing out at anything that comes near, as a sick animal lashes out even at those who might help. In the *emotion* of anger one develops an emotional stance toward a particular object or person that directs behavior in a controlled manner—as an animal might growl menacingly at a tormenter in order to repulse it. The analogous function of rhetoric is to make something seem attractive or repulsive to an audience in order to facilitate productive action. Rhetoric translates impulses into emotions that then become tied to new habits that seek ultimately to reestablish harmony between the organism and its environment and achieve what Burke calls a "reorientation."[124]

Propaganda and the Mass Society

The rhetorical transformation of a situation requires a rhetorical transformation of the self that functions within that situation. Self and situation are inextricably bound within the activity of habit, and the rupture of their habitual connection sparks the rise of impulse, emotion, and consciousness that makes rhetorical persuasion possible. What makes such situations distinctly rhetorical is when they accompany feelings of rupture shared within a community that are incapable of being resolved by conventional or technical means. The *kairotic* moment appears; timely advocacy fills the gap and moves an audience to judgment. Consequently the "self" transformed in a rhetorical situation includes more than the individual speaker or hearer; it includes the communal self known in democracy as the "public." The nature of radical democratic rhetoric thus cannot be understood without interpreting its relationship to how publics are formed, maintained, dissolved, and reconstituted over time.

The philosophical assertion that publics actually exist has always required something of a leap of faith. Given the obvious fact that even the most closely knit group of individuals do not think, feel, or act the same way toward anything, how can we assert—in anything more than a crassly political manner—anything approaching unanimity of attitude or belief? It would seem, as Lippmann ironically suggested, that we might be better off siding with those social theorists "strongly nominalist in their cast of mind" who "look upon the abstract concept of a corporate people as mere words and rather like conjuring up spooks."[125] By "nominalist" Lippmann means someone who believes that things only exists as discrete particulars, and that any term that goes beyond the naming of those particulars functions much as a temporary bin into which a bunch of particular things are arbitrarily thrown and given a label. In rhetorical theory, for instance, Michael Calvin McGee views general terms such as "the public" as shorthand ways of referring to a group of discrete particulars that share no essential relationship. The "people" are at root a "mass illusion," for "the only human reality is that of the individual; groups, whether as small as a Sunday-school class or as big as a whole society, are infused with an artificial identity."[126] In this sense McGee is a nominalist to the extent that he suggests that a public is a mass of individuals temporarily sharing in the same collective fantasy brought into being through rhetorical discourse. As rhetoric is the means by which that fantasy is created and propagated, then, the public is a constitutive product of rhetoric; outside of such rhetorical fantasies, we revert to atomic individuals in a social vacuum.

While such fantasies clearly exist, they fail to account for democratic social life as it exists. What McGee actually describes is the condition of technological societies that are locked within a bleak cycle that vacillates between anarchy and mass delusion, a cycle facilitated by political rhetors who struggle for temporary hegemony over a disorganized mass through systematic propaganda. This is the world described graphically by Jacques Ellul as one that is both an "individualist and a mass society." Although often thought to be contradictory tendencies, Ellul demonstrates they are actually counterparts: "An individualist society must be a mass society, because the first move toward liberation of the individual is to break up the small groups that are an organic fact of the entire society." This breakup of traditional communities and families is often naïvely though to be a source of "liberation" for the individual, but in actual fact the individual is "placed in a minority position and burdened at the same time with a total, crushing responsibility." The result is a paradox—that the individual feels to be a "superman" at the same time that he actually seeks refuge in the propaganda produced for the mass. The culmination of these tendencies is the technological mass society, a society characterized by "considerable population density in which local structures and organizations are weak, currents of opinion are strongly felt, men are grouped into large and influential collectives, the individual is part of these collective, and a certain psychological unity exists. ... Despite differences of environment, training, or situation, the men of a mass society have the same preoccupations, the same interest in technical matters, the same mythical beliefs, the same prejudices."[127]

The bleak uniformity of the mass society is hardly a universal condition of human nature, however. It is the product of specific social conditions that creates such a vast disruption between the organism and its environment that individuals feel completely unhinged from the constraints of habit necessary for sustained communal life. This fragmentation and expansion was, of course, the dominant problem of the public that emerged with modernity around the twentieth century. As Lippmann observed, the "private citizen today has come to feel rather like a deaf spectator in the back row, who ought to keep his mind on the mystery off there, but cannot quite manage to stay awake. ... He lives in a world which he cannot see, does not understand, and is unable to direct."[128] As demonstrated by the totalitarian horrors that soon came about, however, human beings cannot live their lives deaf and asleep. As Dewey writes, the "individual cannot remain intellectually a vacuum. If his ideas and beliefs are not the spontaneous function of a communal life in which he shares, a seeming consensus will be secured as a substitute by artificial and mechanical means."[129] Within the theater of a bewildered public, the propaganda of nationalism helped people see, understand, and act as a "people." But as Dewey notes, this sense of belonging brought about through propagandistic means is artificial, transient, and fickle:

> In consequence, our uniformity of thought is much more superficial than it seems to be. ... Its superficial character is evident in its instability. All agreement of thought obtained by external means, by repression and intimidation, however subtle, and by calculated propaganda and publicity, is of necessity superficial; and whatever is superficial is in continual flux. The methods employed produce mass credulity, and this jumps from one thing to another according to the dominant suggestions of the day. We think and feel alike—but only for a month or a season. Then comes some other sensational event or personage to exercise a hypnotizing uniformity of response. At a given time, taken in cross-section, conformity is the rule. In a time span, taken longitudinally, instability and flux dominate.[130]

This social condition stands in contrast to premodern conditions in which segregated classes and their respective principles and aims could "exist side by side in different strata. . . . Vigor, courage, energy, enterprise here; submission, patience, charm, personal fidelity there." Although society itself was differentiated into a fixed hierarchy that effectively condemned certain classes to perpetual servitude, each class was able to develop its own culture that provided its members a uniform code of conduct that ensured stability and a sense of belonging. This condition started to fracture by the eighteenth century and give way by the nineteenth. Dewey narrates the shift: "Mobility invades society. War, commerce, travel, communication, contact with the thoughts and desires of other classes, new inventions in productive industry, disturb the settled distribution of customs." The result is a predictable divide between the habits of inherited tradition and the demands and impulses brought about by a new environment: "Customs relating to what has been and emotions referring to what may come to be go their independent ways."[131] With one's norms and habits no longer determined by birth, a plurality of identities offers the opportunity to expressed previously suppressed emotions and impulses. At once liberating, it also creates a sense of loss, confusion, and drift, culminating in Lippmann's pronouncement that the public has become a mere phantom that does not know that it is dead.

It is no coincidence, then, that propaganda is associated with the technological society. The success of propaganda is contingent upon a society in which "individuals" are simply components of a uniform mass society. As Ellul points out, the mass "individual" is actually alienated from his or her own desires and possibilities, resulting in that "individual's inclination to lose himself in something bigger than he is, to dissipate his individuality, to free his ego of all doubt, conflict, and suffering—through fusion with others; to devote himself to a great leader and a great cause."[132] Propaganda, as an organized and systematic form of mass persuasion, can thus only be possible in a society made up of individuals capable of acting as a mass.

Rhetoric and Character

The rise of propaganda threatens the tradition of rhetoric in the same way that the technological society challenges the ideals of classical humanism. In other words rhetoric and humanism are linked by certain ethical ideals. The classical rhetorical tradition from Protagoras to Aristotle to Cicero to Quintilian has always championed the ideal of the virtuous autonomous self creating a noble discourse to be delivered to intimate others. One thinks, for example, of articles like the one which appears in the 1923 *Quarterly Journal of Speech Education* essay that begins "One of the greatest needs in the world today is people of character."[133] This is because rhetoric grew out of the Greek *polis* in which the civic ideal was excellence in word and deed. Rhetoric was thus less a means of public suasion than it was a way of establishing personal honor and demonstrating self-discipline in public. It is only by this measurement, after all, that the *Apology* by Socrates could have been handed down as one of the most eloquent rhetorical performances in history.

Of course, such noble aspirations have become severely problematic following what Stewart Hall calls "the critique of the self-sustaining subject at the center of post-Cartesian western metaphysics."[134] Consequently the language of "character" has given way to talk of "subjectivities" or "identities." According to Hall, then, identity is "the meeting point, the point of *suture,* between on the one hand the discourses and practices which attempt to 'interpellate,' speak to us or hail us into place as the social subjects of particular discourses, and on the other hand, the processes which produce subjectivities, which construct us as subjects which can be 'spoken.'"[135] For Hall our subjectivities are the points of articulation that represent the interstices of our web of identities that occurs at any historical moment. Rather than us speaking language, language speaks us.

From this perspective, character in the traditional sense of something stable, internal, and continuous becomes impossible. As Bauman notes, with the eclipse of the humanist subject also goes the ethics of the "pilgrim," or that person who journeys for the purpose of building a coherent self in relation to a fixed ideal. For the pilgrim, "destination, the set purpose of life's pilgrimage, gives form to the formless, make a whole out of the fragmentary, lends continuity to the episodic."[136] In contrast Hall describes contemporary notions of identity as "increasingly fragmented and fractured; never singular but multiply constructed across different, often intersecting and antagonistic, discourses, practices and positions."[137] Trapped as we are within a constant interplay between identification and division, between inclusion and exclusion, pilgrimage becomes simply expressive of another cultural identity. Therefore the "pilgrim" as a representative metaphor for the social actor gives way to what Bauman calls the "stroller," the "vagabond," the "tourist," and the "player," each of whom experience time as "a flat collection or an arbitrary sequence of present moments" that do not accumulate into anything whole or lasting.[138] Their development is not progressive but scattered; they do not travel toward a distant horizon but wander within a maze, and their subjectivities are representative of their momentary efforts to locate themselves at a point.

Yet the self is no more intrinsically a phantom than is the public. The ghostly status of either is a culmination of historical contingency, not metaphysical essence. The key in recovering the insight of classical humanism is to view character not as a natural inheritance but as a work of art. For Dewey, as for Foucault, character is not some romantic essence that lies hidden within the individual soul. Character, like habit, is a product of conscious art. In fact, for

Dewey, "character *is* the interpenetration of habits."[139] One labors to produce character by working to develop a system of habits which interconnect with and reinforce one other with respect to common interests. In this way character is an "abiding unity in which different acts leave their lasting traces."[140] This "abiding unity" speaks not of a transcendental ego but rather the biological and embodied self that persists through time within a constant process of becoming. As Danisch explains via Foucault, the self is an ongoing aesthetic creation that echoes many of the themes of epideictic rhetoric insofar as it is a product on ongoing acts of praise, blame, judgment, and discipline: "Aesthetic self-creation is not equivalent to resistance for Foucault; nor is it a question of simply expressing oneself. Instead, it is a process of understanding the structures and values that order individuals about, of refusing those structures and values, and of using them to produce and to display new ways of living. It is also a way of celebrating the self and thus practicing a kind of epideictic rhetoric that seeks to produce power relations and new forms of agency."[141]

If our lives can, in fact, be a work of art, then the entire basis of character is based on the naturalistic assumption that there exists within us something which endures across situations that both acts and is influenced by action. For Dewey, habit is this "something." Habit reaches down "into the very structure of the self; it signifies a building up and solidifying of certain desires; an increased sensitiveness and responsiveness to certain stimuli, a confirmed or an impaired capacity to attend to and think about certain things."[142] A person with character cultivates and applies certain habits across a variety of different environment in such a way that provides a sense of stability, courage, competence, and focus. Consequently "it demands character to stick it out when conditions are adverse, as they are when there is danger incurring the ill-will of others, or when it requires more than ordinary energy to overcome obstacles."[143] Without character, in other words, one only has the resources of the mask, and a mask is easily shattered in an environment filled with cudgels and easily replaced in an industrial society prepared to sell you a new one.

It is Dewey's emphasis on creating the conditions that make character possible that guides his educational ideal. From Dewey's earliest educational writing, he condemned the fixation on "information" and memorization. A genuine discipline does not enforce obedience through threats of force but provides tools for self-mastery and the mastery of one's situation. As he writes in *Democracy and Education*, "Discipline means power at command; mastery of the resources available for carrying through the action undertaken. . . . Discipline is positive. To cow the spirit, to subdue inclination, to compel obedience, to mortify the flesh, to make a subordinate perform an uncongenial task—these things are or are not disciplinary according as they do or do not tend to the development of power to recognize what one is about and to persistence in accomplishment."[144] The point is that the character of the self—to the extent that the self possesses character—is neither a product of birth nor of discourse but a product of disciplined habits directed toward a goal.

The relationship between rhetoric and character is thus not simply a residue of naïve faith in democracy and the powers of the individual. It is a relationship born out of a mutual emphasis on the significance of the methods of art in creating individuals capable of producing and receiving rhetorical discourse and thereby capable of bringing about what Thomas Farrell describes as a rhetorical culture "in which motives of competing parties are intelligible, audiences available, expressions reciprocal, norms translatable, and silences noticeable."[145] This is a far different society than the one described by Ellul. In a propagandistic society, motives are incomprehensible, audiences are manufactured, expressions are uniform, norms are ephemeral, and cacophony reigns. The pervasiveness of the latter thus stands as a constraint to the realization of the former.

Locating the Public

The notion of the public as essentially a mass illusion parallels the notion of the self as essentially a mask. The two assertions stand or fall together. For Dewey, however, these claims overstate their cases by falling once again into the philosophic fallacy that denies the importance of context and time. It is a matter of common sense, for instance, that "stability of character is an affair of degrees, and is not to be taken absolutely. No human being, however mature, has a completely formed character, while any child in the degree in which he has acquired attitudes and habits has a stable character to that extent."[146] Children, for instance, are notoriously adaptive, blending in to any new situation by altering their behavior to conform to the needs of the social group even when it results in blatant self-contradiction; by contrast, grandparents as a rule are frustratingly consistent in their attitudes even when the practical situation demands a different approach. A child might adopt an identity for the short term but utterly lack character, while a woman of many years may retain a sense of character even after disease has removed any conscious knowledge of identity. The same is thus true of collective associations. A mass of people might come together and form a loose and temporary association based on conscious interests and yet dissolve as soon as the exigency has passed. By contrast a traditional community unified by historical rituals and conventions may retain habitual codes of behavior even when exigent forces might demand adaptation and change. Indeed one of the lasting effects of Dewey's two-year visit to China was his fascination with how the depth of Chinese traditional culture was able to outlast the momentary shifts in state politics and emerge almost unchanged.[147] One thus cannot make blanket assertions of the fragmentation or unity of any self or social group without considering the history out of which they emerge and the context in which they act.

The rhetorical significance of both character and the public is that they provide a basis to understand the nature of both recalcitrance and possibility when it comes to persuasion. The problem for rhetorical theory, in other words, has never been to explain why people do what they do; it is to account for and address situations in which people do not do what we want them to do. Any theory that would posit both self and society as rhetorical fantasies that give order to chaos has no resources to account for why people choose some fantasies over others. Moreover, they are impotent to explain why shifts in cognitive belief often do not result in appreciable changes in action or attitude. The only thing they can say is that certain changes happened and then attribute those changes retroactively to rhetorical causes. However, the mere reinterpretation of past events does not make an art; even a genuine art of history uses theory to improve future practice. Likewise, rhetorical theory must position any rhetorical act with respect to habits—mental, emotional, and physical—that might constrain and enable the accomplishment of some desired end. The point is that once we acknowledge the presence of habits, we are no longer talking just about sutures, interpellations, intersections, or fragments; we are talking about particular and concrete forms of behavior embedded within a self or a society. The rhetorical question is not whether such things essentially exist or not; the question is whether they have existence within the individuals or populations that are at issue within a situated rhetorical context.

An ethical rhetorical theory calls us to address what kinds of habits are necessary to produce a rhetorical democracy that does not dissolve into mass uniformity or chaos. Clearly the kind of "people" articulated by McGee would be incapable of producing anything close to a democracy. They would, instead, approximate the condition of the mass society. Moreover, the very assumption that a public must achieve some kind of uniformity of belief to be a public is itself problematic. As Hauser points out, "The utter diversity of developed societies provides us with daily reminders of our differences," such that "treating 'the public' as if it consists of an entity—an identifiable group with interests that persist across time—compounds the problem of locating its basic character." The only alternative, then, is to view the character of a democratic public in terms of its habits of communication rather than belief. For Hauser the public represents "the interdependent members of society who hold different opinions about a mutual problem and who seek to influence its resolution through discourse."[148] In other words democratic publics have developed the habit of addressing collective problems through cooperative judgment based on communication. This habit persists across differences; it is what unites people in a common endeavor even when their more specific interests stand in tension.

These communicative habits are rooted in the need to cooperatively regulate the indirect and lasting consequences of behavior that result from cohabitation of environment. The character of a public thus derives from what Dewey describes as the natural "fact that all modes of associated behavior may have extensive and enduring consequences which involves others beyond those directly engaged in them." When this fact is not recognized, of course, or the consequences of interconnected behavior are not "intellectually and emotionally appreciated," the shared interest that bring about a public remains inchoate. As an example, Dewey points to earlier periods in which a population lacked a sanctioned legal process to deal with issues of personal injury. At that time resolution of these affairs was the responsibility "of those directly concerned and nobody else's direct business." However, the "consequences of the quarrel did not remain confined to those immediately concerned. Feuds ensued, and the blood-quarrel might implicate large numbers and endure for generations." To break this cycle required a cooperative effort on both sides to regulate action that would better serve the needs of both parties. It thus was the recognition "the harm wrought by it to whole families brought a public into existence."[149] The "shared interest" here is thus not a uniformity of belief or attitude. Quite the opposite, that there were differences between the parties was the motivating force behind the formation of a public who would rely on a cooperative communicative process to solve shared problems without mutual annihilation. To the extent that an increase in the breadth of communication and awareness has brought together individuals, organizations, and nations from across the globe to manage the consequences of interconnected behavior, one can reasonably speak of a "global public" now coming into being.

To speak of the public in such a broad scope does not negate the clear multiplicity of publics that also exist at any given time. The greater the scope of what one encompasses within the idea of a public, the less specific is the nature of that public. At a global scale one can say only that diverse groups of people have recognized their codependency and interconnectedness and developed habits of communication to meliorate the indirect consequences of behavior. Yet as shared interests become more particular to a group, any public necessarily narrows its attention and inclusiveness. Consequently any larger public always consists of a multiplicity of publics that vary depending on the nature of the consequences being regulated. As Westbrook observes, Dewey's study *The Public and Its Problems* "might better have been titled 'Publics and Their Problems,'" for in that book he made it clear that "in any given society *the* Public was, at most, a collective noun designating plural publics that concerned themselves with the indirect consequences of particular forms of associated activity."[150] Included in the rubric of a "public" might thus be an extended family, the chamber of commerce, a social movement, a political interest group, a neighborhood association, or a social networking site. The mark of a public is not simply a collection of people who hold common values, norms, beliefs or interest; it represents that group insofar as they concern themselves with regulating consequences of activity through communicative means.

Unfortunately Dewey created confusion by making this point largely negatively. Instead of advancing the positive claim that a public consisted of publics, he characterized the multiplication of publics as a problem of modernity. With the fragmentation of the local community and increased mobility of the modern citizen, "there are too many publics, for conjoint actions which have indirect, serious and enduring consequences are multitudinous beyond comparison, and each one of them crosses the others and generates its own group of persons especially affected with little to hold these different publics together in an integrated whole."[151] This statement should not be read as a call for a return to a single, monolithic public that represents the general will. As Asen has shown, "Dewey did not object to multiplicity" or support a "reduction of publics or a singular conception of the public" but only wanted to point out that "publics did not interact enough."[152] The issue was fragmentation without subsequent reintegration, culminating in a society of isolated and largely antagonistic groups rather than a cooperative multilayered structure of publics, each with their own unique concerns but sharing a common interest in generating a collective sense of well-being. In Dewey's words the "need is that the nonpolitical forces organize themselves to transform political structures: that the divided and troubled publics integrate."[153] This need led Dewey to address the crucial issue of public communication.

Public Opinion and the Public Sphere

The democratic challenge has always been how to constitute a public that is unified in purpose and method without regressing to a merely mechanical uniformity—to integrate those publics into an interactive whole while still maintaining the diversity and flexibility of its parts. The challenge of a rhetorical democracy, then, is to bring about an enlightened public opinion through the free play of rhetoric in a public sphere. By "public opinion," Dewey simply means "judgment which is formed and entertained by those who constitute the public and is about public affairs."[154] Like the public itself, of course, public opinion is no monolithic entity; it represents a tentative summary of general tendencies. And what marks an "enlightened" public opinion is not how it matches an arbitrary tabulation of morals, facts, and principle, but that it is the result of a free and open process of mutual communication. The formation of democratic public opinion is "a cooperative undertaking, one which rests upon persuasion, upon ability to convince and be convinced by reason," and produces "the common mind, the common intention, resulting from free exchange and communication of ideas, from teaching and from being taught."[155] In sharp contrast to the idea of public opinion as a synchronic slice of the common mind measured by a poll, authentic public opinion can only be interpreted from a developmental standpoint that views it as continuous process of growth and change. Democracy thus places its faith in the long-term ability of public opinion to draw from the resources of rhetoric to form habits of collective judgment that enable an association of interconnected publics to thrive.

Like Habermas after him, Dewey was a firm believer in the power of public opinion, and he never doubted that a truly intelligent public opinion was a possibility, despite consistent evidence that pointed in the opposite direction. By 1930, for instance, he had graphically seen how "comparatively easy it is in any case for a government to control public opinion by propaganda and by shutting out all news and information contrary to its case."[156] Yet Dewey still maintained that democracy was possible despite these barriers. What it required was a unique kind of faith, "faith in public opinion and upon faith that the democratic process will result in the growth of a public opinion which is capable, enlightened and honest."[157] One reason Dewey maintained this faith was simple was that he saw no alternative: "For where there is not public opinion, or where it is not made effective and persistently brought to bear, our affairs remain very largely in the hands of bosses, and thereby represent private interests."[158] Under such conditions, when public opinion lacks coherency and influence, "the need for united action, and the supposed need of integrated opinion and sentiment, are met by organized propaganda and advertising" through which "sentiment can be manufactured by mass methods for almost any person or any cause."[159] In other words, when public opinion lacks the means to form itself, an opinion will be formed for it, but then the "public" will be a public in name only, a mere nominalistic "people" in idea and in practice it will be a mass.

It is thus a mistake to tie the survival of democracy to any particular ideological rhetorical discourse. Indeed some of the most terrific atrocities in human history were justified on the basis of discourses which had the noblest sentiments in their original context, and vice versa. Democracy, as a process, aligns itself primarily with the means by which a public and public opinion comes into existence and maintains itself. This means is the sharing of discourse within an egalitarian public sphere. "The problem under discussion is precisely how conflicting claims are to be settled in the interest of the widest possible contribution to the interests of all—or at least of the great majority," Dewey writes. "The method of democracy—inasfar as it is that of organized intelligence—is to bring these conflicts out into the open where their special claims can be seen and appraised, where they can be discussed and judged in the light of more inclusive interests."[160]

At its most basic level, the idea of the public sphere stands simply for the ability of conflicts to be brought into the open where they can be seen, appraised, and challenged by any member of the public. It is thus synonymous with what Thomas Farrell calls a "rhetorical forum," "within which issues, interests, positions, constituencies, and messages are advanced, shaped, and provisionally judged."[161] Defined in these ways, the conceptions of both Dewey and Farrell differ little from the original liberal notion of the bourgeois public sphere. Dewey, in fact, praises "early liberals" such as John Stewart Mill "for their valiant battle in behalf of freedom of thought, conscience, expression, and communication,"[162] noting that the liberal notion that a representative government should be guided by the principles of discussion, publicity, and liberty of the press is one of the great accomplishments of Western thought.[163] Likewise, Dewey believed the chief virtue of the habit of publicity is that it provides "the opportunity for many silly and many false things to be uttered," for "experience has confirmed the faith that silly things are of so many different kinds that they cancel each other over a period of time, and that falsities come out in the wash of experience as dirt comes out in soap and water."[164] The liberal model merely expands and institutionalizes this notion by making it the basis for law and governance. The bourgeois public sphere represents a washing machine for ideas.

Yet Dewey's notion of the public sphere has a constructive—and rhetorically pertinent—component lacking in that of classical liberalism. For early liberals, writes Dewey, "social arrangements were treated not as positive forces but as external limitations," a perspective which resulted in a failure to "make a distinction between purely formal or legal liberty and effective liberty of thought and action." Their call for the elimination of restrictions was not equaled by a constructive program to give citizens the practical skills of communication and the opportunity to act upon the outcomes of their deliberation. The long tradition of justifying free speech on the basis of individual right while ignoring questions of true access thus had predictable consequences: "Soon after liberal tenets were formulated as eternal truths, it became an instrument of vested interests in opposition to further social change, a ritual of lip-service." The problem with the original liberal doctrine was that while "potent in exposure of abuses; it was weak for constructive purposes"; its proponents "had no glimpse of the fact that private control of the new forces of production, forces which affect the life of every one, would operate in the same way as private unchecked control of political power." As a result the release from the oppressive bonds of state censorship has given way to manipulation of public communication by those already in possession of money and power. The blunt power of the policeman's baton has been superseded by the subtle power "exercised by the propaganda of publicity agents and that of organized pressure groups."[165] This process by which public relations, advertising, and propaganda have come to dominate the public sphere is what Habermas calls "refeudalization," or the shift in content by which "critical publicity is supplanted by manipulative publicity."[166]

Dewey's response to this problem is to promote the development of effective liberty by creating more opportunities for public involvement and advocacy as well as promoting education in the arts of communication. A radical democracy thus commits itself to "extending the application of democratic methods, methods of consultation, persuasion, negotiation, communication, cooperative intelligence, in the task of making our own politics, industry, education, our culture generally, a servant and an evolving manifestation of democratic ideas."[167] In other words *the* problem of democratic publics is a problem of communication, of improving "the methods and conditions of debate, discussion and persuasion."[168] The conditions represent the qualities of the public sphere that allow for greater participation by members of the public, and the methods represent the communicative arts which citizens employ to influence the thoughts and behaviors of others. Rhetoric simply stands for the art most capable of moving an audience to a new judgment in times uncertainty and conflict. The fault of the liberal public sphere is not the presence of rhetoric but its concentration in the hands of a powerful minority. In a radical democracy, rhetoric would not shrink out of fear of being manipulated by the few but would proliferate out of hope of being inspired by the many.

Constitutive Rhetoric

Because Dewey viewed the public as an interactive and functional entity, the process by which Dewey imagines that democratic publics are constituted thus differs significantly from the current notions of "constitutive rhetoric." For Dewey, publics form whenever an interconnected group of individuals are persuaded to develop collective habits of communication and judgment in order to resolve problems in such a way as to promote some shared interest. In what now goes by the name "constitutive rhetoric," however, the very existence of deliberate persuasion and autonomous judgment are called into question. As Maurice Charland argues, they both imply "the existence of an agent who is free to be persuaded."[169] Consistent with deterministic theories of the self, Charland interprets rhetorical audiences are always already "constituted as subjects through a process of identification with a textual position." For him, therefore, audiences "do not exist outside rhetoric, merely addressed by it, but live inside rhetoric." To be a "subject" living "inside rhetoric" means that an individual is not a natural but a textual being. As Charland makes clear, the "subject is a position within a text. To be an embodied subject is to experience and act in a textualized world." Constitutive rhetoric thus refers to the process of merging different subject positions into a collective identity by interpellating people as political subjects within some ideological narrative. A rhetor does not persuade organic selves to form a public; one hails a collection of what Charland calls "paper beings" to become a "mass."[170]

By contrast a naturalistic ontology of becoming views the rhetorical formation of new publics as a process of transforming habits. This view accepts the importance of prior rhetorical discourse in forming our sense of self and structuring our attitudes toward our environment, but it sees that self as a product of art formed through the productive transaction between communication and experience. Our selves are not simply vessels for texts, such that we wander through a discursive world passively absorbing and regurgitating rhetorical narratives. We are organic beings who use the resources of language and communication to adapt to a changing natural environment. Moreover, people are stubbornly resistant to change and skeptical of idealistic narratives that would force them to alter their preexisting habits. New publics only come into being through a long rhetorical struggle, and only then once their environment has changed such that old habits become obsolete. This is not so much the effect of a "changing concrete world" as it is a changing relationship between an organism and its environment. Recalcitrance is not simply that two cognitive meanings will not fit together; recalcitrance also happens when we no longer can feed our family, succeed at our careers, protect our nation, or achieve social justice. Constitutive rhetoric is the effort to overcome such recalcitrance through the formation of a new conjoint effort and endeavor motivated by the redefinition of collective identity.

A democratic constitutive rhetoric simply makes the formation of such an identity a collaborative effort rather than the responsibility of a single authority. Diverse rhetorical narratives of shared interest and identity may each struggle individually for totalizing hegemony, but only in moments of intense crisis does any one discourse achieve such a totalizing effect—and even then for only a short period marked usually by a violent outburst of energy. The common error is to take these extraordinary contexts to be the norm, such that the rhetorical constitution of publics becomes an all-or-nothing affair. More often, the cumulative effect of democratic rhetorical advocacy on social identity is to produce something of a bricolage produced through selective judgment. Long-term and stable publics come into being by piecing together aspects of numerous narratives in order to develop a loose sense of collective belonging that satisfies the emotional and practical needs of a diverse population while still allowing room for difference. Whatever the nature of the public, however, its rhetorical formation cannot be understood outside of the historical, social, and natural context that gives meaning to public experience. In other words publics come into being for reasons beyond the fact that someone stands up and says, "Hey, you there!"[171] Such an exclamation might get people to turn their heads, but it certainly is not sufficient make them cast off the burden of an old subjectivity to become a martyr for the cause.

The problem with the whole idea of "constitutive rhetoric" as something separate from commonplace rhetorical practice is that it assumes a binary where none exists. Clearly one can point to matters of degree, such that certain rhetoric tends to praise Athenians before Athenians while the other seeks to create the very idea of what it means to be an Athenian. Yet both are still communicative acts, and the very nature of communication is that it "modifies the disposition of both the parties who partake in it."[172] Every act of communication requires an individual to give form to what had previously been formless, and in doing so changes the attitude of that person toward his or her own experiences as they relate to the experiences of others. As Dewey writes, the "remaking of the material of experience in the act of expression is not an isolated event confined to the artist and to a person here and there who happens to enjoy the work . . . it is also a remaking of the experience of the community in the direction of greater order and unity."[173] This is what it means to have a communicative transaction. According to Stephen Fishman, it means a refusal to view "writers, cultures, and texts as static and independent of one another." Rather, it reveals that "the individual's writing is always a mutual reshaping of author, culture, and text" and that the process of writing and "revising is a double-barreled task, a matter of conserving and reforming, of challenging and building upon our familiar ideas in ways which enable us to modify and enrich them."[174] To make a rhetorical act is always already to be caught up in a mutual transaction. The only way it could be otherwise would be to view oneself as a god.

Equally important within this communicative transaction, however, is the environment in which it takes place. Communication is not simply an exchange between disembodied minds trading thoughts about a text. It involves organic beings adapting to a changing environment by reflecting upon and molding shared experience. Rhetorical acts thus engage in a total process of becoming in which self, other, world, and text transact with one another through time. As Larry Hickman has argued, Dewey's interpretation of communication was heavily influenced by his naturalistic interpretation of *technē*, inspired by Darwin, which saw all human creations, from technology to the sciences to the fine arts to philosophy, as productive skills "brought to bear by human beings on the project of *altering* their environments and *accommodating* themselves to those environments." Thus, Hickman concludes, for Dewey "ideas, knowing, and active engagement with experiential contexts are artifacts of inquiry in just as important a sense as are works of art that are made of canvas and paint, stone, metal, plastic, steel, or shoe leather."[175] From Hickman's perspective, then, the fact that rhetoric puts ideas to work, draws from and forms our ways of knowing, and promotes active engagement with others in a shared environment makes rhetoric itself a kind of technology. To alter the relationship between an audience and its social environment is to create a kind of "tool" for changing the events and objects of experience; and it is, finally, only through the artistic use of tools that one can constitute anything.

Assembling Social Democracy

What would a successfully constituted public look like? Perhaps nothing dates Dewey's prose as much as the language he uses to describe his vision for a perfected democracy. Using capitalized terms that today give the impression of monolithic ideals, Dewey describes in *The Public and Its Problems* what he calls "the conditions which must be fulfilled if the Great Society is to become a Great Community; a society in which the ever-expanding and intricately ramifying consequences of associated activities shall be known in the full sense of that word, so that an organized, articulate Public comes into being."[176] Without fully understanding what Dewey means by these terms, one could easily conclude that his vision is one of an undifferentiated public whose members all share the same goals, values, and attitudes, culminating in a "Great Community" that aspires toward a Hegelian absolute in which the concrete individual and abstract universal become fused in a idealistic state. However, despite Dewey's unfortunate habit of slipping back into the Hegelian language of his youth, what he meant by "Great Community" was something far more subtle and contemporary. As Peters characterizes it, Dewey's solution to the problems of modern life amounted to "a patchwork of interlocking face-to-face setting that somehow added up to a national conversation, thus reconciling town-meeting practices with continental scope."[177] But even this description does not address the full complexity of his social theory, for it black-boxes his method with the word "somehow." A more accurate account might be found in the work of Bruno Latour, who follows Dewey in defining politics as "*the progressive composition of the common world.*"[178] In other words politics is the method by which be assemble, dissemble, and reassemble the public over time.

What Latour highlights is a point that Dewey made in his earliest writing on democracy, that the public is not something that results from the so-called interaction between the "individual" and the "social." This dialectical framework assumes, quite falsely, that there exist discrete individuals apart from association as well as social "forces" that stand outside and above individuals. The pervasive use of the term "social" (along with the term "discourse") to stand in for some ubiquitous and invisible "stuff" is the reason Latour decided that "the word 'collective' will take place of 'society.' Society will be kept only for the assembly of already gathered entities that sociologists of the social believe have been made in social stuff. Collective, on the other hand, will designate the project of assembling new entities not yet gathered together and which, for this reason, clearly appear as being not made of social stuff."[179] Latour's point is that "society" represents not a force but a product; it is something to bring into existence by creating working relationships between parts, much like a garden, a car, Thanksgiving, or a family. "Collective" simply represents the artistic endeavor of bringing-into-being—that is, of becoming.

Dewey's vision for the democratic collective involves three components—localities, universals, and networks. In *The Public and Its Problems*, for instance, he envisions a new form of social organization that balance the need for maintaining traditional local communities—what Dewey calls the "contiguous associations of the past"—while promoting a more universal perspective that makes them more "responsive to the complex and world-wide scene" in which they are now enmeshed. The basic outline of this new community at first appears simple: "While local, it will not be isolated. Its larger relationships will provide an inexhaustible and flowing fund of meanings upon which to draw, with assurance that its drafts will be honored."[180] This seems little more than a restatement of the popular dictum to "think globally, act locally." But it is this and more. After all, being able to "think globally" is not simply an act that can be done from sheer strength of will. Thinking globally requires the skills and resources to develop an understanding of a complex environment—just the capacity that Walter Lippmann had called into question because of the limitations of both human nature and the mass media.

The more radical aspect of Dewey's proposal comes in the metaphor of a national "bank," a metaphor that helps open up the black box of social democracy. What Dewey means by a national bank is a network of overlapping public spheres that contribute to a common body of social knowledge. He envisions a series of local communities that "draw" resources from the bank in order to "fund" local projects and in turn receive the fruits of the investment in terms of such things as art, science, and industry. Under such a situation Dewey hopes that "the vast, innumerable and intricate current of trans-local associations [will] be so banked and conducted that they will pour the generous and abundant meanings of which they are potential bearers into the smaller intimate unions of human beings living in immediate contact with one another," culminating in local communities that are "stable without being static, progressive without being merely mobile." Dewey's "Great Community" is not simply a larger version of a local community but represents a network of national communication that does "its final work in ordering the relations and enriching the experience of local associations."[181]

Bruno Latour gives the name "oligoptica" to these local sites of communal association. This term is designed as a point of contrast to the notion of "panopticon," which refers to a site which sees everything all at once. According to

Latour, "They do the exactly the opposite of panoptica: they see much too little to feed the megalomania of the inspector or the paranoia of the inspected, but what they see, they see it well—hence the use of this Greek word to designate an ingredient at once indispensable and that comes in tiny amounts (as the in the 'oligo-elements' of your health store). From oligoptica, study but extremely narrow views of the (connected) whole are made possible—*as long as connections hold.*"[182]

That added modifier, "*as long as connections hold,*" is central to the democratic functioning of such "oligoptica." For without the ability to connect to other social universes, they would be locked into a stagnant tunnel vision. But in a genuinely networked society, "macro no longer describes a *wider* or a *larger* site in which the micro would be embedded like some Russian Matryoshka doll, but another equally local, equally micro place, which is connected to many others through some medium transporting specific types of traces."[183] The difference is crucial, for it distinguishes a genuinely democratic public from more feudal structures that are ranked hierarchically.

The possibility of Dewey's great community is thus contingent on the existence of oligoptic associations and communicative networks. In the first case the recovery of "the vitality and depth of close and direct intercourse and attachment" is made possible through the "reconstruction of face-to-face communities." In the second case the ability for "free and full intercommunication" on a national scale is made possible through the structures of the public sphere.[184] Of the two factors necessary for the great community, the recovery of face-to-face communities has drawn the most attention from contemporary interpreters. The reason for this attention is that Dewey places upon the face-to-face community the great burden of providing an answer to the fear that industrial age is replacing the intimacy of local communities with a faceless system of mechanical organization established for purely external ends. Similarly Dewey warns that "enormous organization" has led to the "substitution of impersonal bonds for personal unions," culminating in "a flux which is hostile to stability." Rational and mechanical forms of organization have become ends in themselves, "hampering the free play of artistic gifts, fettering men and women with chains of conformity, conducing to abdication of all which does not fit into the automatic movement of organization as a self-sufficing thing." However, Dewey does not believe such a fate inevitable. Rather than having to exist only as an end-in-itself, "organization as a means to an end would reenforce individuality and enable it to be securely itself by enduing it with resources beyond its unaided reach."[185] To become a "means to an end," however, social organization had to be put in the service of community life rather than exploiting its resources for purely material gain.

The importance Dewey places on such face-to-face environments is derived largely from his naturalistic premise that humans are biological beings that have an instinctual desire for physical closeness and intimacy. As he explains, "There is something deep within human nature itself which pulls toward settled relationships" such that "vital and thorough attachments are bred only in the intimacy of an intercourse which is of necessity restricted in range."[186] Unfortunately Dewey's observation of this consistent trait of human nature has been seen as a metaphysical statement about the nature of consciousness. Asen, for instance, draws from Derrida to argue that "Dewey's insistence on face-to-face communication promised an unattainable mode of interaction: an ideal of direct, unmediated communication with another" that betrays "a belief in a direct route to human consciousness."[187] Once again we find the accusation that Dewey's theory is limited as a result of a naïve attachment to classical humanistic ideals of the autonomous subject and the vision of pure communication.

However, when Dewey asserts that "democracy must begin at home, and its home is the neighborly community," he is not claiming that face-to-face communication is a transparent bridge between minds; he is saying that face-to-face communication, because of the experience of physical closeness, has the practical effect of building emotional ties to other people and environments that make for a deeper, richer, and more lasting impact on our thoughts, habits, and feelings. There are three practical consequences that such a process has for the possibility of democracy. First, community interaction builds character: "This is why the family and neighborhood, with all their deficiencies, have always been the chief agencies of nurture, the means by which dispositions are stably formed and ideas acquired which laid hold on the roots of character." Without such face-to-face interactions, the development of stable character is severely handicapped, as it is either fragmented by increased mobility or standardized by the pressures of mechanical organization. Second, the intimate relationships one builds through face-to-face dialogue create the possibility of human understanding that is necessary if one is to become a sympathetic member of a more global community. As Dewey explains, "It has also been said that if a man love not his fellow man whom he has seen, he cannot love the God whom he has not seen. The chances of regard for distant peoples being effective as long as there is no close neighborhood experience to bring with it insight and understanding of neighbors do not seem better."[188] Thus a rich community life, particularly when it includes a diverse membership, is vital for the creation of a larger social organization that requires an ability to sympathize and understand people of different backgrounds.

Lastly, face-to-face dialogue is inherently richer than mediated forms of communication. As Dewey famously observed, the "winged words of conversation in immediate intercourse have a vital import lacking in the fixed and frozen words of written speech," for "the connections of the ear with vital and out-going thought and emotion are immensely closer and more varied than those of the eye." Although Dewey's differentiation between hearing and vision is questionable, the basic proposition that face-to-face dialogue has the potential for more lasting and deeper impact on our experience than conversations in print or voice is a well-established fact. This does not diminish the importance of dissemination as a form of communication but merely insists that "publication is partial and the public which results is partially informed and formed until the meanings it purveys pass from mouth to mouth," for then "there is no limit to the liberal expansion and confirmation of limited personal intellectual endowment which may proceed from the flow of social intelligence when that circulates by word of mouth from one to another in the communications of the local community."[189] Dewey's belief in the importance of face-to-face dialogue likely originated in own rural upbringing, but it is important to recognize that this belief was reinforced by the hard realities of war and oppression. Given the situation Dewey describes, it is hard to see how protests of the "metaphysics of presence" have any bearing on the practical importance of face-to-face dialogue to the formation of a genuine public opinion:

> When I think of the conditions under which men and women are living in many foreign countries today, fear of espionage, with danger hanging over the meeting of friends for friendly conversation in private gatherings, I am inclined to believe that the heart and final guarantee of democracy is in free gatherings of neighbors on the street corner to discuss back and forth what is read in uncensored news of the day, and in gatherings of friends in the living rooms of houses and apartments to converse freely with one another. Intolerance, abuse, calling of names because of differences of opinion about religion or politics or business, as well as because of differences of race, color, wealth or degree of culture are treason to the democratic way of life. For everything which bars freedom and fullness of communication sets up barriers that divide human beings into sets and cliques, into antagonistic sects and factions, and thereby undermines the democratic way of life. Merely legal guarantees of the civil liberties of free belief, free expression, free assembly are of little avail if in daily life freedom of communication, the give and take of ideas, facts, experiences, is choked by mutual suspicion, by abuse, by fear and hatred. These things destroy the essential condition of the democratic way of living even more effectually than open coercion which—as the example of totalitarian states proves—is effective only when it succeeds in breeding hate, suspicion, intolerance in the minds of individual human beings.[190]

In terms of rhetorical democracy, Dewey's attention to the importance of gatherings of friends and neighbors to discuss the "uncensored news of the day" points to the importance of having an autonomous audience able to understand, debate, and respond to discourse about political affairs. Lacking such an audience, made possible largely through the existence of face-to-face communities, or lacking such a public sphere in which individual have an opportunity to expand the horizon of their social understanding, a "public" exists only in name only. In fact it exists as either an atomized mass of disconnected individuals or a fragmented collection of "antagonistic sects and factions," both of which are rendered impotent to function as a group to form and act upon public opinion. To be a democratic public is thus to do more than proclaim oneself a "people," it is to be able to work collectively together through networks of communication toward a common aim of transforming the common world.

Intelligence and Freedom

Once emancipated from laizzez-faire notions of rhetorical democracy, the ethics of rhetoric take on a much more substantial form. It is not enough to advocate, as in classical liberalism, the creation of an unrestricted public sphere in the hope that the truth will win out. Clearly the creation of such egalitarian rhetorical forums are necessary for promoting critical discussion through competing rhetorical claims. "Discussion," Dewey writes, "as the manifestation of intelligence in political life, stimulates publicity; by its means sore spots are brought to light that would otherwise remain hidden. It affords opportunity for promulgation of new ideas ... [and] it is an invitation to individuals to concern themselves with public affairs." What Dewey rejects is the belief the liberal notion that public discussion, left to its own affairs, is sufficient to produce the kind of intelligent collective judgment adequate for the problems of a global age. Indeed, "discussion and dialectic, however indispensable they are to the elaboration of ideas and policies after ideas are once put forth, are weak reeds to depend upon for systematic origination of comprehensive plans, the plans that are required if the problem of social organization is to be met."[191] More than simply opening up the public sphere to open discussion, Dewey suggests the need both for the systematic development of practical ideas along with the further cultivation of the creative arts.

Dewey's notion of a radical democracy is thus not synonymous with what we might associate with a rhetorical democracy; it is a fusion of the methods of rhetorical democracy with the ideals of a rational society. On the one hand Dewey accepted the rationalist notion, stemming from Plato, that intelligent social judgment needed to draw on more than simply the resources of *doxa*. For him social intelligence cannot be "identified simply with discussion and persuasion, necessary as are these things," for discussion and persuasion without the application of scientific method "in the invention and projection of far-reaching social plans" leaves social intelligence "inchoate."[192] Indeed the populist faith that wisdom will spring spontaneously from the people is itself grounded in the metaphysics of idealism. "The idea that the conflict of parties will, by means of public discussion, bring out necessary public truths," Dewey argues, "is a kind of political watered-down version of the Hegelian dialectic, with its synthesis arrived at by a union of antithetical conceptions."[193] On the other hand, Dewey promoted the creative, critical, and individualistic spirit of rhetorical democracy that emerged from the Sophists. Democratic publics thus "cannot give up the policy of depending upon voluntary and private initiative and effort; upon the processes of persuasion and conviction, discussion, publicity, and exchange of ideas so as to form public opinion."[194] The communicative practices that make up a rhetorical democracy do not need to be rejected, they only need to be supplemented by "a greater recognition of responsibility to the common weal in carrying on these operations."[195] We stand stronger pooling our resources together than we do merely standing next to one another.

A radical democracy thus attempts to find a balance between the Platonic love of philosophical wisdom and the Sophistic commitment to creative art. Effective liberty, in this framework, comes about when members of the public are able to draw from more than just their limited personal experience to advocate for changes in a complex social environment. Individual rhetors must have access to the full resources of the arts and sciences such that they are able to advocate for collective action that serves the needs of a wide and diverse public. Indeed such access is necessary if one is to be able to influence actors beyond one's immediate environment. To persuade one must understand, even if that understanding is purely emotional. Persuasion in an interconnected age thus requires something other than sheer ejaculation of sentiment and opinion. It requires an intelligent and sympathetic appreciation of the relationships being people and their environments such that one's discourse is able to speak to and potentially transform their habits, impulses, emotions, and consciousness. This challenge was difficult enough in the time of Gorgias, but even he would have a difficult time in a global environment living up to his reputation as apprentice to a mighty lord. The locality that built him a golden statue exists no longer; one now has a public that extends across the globe and can communicate more rapidly than classical Greeks who lived on opposite sides of Athens.

Just as the ethics of democracy demands that we attend to the expansive and long-term connections between individuals and publics as they act together in a common world, so too does the ethics of rhetoric demand that our discourses transcend the limitations of narrow self-interest by criticizing, contributing to, and drawing from the resources of common knowledge. This is why, as Bruno Latour points out, arts like the "social sciences are so indispensable to the reassembling of the social. Without them we don't know what we have in common, we don't know through which connections we are associated together, and we would have no way to detect how we can live together in the same common world."[196] Latour goes on: "No one has made the point as forcefully as

John Dewey did with his own definition of the public. For a social science to become relevant, it has to have the capacity to renew itself—a quality impossible if a society is supposed to be 'behind' political action. It should also possess the ability to loop back from the few to the many and from the many to the few. . . . One must practice sociology in such a way that the ingredients making up the collective are regularly refreshed."[197]

Based on this proposition one can see how fruitless the continued tension between such fields as "science" and "rhetoric" is. As Latour points out, the "difference is not between those who know for certain and those who write texts, between 'scientific' and 'literary' minds . . . but between those who write *bad* texts and those who write *good* ones."[198] And a good text is that which makes rich connections between people and things in a shared environment such that collective associations can become richer, more intelligent, and more satisfying.

Summary

Dewey's appeal to intelligence often overshadows the clear necessity for rhetoric in the development of a social democracy. Yet in a world marked by constant becoming—of rises and falls, of perching and flightings, of peace and strife, of stability and change—rhetoric emerges whenever the past resources of intelligence are insufficient for collective judgment and when moral conflict forces upon us a choice. This point was first made most forcefully by Aristotle and remains true: "[Rhetoric] is concerned with the sort of things we debate and for which we do not have [other] arts and among such listeners as are not able to see many things all together or to reason from a distant starting point. And we debate about things that seem capable of admitting two possibilities; for no one debates things incapable of being different either in past or future or present, at least not if they suppose that to be the case; for there is nothing more [to say]."[199]

For Aristotle, as for the Sophists, rhetorical ethics inevitably revolve around the kind of actions taken in moments of *kairos*. Dewey defines the ethical nature of *kairotic* judgment as follows: "The right time, occasion, person, purpose and fashion—what is it but the complete individualization of conduct in order to meet the whole demands of the whole situation, instead of some abstraction? And what else do we mean by fit, due, proper, right action, but that which just hits the mark, without falling short or deflecting, and, to mix the metaphor, without slopping over?"[200] There are, of course, *kairotic* moments outside of rhetoric, but when such moments are shared by a public in exigent circumstances, rhetoric is not far behind.

The larger ontological question of this perspective arises once one explores more concretely the relationship that exists between what Dewey calls the "individualization of conduct" and the "demands of the whole situation." If we take the invention and enactment of a persuasive message to represent the individualization of conduct in a rhetorical act, to what rhetorically does the "whole situation" refer? Ethically the latter question is of decisive importance, for its determination establishes the criteria by which we judge a message to have hit the mark, and without a target toward which to aim, we are simply flailing about aimlessly in the dark. As usual, convention presents us with two possible extremes. At the one end the "whole situation" is said to be contained completely within the *kairotic* moment itself. As a Sophist in a court of law, the ethical measure one's rhetoric is determined by what was accomplished or lost within the hours or minutes that decided a trial. At this extreme, which we might label "circumstantial ethics," judgment is a wholly circumstantial and contingent affair that forces one to rapidly evaluate a changing situation that lacks clarity both in precedent and consequence. At the other end, the "whole situation" represents the universe as it is projected into infinity. Like a biblical prophet before Caesar, the ethical measure of one's rhetoric is determined by a set and unchanging standard of right and truth that applies equally to all times and places. At this extreme, one might call it "transcendental ethics," a uniform judgment is demanded, even if it flies in the face of appearances. One must instead rely on principles that conform to a universal code, for only by adhering to that code do we keep ourselves in line with truth.

The problem with both approaches is that they are equally locked within the logic of being. This logic is obvious in transcendental ethics. The being exists in universal truth propositions that describe a fixed moral universe. Yet the logic of being also exists in the extremes of circumstantial ethics. Although denying the existence of transcendental morality, it nonetheless denies the principles of continuity and transaction that characterize the ontology of becoming. Instead of viewing self, other, and situation as objects which continue through time, their existence is frozen within the atomic moment. They are thus condemned to being events with neither histories nor futures. Moreover, even though they exist in the moment, they are effectively treated as if they were, themselves, transcendental qualities. As with neo-Aristotelianism, orators and audiences emerge into an objective situation fully formed, and the gauge of any "success" is determined by how a message adapts to the fixed characteristics of those events. In other words neo-Aristotelianism adopts the methods of transcendental ethics but simply narrows the universe to a point in time. But this is as useless a criteria for judgment as is infinity.

By contrast, in Dewey's naturalistic ontology of becoming, ethics represents a reflective process whereby one attempts to gauge the effect of one's actions within a total transaction of self, other, and situation as it occurs over a "bounded" span of space and time. In this view there is no essential ethical conflict here between "desire" (as represented by extreme circumstantial ethics) and "reason" (as represented by transcendental ethics). There is rather a challenge to reconcile two rational desires—"between a desire which wants a near-by object and a desire which wants an object which is seen by thought to occur in consequence of an intervening series of conditions, or in the 'long run.'"[201] Circumstantial ethics is thus correct to emphasize the legitimacy of personal desires in gauging the success or failure of some action, while transcendental ethics is correct in emphasizing a broader view of one's responsibilities as determined by rational thought. When brought together, the pragmatic question then becomes how "long" one's view should be in any given act such that any decision is based on a total evaluation the consequences of one's actions within a larger but bounded environment. The function of ethical theory is not to give a catechism; it is to help us construct an environment that helps us determine the conditions that must be met in order to satisfy the ethical demands of both desire and reason. Thus rhetoric is a quintessentially ethical endeavor insofar as it always struggles to balance both tendencies within exigent moments of crisis.

It is this intimate connection between rhetoric and *kairos* that has linked the rhetorical tradition—far more than the philosophical tradition—with the ontology of becoming. John Poulakos forcefully makes this point in defining what he calls the "rhetorical orientation" stemming from the Sophists as opposed to the "philosophical orientation," which drew its inspiration from Plato. In the latter view arts such as rhetoric are merely knacks for getting by in a world of appearances; the genuine goal is the "pursuit of *episteme*, a pursuit whose ultimate end is the discernment of divine intelligence through the disciplined study of the laws of the universe." Thus it is not that the philosophical orientation denies rhetoric; it merely relegates it to a ladder to be thrown away once the peak of Enlightenment has been reached. In contradistinction, the

> rhetorical orientation had advanced the anthropocentric view, a view that situates man amidst fellow human beings and construes him as a spring of insight and resourcefulness, serving necessity and pursuing pleasure in the face of changing appearances and trying circumstances. Effectively this view had granted validity to human inventiveness, promoted faith in progress, and valued achievement in the arts. On a parallel line, it had stipulated the condition of limited and incomplete knowledge, that is, the condition of *doxa* as well as the factors that shape it, e.g., individual sense-perception, and collective common sense. At the heart of the rhetorical orientation lay the human capacity to create in and through language interested visions of order and to share them with others.[202]

In our terms Poulakos associates rhetorical orientation with the ontology of becoming and the philosophical orientation with the metaphysics of being. However, this should not be interpreted as a disparagement of philosophy as a discipline. Indeed, from the rhetorical orientation, philosophy, too, is an art of becoming capable of transforming society.[203] It simply uses different tools in different contexts. Indeed, to assume otherwise is to render a "philosophy of rhetoric" an oxymoron.

Rhetoric, in short, is a creature of crisis, whereas philosophy is a lover of continuity. Philosophy attempts to formulate relatively universal patterns in human behavior through a diachronic study of the human conditions; rhetoric situates itself into the contingent upheavals of social life that punctuate historical time. A philosophy of rhetoric, then, seeks to understand these discontinuities within a continuous history, to show how even in the particular moment are recurrences that resonate with the past and will carry forward into the future. To adapt an Aristotelian dictum, philosophy can be considered the counterpart of rhetoric.

This is why someone such as Kenneth Burke can, at one time, write *Attitudes toward History*, which "deals with characteristic responses of people in their forming and reforming of congregations," while, at the other, pen *A Rhetoric of Motives*, which leads us "through the Scramble, the Wrangle of the Market Place, the flurries and flare-ups of the Human Barnyard, the Give and Take, the wavering line of pressure and counterpressure, the Logomachy, the onus of ownership, the Wars of Nerves, the War."[204] These neither represent contradictory trajectories nor are they just manifestations of a single "rhetorical" interest. They are, rather, two discrete ways of examining the human condition whose conversation is necessary for understanding long-term social change. In other words, if rhetoric is necessary, it is not because it is totalizing, it is because it represents a part of an interconnected whole.

If, as Danisch argues, Dewey outlined a philosophy that makes rhetoric necessary, it falls to rhetoricians to clarify not only why it is necessary but also how it informs a philosophy that often ignores its presence.[205] Once this project is engaged, it becomes all the more clear that it is insufficient to parrot the liberal point that democratic growth simply requires more open-minded tolerance of bad rhetoric in the hope that the dirt will come out in the wash. Nothing could be more naïve in a technological society in which it is the business of propaganda to keep people vacillating between neurotic agitation and mechanical uniformity. Plato has a point when he says that nothing much will grow out of rhetoric when it wallows in the pains and pleasures of the immediate moment. The constitution of an ethical society also requires the development of an ethical rhetoric produced by disciplined individuals within stable and interconnected communities that draw from the best available knowledge in order to bring about a better world.

The question for a postmetaphysical rhetorical theory is how to promote such rhetoric without falling back into an idealistic conception of the good.

How do we construct an experimental vision of the good, of what Dewey calls that end "which satisfies want, craving, which fulfills or makes complete the need which stirs to action," in a world fraught with becoming?[206] The answer to this question leads us to consider the relationship between rhetoric and the other two dominant arts of becoming—the logic of inquiry and the art of aesthetic experience.

2 The Rhetoric of Inquiry

IF INQUIRY REPRESENTS A DISCIPLINED ACT of concentration, rhetoric has traditionally been seen as its polar opposite—an unruly distraction. The Platonic caricature of rhetoric, in other words, has always associated it with a knack for manipulating circumstances for one's own benefit. Concerned with promoting expediency and accumulating power in the short term, it focuses its attention only on the contingencies of the moment and exploits the weaknesses of the other in order to serve the pleasures of the few or the one. Naturally the moralistic response to the supposed baseness of rhetoric has been to make it subservient to a higher discourse—to make it a means of disseminating the good. Plato simply pushed this logic to the extreme in the *Republic* when he suggested banning all poets except those sanctioned by the state. His method was simple and universal—to "supervise the storytellers" and "select their stories whenever they are fine or beautiful and reject them when they aren't."[1] This is not a sweeping condemnation of the arts, as is commonly supposed; it rather sees arts like rhetoric as vehicles whose value in any particular action must be judged on the quality of the content delivered.

The caretakers of rhetoric have typically been one of two institutions—science or religion. What binds these two institutions together is that they stand for a commitment to the discovery and formulation of higher laws that approximate the nature of being through the language of logic. This commitment unites them despite significant differences concerning the method of discovery and the fallibility of their principles. As John Ziman observes, "'Sciences' and 'religions' are very much alike, in that they are general systems of belief from which people seek guidance in their life-world thoughts and actions."[2] Put another way, science and religion both represent coherent bodies of knowledge that can be expressed in propositional form and can assert degrees of correspondence to stable aspects of the world. Consequently, even when science abandons the absolutism of traditional religion and adopts an experimental attitude, the fact that it retains its commitment to logical coherence, consistency, and veracity gives it common aim with institutional religion. This makes both science and religion look askance at rhetoric, which by nature tends to adapt its content organically to a situation. The rationalistic project, then, has always been to constrain this tendency toward circumstantial adaptation by forcing rhetoric to employ argument by principle drawn from preexisting regimes of logical truth—both empirical and moral.

We find this subordination at work even in one of rhetoric's most articulate supporters, Richard Weaver. In *The Ethics of Rhetoric,* Weaver labors to advance the virtues of rationalism through the lens of rhetoric. For Weaver the central tension in rhetoric lies between those who would argue from circumstance and those who would argue from definition. In the argument from circumstance, one favors urgency and expediency over patience and perspicacity, leading to impromptu rhetorical responses to existing tangible facts in the assumption that they stand as exceptions to the rule. By contrast argument from definition rejects the idea that there are exceptional facts that require unique responses; it poses instead "that there exist classes which are determinate and therefore predictable" and therefore suggests that any virtuous rhetorical response must proceed from arguments which speak to "the nature of the thing" in its universal character. The advantage of employing argument from definition is that it allows a rhetor to step outside of the immediate push and pull of circumstance; it thus relies on the "habit of viewing things from an Olympian height."[3] For Weaver, whatever short-term gain one acquires through argument from circumstance is thus surpassed by the long-term accomplishments of the triumph of principle.

This attitude subordinates rhetoric to logic for the same reason that Hegel could simultaneously praise and subdue the Sophists. For Hegel the Sophists were valuable only insofar as they saw things from different perspectives and continued the progressive advance of spirit, yet their contribution was historical only. As Poulakos observes, "Hegel did not so much rehabilitate as philosophize the Sophists," for on account of his "intellectual totalitarianism, their personalities are dismissed or crushed under the weight of the One."[4] Likewise, Weaver praises rhetoric for advancing new definitions, but ultimately it is the definitions, not the rhetoric, which do the work of the good. Weaver can hold this attitude because he understands becoming in terms of our inevitable growth toward being. Hence, his "true conservative" is "one who sees the universe as a paradigm of essences, of which the phenomenology of the world is a sort of continuing approximation." The conservative rhetor, in other words, perceives the universe as an evolving logical form—as "a set of definitions which are struggling to get themselves defined in the real world."[5] The ethics of rhetoric thus amounts to logical piety. For him the ultimate end of rhetoric is the construction of a logical system of principles that achieves an "ordering of our own minds and our passions" and conforms to the moral laws of the universe.[6] There is need for rhetoric only because this ordering comes about through a dialectical process by which political parties oppose one another on the basis of principle. For Weaver, then, rhetoric helps move us out of old definitions and into new ones, but its ethical status ultimately rests on the logical definitions it supports and builds.

Weaver's framework really only differs from the traditional binary between rhetoric and logic by emphasizing the temporal aspect of growth. Yet because the "end" is still the correspondence between logical principles and metaphysical being, it remains locked with a dualistic understanding of language. Within this dualism, logic represents the rational representation of the laws of being while rhetoric represents the strategic efforts to arouse the passions for the sake of manipulating action in the world of appearances. This sharp distinction found its most vigorous expression in Peter Ramus. For him the "whole of dialectic concerns the mind and reason, whereas rhetoric and grammar concern language and speech," meaning that "invention, arrangement, and memory belong to dialectic, and only style and delivery to rhetoric."[7] Put another way, dialectic reigns in the kingdom of the mind through the power of logos, allowing rhetoric to have sway only in the fiefdom of the body through the use of pathos. For Ramus, to make logic a tool of the body would be to corrupt the instrument and abandon all hope of discovering or conveying the truth. Like Plato and Weaver, Ramus sees some value in rhetoric, but only when it remains pious to its more dominant counterpart.

Rhetoricians frustrated at being under logic's heel can, of course, simply turn Weaver's world upside-down and crown rhetoric king. One sees this strategy at work in the "rhetoric as epistemic" tradition. In Robert Scott's foundational essay, he rejects the analytic ideal of a "timeless" language of prior and immutable truth to be a philosopher's fantasy. This is because for Scott the universe is a contingent rather than a stable affair; a rhetor must therefore "consider truth not as something fixed and final but as something to be created moment by moment in the circumstances in which he finds himself and with which he must cope." What Weaver champions as argument from definition is thus reduced, in Scott, to another species of argument from circumstance, for while humans "may have recourse to some universal ideas in which they are willing to affirm their faith," these ideas "must enter into the contingencies of time and place and will not give rise to products which are certain."[8] Given the unpredictable flux of things, logic as a way of knowing through propositional representation is considerably limited; it is rhetoric as a form of action that produces knowledge. In other words rhetoric is epistemic because it helps us navigate the world of practice in a way that obeying the dictates of formal logic does not.

The problem with the view of rhetoric as "epistemic" is that it largely buys into Weaver's dualistic framework; it simply takes the other side. By fixating on the critique of realism and logic, they leave in place the notion that rhetoric is a kind of loose reasoning through style. The only difference is that logic is now revealed to be no better in substance, thereby proving its rhetorical nature. Following this reasoning, rhetorical critics thus become hunters of hidden tropes and figures that serve to unmask the pretenses of realism. Alan Gross's *Rhetoric of Science*, for instance, largely functions as a guide to identifying rhetorical forms. If "science is about such 'fictions,'" he says, "rhetoric has a central role in its analysis; and the proper deployment of the central concepts of rhetoric—style, arrangement, invention—will yield an appropriate intellectual harvest."[9] This focus on identification and categorization as the primary tools of the rhetoric of science then reappears in the introduction to *The Rhetoric of the Human Sciences* by John Nelson, Allan Megill, and Donald McCloskey. For these authors, rhetoric appears in the form of rhetorical "devices". First, they assert that every "scientist or scholar, regardless of field, relies on common devices of rhetoric: on metaphors, invocations of authority, and appeals to audiences—themselves creatures of rhetoric." And second, they say, "every field is defined by its own special devices and patters of rhetoric—by existence theorems, arguments from invisible hands, and appeals to textual probabilities or archives—themselves textures of rhetoric."[10] Rhetoric exists, in other words, when logical coherence, rigor, objectivity, reference, and truth are absent. And since they are always absent, rhetoric always exists.

Left untouched, however, are two basic principles: Logic can exist only as the dualist interprets it to be, and the fate of rhetoric is determined by whether one accepts or rejects that definition. Yet these principles are themselves the problem. Notable about Scott's essay is the effort expended on debunking the analytic ideal of logic in order to liberate rhetoric. Yet in doing so, Scott somewhat carelessly leaves behind him the skeletal remains of an eviscerated logic alongside its broken body of truth. Rhetoric triumphantly marches into the future ready to face contingency, but it remains unclear with what weapons rhetoric is to fight this battle. Having gained "knowledge" from past rhetorical actions, has it become wiser with respect to the future? This remains opaque, for to assume such wisdom is to assume stability and continuity in a universe of flux. And even if such permanence existed, it equally remains unclear how language could ever faithfully represent its qualities absent the power of logical form. Scott's moral agent thus becomes Weaver's circumstantial rhetor—someone with their eyes so fixed on the ground that they cannot see the forest for the trees. A state in which rhetoric is subordinate to logic may make rhetoric empty, but without logic, it may very well be blind.

As long as logic is either praised or condemned in its current form, our understanding of rhetoric will vacillate between the spectrums of the empty and the blind. The fact is that the arts of logic and the arts of rhetoric are not antagonists. The fate of one is tied up with the fate of the other. To view them as complementary, however, we must get beyond the dualistic notion of logic as the linguistic representation of atomic facts that are linked through propositions into a global representation of the universe. Such a view explodes the least persuasive ideas of Aristotle and formalizes them into a bureaucratic ideal of truth. To recover a more practical view of logic thus requires us to return, once again, to the Sophistical context in which the power of logos becomes subjected to reflective inquiry. For the Sophists, rhetoric and logic are closely aligned in practical aim, but they employ different methods to achieve their goals. It is this difference in method, and not in epistemological status, in which we discover the function relationship between the two forms of logos.

This reconceptualization of logic as a form of inquiry within the ontology of becoming thus provides a way to address the tense and often problematic relationship between rhetoric and science. This is because what John Ziman calls the "Legend" of science is built upon the ground of metaphysical logic. In short, when science is viewed as a method of "guaranteed, unassailable competence," logic is viewed as the receptacle for empirical truths that represent the laws of being.[11] Science, of course, differs from formal logic because it adds an empirical component; "logical empiricism" thus stands for the method by which observations of empirical data are organized into logical categories and formed into universal laws. Yet empirical data is often treated in the legend the same way as rhetoric—as a ladder to be thrown away. Once the logical law is formulated, what observers saw in the field or in the laboratory becomes primarily material for historians. In the legend science begins and ends with logical propositions that seek more accurate approximation of being, even while admitting that this perfect representation will take time and be riddled with error.

To view logic primarily as an art rather than an episteme is to challenge the legend at every point by aligning it with the productive agenda of the ontology of becoming. Most important, to use Ziman's words, this shift in orientation renders scientific rationality "no more than *practical reasoning* carried out as well as possible in the context of research."[12] The phrase "no more" is not to be taken as an insult; in a world of becoming, nothing is more crucial to social progress that the development of practical reasoning that can address situations of enormous breadth and complexity. A related point is also made by Latour in his distinction between "Ready Made Science" and "Science in the Making." For Latour we often interpret science retrospectively, leading to the assumption (which is another form of the philosophical fallacy) that the cause of one's discovery was the discovery itself. However, when viewed as an ongoing process, science *becomes* as a result of the interplay of interests, contingencies, institutions, objects, and messages. Within this temporal discipline, rhetoric is not only present but necessary; for how else can the weaker argument be made the stronger? With respect to the Janus face of the two perspectives on science,

Latour writes, "One mouth says: 'science is truth that authority shall not overcome'; the other asks: 'how can you be stronger than one thousand politicians and one thousand philosophers?' On the left side rhetoric is opposed to science just as authority is opposed to reason; but on the right, science is a rhetoric powerful enough, if we make the count, to allow one man to win over 2000 prestigious authorities!"[13]

Once again it is important not to misinterpret Latour as implying that science is nothing more than a rhetorical struggle for power. Like Ziman, Latour views science, at its best, as an institutional method of producing a kind of reliable knowledge that is impossible to achieve through other means. To say that science relies in part on rhetorical discourse for its ability to produce new knowledge claims is neither to reduce knowledge to politics nor to assert the weaker claim that one is warranted to study "rhetorical aspects" of technical literature, as "if the other aspects could be left to reason, logic and technical details." Rather, Latour argues that the "difference between the old rhetoric and the new is not that the first makes use of external allies [such as passion, style, emotions, interests, lawyers' tricks and so on] which the second refrains from using; the difference is that the first uses only a *few* of them and the second *very many*."[14] In other words science does not strip itself of rhetorical influence; rather, it actually *multiplies* rhetorical influences in such a way that culminates in a product that is complex instead of simple, broad instead of narrow, holistic instead of partial, far-reaching instead of crude.

Because of the institutional complexity of modern science, recovering the productive and necessary relationship between rhetoric and science is a daunting task. Therefore, this chapter begins by exploring the relationship between rhetoric and logic as it originated in the Sophistical era of classical Greece and continues to evolve in modern democracies influence by institutional science and industrial technology. As the tradition of Western science grew out logic, particularly as defined by Aristotle, finding the continuities and ruptures between these two arts provides a richer perspective on the contemporary relationship between rhetoric and science. Tracing the components of this relationship enables us, in turn, to better comprehend the ethical responsibility of a rhetor who must address a problems of contingency with one eye toward past wisdom and the other toward future possibility. In short, a radical rhetoric for the global age must be able to both contribute to and draw from scientific knowledge if we are to transcend partisan interests and interpretations in the making of a common world.

Logos, Logic, and Rhetoric

The Sophists were practitioners of logic as much as of rhetoric. Indeed, for Dewey, the Sophists were not so much rhetoricians as protologicians. By teaching citizens the ability to reason independently from the constraints of traditional ritual and habit, the Sophists not only provided "training in ability to speak in private groups and in the public forum" but also "formed the beginnings of a kind of practical logic."[15] Both rhetorical and logical theories thus share a common origin in the Sophists when the "ordered development of meanings in their relations to one another" becomes an engrossing interest on its own account.[16] In Dewey's history, "the first step, the one that costs and counts, was taken when some one began to reflect upon language, upon logos, in its syntactical structure and its wealth of meaning contents."[17] This first step was taken in classical Greece because of the shift toward democratization, which began to disrupt traditional ways of talking about the world. For Dewey the Sophists were thus "symptoms of the change from the regime of custom to the regime of analysis and reflective thought" who embodied "a certain opposition between social customs organized in institutions, and the procedure of critical, analytical intelligence."[18] The Sophists responded to this change by developing the art of practical logic that the political environment of Athenian democracy demanded. Dewey explains:

> The conditions under which logical theory originated are indicated by the two words still generally used to designate its subject matter—logic and dialectic. Both of these words have to do with speech, not of course with speech in the form of mere words but with language as the storehouse of the ideas and beliefs which form the culture of a people. Greek life was peculiarly characterized by the importance attached to discussion. Debate and discussion were marked by freedom from restrictions imposed by priestly power and were emphasized with the growth of democratic political institutions. In the Homeric poems the man skilled in words which were fit for counsel stands side by side with the man skilled in martial deeds. In Athens not merely political but legal issues were settled in the public forum. Political advancement and civic honor depended more upon the power of persuasion than upon military achievement. As general intellectual curiosity developed among the learned men, power to interpret and explain was connected with the ability to set forth a consecutive story. To give an account of something, a logos, was also to account for it. The logos, the ordered account, was the reason and the measure of the things set forth. Here was the background out of which developed a formulated theory of logic as the structure of knowledge and truth.[19]

The tragic element in this narrative of common origin is that it soon resulted in an impassible divide between logic and rhetoric. The radical quality of the Sophistical revolution is that it had recognized the "power of language to generate reasoning and, through the application of the meanings contained in it, to confer fuller and more ordered significance upon existence." The Sophists saw language, in all its forms, as helping bring about a more ordered and enriched social experience. Yet the revolution was stifled by the "hypostization of Reason." The revolution became a tragedy as soon as the Sophistical emphasis on using logic as the logos of practical reason gave way to the study of logic as the logos of pure reason. Assisted in no small part by Plato, logic became the antithesis of rhetoric rather than its facilitator. Whereas rhetoric dwelled in the corrupted realm of *doxa,* logic walked the halls of *nous,* in which Logos existed "untainted by need for anything outside itself and hence independent of all operations of doings and making." This distinction between rhetoric and logic, between logos and Logos, was, of course, a distinction "derived from and controlled by a class-structure of Greek society" in which "active or 'practical' participation in natural processes were given a low rank in the hierarchy of Being and Knowing." Yet the consequences for logical theory were disastrous, for "it held back for centuries the development of inquiries of a kind that are competent to deal with the problems of the existent world."[20] In other words it prevented the recognition that logic, like rhetoric, is an art of productive transformation that we use to adapt to a changing environment.

Yet if not the division between the rational mind and the emotional body, what distinguishes logic from rhetoric? Reading Dewey's account of the Sophists, it is difficult to tell where logic ends and rhetoric begins, as both deal with the production of a "consecutive story" and "ordered account" that is delivered in a public forum for the purposes of advocating social judgment. Logic, like rhetoric, is *inherently* practical, just as rhetoric, like logic, deals with issues of coherence and order. Both are forms of discourse that arise in response to problematic situations and manipulate symbols so as to provide practical meanings that lead to consummatory ends. This practical orientation is what makes both logic and rhetoric share status as an art in the Greek sense of *technē*. For Dewey logic does not stand apart from the rest of the "the mechanical and industrial arts" that flourished during the Sophistical movement. In his characterization of the Sophists, for instance, he includes skill in the art of logic with "defense of persuasion, of writing dramas, athletic arts, dyeing, bleaching, [and] metal working."[21] It was their dedication to the teaching of practical arts based upon experimental knowledge that made the Sophists such modern thinkers. Logic and rhetoric were simply two such arts which concentrate their attention on the practical use of logos.

What, then, is the difference between the two forms of logos? Determining their difference takes us back to Aristotle's distinction between rhetoric and dialectic. For the great categorizer, rhetoric and dialectic are counterparts, not opposites, for both are equally employed as people "attempt to discuss statements and to maintain them, to defend themselves and to attack others."[22] Moreover, Aristotle rejects the notion that appeals to emotion or the use of flowing style are the essential marks of rhetoric. They are, in his words, "non-essentials" that deal more with the personal appeal or poetic expression than the facts of the situation.[23] Like logic, then, the true substance of rhetoric is found in its form of reasoning. The difference is that whereas dialectic seeks the construction of syllogistic proofs, rhetoric employs enthymemes, which are more aesthetic and persuasive forms of demonstration in which speaker and audience cooperate in the construction of a practical judgment about some aspect of a shared situation. Drawing from and expanding upon Aristotle's insights, Farrell shows how the power and character of rhetoric derives from its ability to use enthymematic reasoning to harness the latent capacities of social conversation and channel them into productive action. For him,

> it is the *enthymeme*, as a middle-range inferential prototype of rhetorical practice, that allows conduct to become obligatory through an entwinement of situated interests and perspectives. The end result suggests that the reflective capacity of rhetoric is embedded in the reflective capacities of conversation in general—not only conversation as argument-constituted communicative action, but conversation as the sloppy, playful, give-and-take of ordinary life, distortions and all. Generally speaking, rhetoric emerges in discourse as a reflective and anticipatory choice among options imposed in a moment of uncertainty or contingency. The discursive impetus behind rhetoric is often intentional; it is always accountable, even as its successful enactment is always collaborative, bound up with the confirmation and commitment of others.[24]

The only characteristic in Farrell's description that distinguishes rhetoric from logic is its *kairotic* quality. After all, logic, no less than rhetoric, is intentional, accountable, collaborative, practical, reflective, and bound up with the confirmation and commitment of others. But only rhetoric "emerges in discourse as a reflective and anticipatory choice among options imposed in a moment of uncertainty or contingency" within the "sloppy, playful, give-and-take of ordinary life, distortions and all."[25] In Dewey's terminology logical theory differs from rhetoric only in the means by which it pursues the common goal of collective practical judgment. Whereas rhetoric finds its habitation in the moment of contingency and crisis, logic approaches inquiry as a longer term, intermediary process that requires a detailed analysis of "the relations of propositions to one another." As a result it relies less on the informal connections made by a situated audience and more on formal connections "expressed by such words as *is, is-not, if-then, only (none but), and, or, some-all*" and all others that deal with "affirmation-negation, inclusion-exclusion, particular-general" and the like.[26] Logical theory is thus an "inquiry into inquiry,"[27] and as such it allows us a place of reflection to step away from the turbulence of the public forum and examine the character of logical forms apart from the immediate demands of social judgment so as to better development lasting judgments in the long term. To define rhetoric as a kind of "applied logic" thus misses the point, for it assumes the existence of a realm of "pure" symbolic relations that only incidentally might be put to use in concrete matters. Once logic is seen for what it is—an extension of our natural ability to resolve problematic situations through the use of intelligent foresight—then the traditional problems of realism, idealism, and skepticism dissolve away; "applied" logic becomes "the sole genuine logic."[28]

If we use an example from cartography, logic endeavors to build a map of the landscape, charting out the connections, causations, and consequences between objects and events that are relevant to an eventual judgment. It thus orders a disordered situation, bringing clarity through breadth of vision and depth of insight. Logic is thus always practical insofar as it enables the restoration of equilibrium to a disturbed environment, but it becomes rhetorical once any part of this account becomes used to direct attention, interest, and energy within a situated moment of urgency and uncertainty in which one must fight, negotiate, or flee. In those contexts the patient and lengthy exposition of meaning-relationships becomes condensed into a point and fused with contingent elements of shared experience. Rhetoric thus emerges at the limits of logic to sufficiently address a moment of crisis, necessitating the creation of discourse which ultimately inhabits the particular rather than the universal. Historians, sociologists, politicians, cartographers, and military strategists may assist in judgment by constructing symbolic environments using the tools of logic, but there comes a moment when these resources are impotent to force a choice between competing moral ends. It is within these crises of judgment that rhetoric calls us to act. Yet our action is not a blind flailing about. Especially in a complex modern environment, rhetoric still draws from the resources of logic, particularly in the form of modern science, even as its activities serve to contribute to the further development of those resources.

The Colonization of the Lifeworld

If the paradigmatic rhetorical discourse is the impromptu speech given to resolve a specific moment of crisis, the paradigmatic logical discourse is the theoretical system developed to provide general guidance across diverse situations. In other words the paradigm of logic is science. In the Western tradition science began with the Presocratics in the sixth century B.C. According to

Eduard Zeller, the Presocratics "set in the place of a mythological world a world of ideas built up by the strength of independent human thought, the logos, which could claim to explain reality in a natural way."[29] This movement did not simply signal an intervention into the world of "ideas"; it set into motion the project of scientific rationality that challenged traditional beliefs and sought control of nature through empirical inquiry. Today we might find amusing Thales discovery that "all is water," but that declaration had a dramatic impact on his culture. On the one hand, Herodotus writes that being a man of a great mathematical and practical mind, Thales was able to use his practical knowledge of water to assist an army's fording of a river by cutting a channel to divert and thereby reduce its flow.[30] On the other hand, Herodotus attributes to Thales a theory that accounts for the flooding of the Nile not by the will of gods but by the Etesian winds, which obstruct its current.[31] Thales's aquatic metaphysics thus transformed both the social and natural environment in tangible ways, regardless of whether or not we hold his theory to be "true." In other words his logical discourse made meaningful changes in the realities of people's experience.

Yet efforts of this kind to explain natural phenomena through material causes challenged the conventional myths of Greek society in such a way as to cause people discomfort and resentment. In Aristophanes's *Clouds*, for instance, the ironic character of Sokrates explains rain as a result of water-saturated clouds colliding rather than "just Zeus pissing through a sieve."[32] In a telling portrait, Sokrates runs a school called the "Thinkery" in which he spends most of his time scanning the heavens while crouched in a basket that is hoisted by a crane. These types of reactions showed the consternation that the rise of science affected in a traditional culture, particularly when its conclusions seem to have come from "above" to enlighten a population who may not have asked for it. Moreover, it shows how the Greek public came to look skeptically at the flurry of efforts to find the ultimate metaphysical basis of existence. Consequently Sophists such as Protagoras stood to gain by being "in the vanguard of the humanistic reaction against the natural philosophers, whose contradictory speculations were bringing them into disrepute among practical men."[33] They looked askance at philosophies that are so detached from everyday practice as to be useless.

This tension between science and culture continues unabated today. Indeed the tensions are in many ways much greater because of the institutionalization of science, which occurred with the rise of modernity and the increasingly close relationship between science and industry. The effect is what Jürgen Habermas has called the "decoupling" of the system and lifeworld. In traditional societies, what exists is only a "lifeworld," which represents the "complex of interpenetrating cultural traditions, social orders, and personal identities"[34] that exists insofar as they draw their vitality from "a reservoir of taken-for-granteds, of unshaken convictions that participants in communication draw upon in cooperative processes of interpretation."[35] Modernity permanently disrupts this continuity. The rise of global and pluralistic societies fragments and expands the local community and besets it with problems that are too complex and far-reaching for the resources of an unreflective lifeworld to handle. Consequently, rational and independent systems of largely strategic action develop free from the constraints of social norms so as to confront problems in the objective world.[36] Systems like religion and education take over the lifeworld functions of cultural reproduction and socialization, while systems like science and law inform our ideas of truth and rightness.[37]

The danger inherent in this "decoupling," particularly with regard to science, is the potential "colonization" of the lifeworld by the very system that grew out of it. The realm of "fact," now dominated by the discourses of the system, detaches from the realm of "validity," still retained by the lifeworld, and then imposes itself back upon it. The language of "realism," of a world viewed as the objective and exclusive property of scientific research, then became what McGuire and Tuchanska describe as the "capping-stone that gave science the status of a totalizing form of cognition."[38] The practical effect of this transformation of scientific cognition into a totalizing form of cognition thus served to undermine the original, practical and democratic purpose of science as envisioned by the Sophists. As reflected in the critical tenor of much science studies, the modern fear is that science too easily translates into an ideology that empowers narrow institutional interests over the public good. In Habermas's account science produced instead a "technocracy" oriented not "toward the *realization of practical goals* but toward the *solution of technical problems*."[39] By accepting this technocratic ideology, a public thereby detaches "society's self-understanding from the frame of reference of communicative action and from the concepts of symbolic interaction and replace it with a scientific model."[40] G. Thomas Goodnight describes this process in terms of the erosion of the public sphere, which occurs as "issues of significant public consequences, what should present live possibilities for argumentation and public choice, disappear into the government technocracy or private hands."[41]

It is only from this modern problem of technology unhinged, of the rampant exploitation of instrumental reason by amoral or immoral agencies of power, that the metaphysics of "realism" becomes a rhetorical problem. This metaphysics serves to legitimate technocratic exploitation through an artificial distinction between "pure" and "applied" science that severs the connection between theory and practice. The problem with defining "applied" science in this way is that it effectively strips theoretical science of its ethical qualities and responsibilities. According to Dewey, as a result of this division, "applied science has been so largely made an equivalent of use for private and economic class purposes and privileges . . . [that] the consequences is in so far disastrous both to science and the human life."[42] Realism may give philosophical cover for these consequences, but the consequences themselves are most definitely real.

It was Dewey's recognition of this colonization of lifeworld by the instrumental imperatives that made him demand a more intelligent and democratic management of science. For him it is not enough to expose the workings of power. One also had to find an alterative way of channeling that power for productive ends. The inability or unwillingness to do so would culminate in the stripped-down world of purposive-instrumental rationality that Max Weber called the "iron cage," which was a world run by "specialists without spirits, sensualists without heart."[43] For Dewey we thus face a choice between using knowledge and being used by it. For at present,

> the application of physical science is rather to human concerns than in them. That is, it is external, made in the interests of its consequences for a possessing and acquisitive class. . . . Knowledge divided against, itself, a science to whose incompleteness is added an artificial split, has played its part in generating enslavement of men, women and children in factories in which they are animated machines to tend inanimate machines. It has maintained sordid slums, flurried and discontented careers, grinding poverty and luxurious wealth, brutal exploitation of nature and man in times of peace and high explosives and noxious gasses in times of war. . . . The ultimate harm is that understanding by man of his own affairs and his ability to direct them are sapped at their root when knowledge of nature is disconnected from its human function.[44]

What Dewey describes as the division between pure and applied science is, in effect, what Ziman calls the division between "academic" and "industrial" science. On the one hand academic science views itself as pursuing "basic" research that focuses solely on the "advancement of knowledge" that is "useless," "curiosity-driven," and propelled entirely by the "personality of the researcher."[45] As Ziman points out, this inspiring vision of the heroic researcher searching for truth is itself a part of the "Legend," but he does acknowledge that academic science nonetheless represents an institutional culture still largely guided by the Mertonian norms of communalism, universalism, disinterestedness, originality, and skepticism. On the other hand, industrial science is proprietary, local, authoritarian, commissioned, and expert, and it only pursues research "which is *commissioned* to achieve practical goals, rather than undertaken in the pursuit of knowledge."[46] This division is never as stark as the legend makes it out to be, but it is institutionalized enough in actual practice to create a divide between basic research, which grows out of universities and is driven by the acclaim given to published research, and industrial science, which occurs in the private and largely corporate research laboratories and is driven by the profit that comes from patented technology. The result is that the basic research done in the name of "useless" knowledge is often either genuinely useless or is used by industrial science to serve narrow practical interests.

Dewey's vision is in many ways continuous with the method of Protagoras's "wise man"—to find a way to create a science that was applied "in" life rather than just "to" life. For Dewey, the genuine interests of science are "served only by broadening the idea of application to include all phases of liberation and enrichment of human experience."[47] A truly "pure" science, in other words, liberates experience by functioning as a conduit through which tentative solutions to complex social problems are constructed, and it enriches experience by expanding the scope of our imaginations beyond our immediate context. In other words, at its best "scientific inquiry is an art, at once instrumental in control and final as a pure enjoyment of mind." By calling science an "art," of course, Dewey returns to the Sophistic notion of *technē* in which "art is a process of production in which natural materials are re-shaped in a projection toward consummatory fulfillment through regulation of trains of events that occur in a less regulated way on lower levels of nature."[48] Science liberates us by making the familiar strange, pursuing the meaning of that strangeness through rigorous method, and then applying that knowledge back to the familiar to make it "better."

The Rhetoric of Science

In one way the rhetorical response to the colonization of the lifeworld has followed the lead of Dewey and Habermas by critiquing the technocratic ideology, particularly as it is grounded in the metaphysics of realism, which legitimates the consolidation of power in elite hands. As Alan Gross rightly points out, the "sciences create bodies of knowledge so persuasive as to seem unrhetorical—to seem, simply, the way the world is." A rhetorical redescription of science for him thus has an emancipatory *telos,* to unmask the "arrogance of experience" in "their attempt to circumvent in their own interests the checks and balances of an open society." Put under suspicion, then, are traditional scientific claims to be discovering something true and enduring about the natural world of events and objects. To accept this possibility is to give too much ground to "realism" and thereby reinscribe the hegemony of technocratic discourse. This position is explicit in Gross when he argues that a "complete rhetoric of science must avoid this accusation: after analysis, something unrhetorical remains, a hard 'scientific' core."[49] For Gross, only by a complete rhetorical interpretation of scientific explanation does a complete rhetoric of science become possible.

In another way, however, the rhetorical response makes a significance departure from Dewey's reconstructive project. For instance, although admirable for its emancipatory ends, Gross's critical project of rhetorical redescription fails to develop adequate means to accomplish that end. As Leah Ceccarelli observes, a narrow focus on "only the 'hard case' of the scientific truth claim does more to reify science as a purely cognitive enterprise than it does to open science to the illumination of rhetorical scrutiny."[50] This effect is particularly evident in Gross. For him rhetoric as a discipline is focused specifically on starring aspects of texts, fully acknowledging that the texts of the sciences "depend heavily on a set of practices well outside the scope of rhetorical analysis."[51] This bracketing is necessary, for Gross, in highlighting the way texts—from research reports to structural paradigms—are constructed to function as persuasive documents. This disciplinary focus, in turn, is legitimized by the fact that truth claims are entirely cognitive affairs that rely on linguistic representations to produce consensus in belief. In accord with logical empiricism, Gross asserts that experiences, once they are had, are disposable, for when "experiences are represented in our belief system, they *are* in our heads and nowhere else."

This does not mean Gross denies the commonsense "brute facts" that govern our practical activities. He merely wants to assert that these activities are not really cognitive "facts" but are only activities of the body. "Facts," therefore, are linguistic propositions that can be asserted or rejected insofar on the basis of a theoretical framework of understanding. To the degree that those frameworks are created rhetorically, the facts that derive from those frameworks are rhetorical. "While our sentences about the world are caused by objects and events in the world," he explains, "it is we and not the world who attribute meaning to those objects and events. . . . Facts are not in the world but in our heads; they are by nature linguistic—no language, no facts. By definition a mind-independent reality has no semantic component. It can neither mean nor be incorporated directly into knowledge. Incorporation by reference is the only possibility."[52] The problem with this interpretation, as indicated by Ceccarelli's criticism, is that it remains completely outside the ontology of becoming in which knowledge functions as an art of transforming experience. Indeed, in Gross's account, the primary causal agent is neither texts nor human beings but "objects and events in the world." In effect Gross creates a one-way street from being to experience to rhetoric to sentences to facts. Once facts end up in the vacuum of the mind, however, it is unclear what role they play beyond crashing against one another on the backs of rhetorical tropes and figures.

However, not even Gross seems satisfied with a rhetorical account of science that restricts itself to deconstruction of isolated texts. In a striking change of tone, Gross concludes his most recent book with an analysis of "Science and Society" in which he explores how scientific facts are implicated in controversies that challenge "an existing moral order." Drawing from the work of Victor Turner, Gross explores how science functions in public controversies which are "social dramas" that involve "real-life sequences of events that share a common underlying dramatic structure." In the first act, the Breach, agents bring an "underlying social conflict vividly to public attention." In the second act, Crisis, the conflict organizes publics into conflicting or antagonistic parties. And in the third act, Redressive Action, society "adjudicates rival claims in such arenas of redress as legislatures, regulative bodies, and judiciaries." Using these categories, Gross explores how an explosion at a West Virginia coal mine led to a political movement by coal workers to change the laws regarding the regulation for coal dust levels and compensation for black lung disease, in part based upon a new ecological model of health and disease that accounted for environmental conditions. Gross thus offers a conclusion that departs radically from the confines of the text: "In the case of black lung, the miner's discontent created a breach in the social fabric, a prolonged reflective moment in which Habermas's emancipatory interest, embodied in a rhetoric of talk and action, transformed an existing moral order. This transformation altered the understanding of occupational disease, substituting and ecological for a biomedical model. More importantly, the miners' action democratized the process whereby disease is defined. In the case of the biomedical model, the needs of the physicians and their employers were satisfied; in the case of the ecological model, the needs of the miners."[53]

Notable about this dramatic representation of scientific controversies is how texts no longer exist outside of "practice" and how facts are no longer just in the "mind." Instead texts and facts only find meaning within situational contexts of judgment that occur over a temporal horizon of becoming. This interpretive attitude appears in the work of Celeste Michelle Condit in her analysis of the shifting meanings of the "gene" both in public discourse and in institutional scientific practice. For Condit there are two false binaries which rhetorical theory needs to confront. First, no clear hierarchy exists between public and scientific discourse; in actual fact, "public discourse guides and supports (or prevents) science every bit as much as the reverse." Second, science tends to enter the public arena when it relates to our "shared determinations of how we should live together." This does not mean, however, that public rhetoric is simply "added on" to some pure scientific text. As Condit emphasizes, "public rhetoric" is not what is leftover after the science, logic, action, and other substance is left out, as is implied by the frequent misuse of the phrase "mere rhetoric." Rather, public rhetoric consists of the set of communicative interactions through which members of a community share with each other their good reasons for choosing courses of action together, where these good reasons include evidence and logic, but also, necessarily, social values and affective relationships and identities. For Condit, then, scientific and public discourse are distinct but overlapping entities that converse with one another through time in search of "shared determinations of how we should live together."[54] To study the rhetoric of science is to explore the different rhetorical formations that compete with one another for institutional support and public authority in an ever-changing social environment.

It is from this transactional perspective that a truly democratic rhetoric of science returns to its authentically Sophistical roots. In Dewey's narrative, Sophists like Protagoras were less interested in metaphysical doctrines and more interested in developing "inventions, tools, techniques of action and works" that might "cooperate with nature and render it amenable to human happiness."[55] Rather than seek to discover (or debunk) the pure logic of being to find the truth, they strived to produce a practical logic of becoming to constitute a pleasurable life. For achieving the goal of an authentically "pure" science takes more than simply a nominalistic critique of realism. Criticism may pierce the ideological mask of technocracy, but it does little to promote active reconstruction in science. That can come only through a broader understanding of the origin and function of science in a modern technological and global society. Dewey's work provides a framework for that rhetoric that resonates with the social and historical approach taken by Habermas. By viewing science as an institutionalization of the procedures of experimental logic, Dewey provides a pragmatic distinction between logic and rhetoric that also allows us to see their interactive and function relationship in the world of practice. From this perspective rhetoric arises both at the points of intersection between science and society as well as the moments of conflict between the differing lifeworlds within science itself. Recovering the situational and instrumental essence of rhetoric leads to a more genuinely democratic and liberating rhetoric of science that both challenges realist hegemony and advances the project of practical and cooperative judgment.

Naturalism in Logic

From the perspective of the ontology of becoming, a rhetoric of science moves beyond the critique of realism to ground itself within the temporal, spatial, and communicative relationship between science and common sense. Understanding this relationship, however, requires a deeper appreciation of the naturalistic roots of logic as a functional expression of our naturalistic relationship to our environment. This appreciation is important because the very word "logic" denotes a system of abstract symbols such as algebra that have only a mental, not physical, existence. Likewise, scientific knowledge, as a form of logic, is said to exist in a purely cognitive realm of *episteme* that exists parallel to the emotional and physical realm of *doxa* and *nomos*—of common *sense*. The dualism that divides science from common sense is thus an extension of the dualism that separates logic from rhetoric—the dualism between mind from body.

Dewey's naturalism strikes at the heart of this dualism by viewing "mind" as a functional organ of the body in the way like our other sensory or motor organs. For Dewey "rational operations grow out of organic activities, without being identical with that from which they emerge."[56] This nonidentification is precisely what gives logical forms their power; by growing out of organic activities and then being transformed in reflection, rational operations can then be used as tools to direct further activities. Logic within this postulate is a higher activity of the organ of mind that shares with the other biological activities and forms the same basic goal—the adjustment of the whole organism to its environment. The difference is that logic adopts the route of symbolic abstraction to resolve problems in that environment whereas other activities are more direct. Yet even in abstract, logic remains continuous with biological operations.

To exemplify how rational processes grow out of biological contexts, Dewey uses the example of "hunger." In all organisms the experience of hunger comes about by an imbalance in the digestive system, usually caused by lack of nutrition, which affects the performance and health of other organs. In hunger, therefore, a "state of tension is set up which is an actual state (not a mere feeling) of organic uneasiness and restlessness. This state of tension (which defines need) passes into search for material that will restore the condition of balance." Hunger is not simply the psychological feeling of an isolated subject, it is a state of tension that involves the total relationship between an organism and its environment. However, the subsequent behavior of that organism to that state of tension, to the need to *eat*, differs depending on the capacities of the organism. In simple-cell organisms, one sees such actions as "the bulgings and retractions of parts of the organism's periphery so that nutritive material is ingested," which in turn leads to restoration of balance, to fulfillment.[57]

In higher, more complex organisms, the process has more intermediate steps; "the activity of search involves modification of the old environment, if only by a change in the connection of the organism with it."[58] Ants do not simply "bulge" but develop complex instincts over time that lead them to construct shelters, search for good, and organize foraging parties. Higher mammals such as primates then differ from ants in being able to adapt more flexibly to environmental and social situations. By drawing from the resources of imaginative reason and social gestures of communication, they are able to hunt collectively and develop basic tools to modify their environment. With all organisms there is a desire to return to a state of fulfillment, but the time between agitation and satisfaction grows wider and involves more intermediary steps as organisms develop capacities to more thoroughly modify environmental conditions. In this sense the sciences of agriculture and the economic systems, at least in their functional capacity, that support differ only in degree from the systems of cultivation that go on within the tunnels of anthills.

The parallel between logical theory and the bulging of a microorganism does not imply that microorganisms possess logic, but rather than logic is a continuation of the basic function of biological habits. In all organisms with the capacity to learn, habits represent the complex of adjustments that they use to maintain or restore equilibrium. As "the basis of organic learning," habit stands for a series of coordinated actions that originates in need or desire and ends in consummatory satisfaction. Thus in "habit and learning the linkage is tightened up not by sheer repetition but by the institution of effective integrated interaction of organic-environing energies—the consummatory close of activities of exploration and search."[59] A dog's habit of curling up at the foot of the bed at night for security and warmth is thus no different in kind than an engineer's habit of using pi in the formulas used to design parts for a space shuttle. Both are habits of thought and action that originate in a problem and are directed toward a consummatory end. Dewey's point is that the practice of logic should be understood within the basic need-satisfaction continuum that distinguishes living from nonliving entities.

The crucial difference between the habits of dogs and engineers, the difference that also informs our understanding of rhetoric, is that the habits of the latter are focused largely on habits of thought that center on the manipulation of symbols. The problems that occupy the mind of an engineer do not stem from the biological environment but from the cultural and discursive ones. The obvious fact is that the activities of human beings are "determined not by organic structure and physical heredity alone but by the influence of cultural heredity, embedded in traditions, institutions, customs and the purposes and beliefs they both carry and inspire." Recognition of this fact then leads to the inevitable focus on language and communication as the primary means by which a culture is formed, maintained, and transformed. As Dewey never tires of pointing out, communication is "the making of something common." To "make common" does not mean to place in individual minds an equivalent cognitive meaning or reference but to create common "agreement in *action;* of shared modes of responsive behavior and participation in their consequences."[60] Through a conjoint community of functional use, linguistic symbols take on conventional meanings that establish common attitudes toward the events and objects that populate a social environment.

Often, then, problems arise not because of biological conditions but as a result of conflict within the symbolic realm of language itself. A dog is unlikely to be distraught while lying on a soft rug at the feet of its owner. An engineer, however, concerned about generating consensus about a design plan, may be overcome by anxiety over an unsolved equation even while watching the sun set.

She then might begin to develop arguments for how to persuade her colleagues to adopt a new method of inquiry when they meet again in the morning.

Science simply institutionalizes the reflective and experimental process of logical thought as it goes on in the human individual. Similar to how logic functions in individual consciousness to bring order to a problematic situation and direct future experience, science reacts to problems in common sense by using the tools to theoretical abstraction to provide richer resources for collective judgment. Scientific subject matter and procedures not only grow out of common sense but also react into it "in a way that enormously refines, expands, and liberates the contents and agencies at the disposal of common sense."[61] This occurs in both the context of everyday technology and the very way we understand ourselves and our world. Technology may lift human beings into space, but scientific understanding provides the unique sense of wonder when observing the unblemished stars through the window of the shuttle. Herein lies what he calls the paradox of theory and practice—"that theory is with respect to all other modes of practice the most practical of all things, and the more impartial and impersonal it is, the more truly practical it is."[62] The reason for this paradox only becomes apparent when one understands that the "depersonalizing of the things of everyday practice becomes the chief agency of their repersonalizing in new and more fruitful modes of practice."[63] What Dewey refers to here is the often unrecognized "final cause" of science—the liberation and enrichment of human experience. Only through the liberation of meanings from the context of commonsense usage are such novel and more far-reaching ways of interpreting our world made possible such that science attains its status as "pure."

Science and Common Sense

For Dewey genuine reconstruction in knowledge comes about through changes in the forms of communication between science and common sense. The relationship between these two spheres roughly parallels the relationship between logic and experience. Similar to Habermas's concept the lifeworld, Dewey's interpretation of common sense represents a "set of meanings which are so deeply embedded in its customs, occupations, traditions and ways of interpreting its physical environment and group-life, that they form the basic categories of the language-system by which details are interpreted." What characterizes common sense is that it deals with issues of "use and enjoyment" that are directly implicated in the ordinary affairs of life.[64] As such common sense is highly qualitative and teleological; it deals with things in their unique relationship to people's situated needs and desires.

By contrast science represents a specialized community of inquirers who rely on the language and methods of logic to produce warranted assertions that enable judgment in problematic situations which cannot be adequately settled by conventional methods. Consequently science can only develop a unique perspective on this subject matter by stripping its discourse of qualitative and teleological aspects and replacing them with accounts that rely on magnitude, mathematical relations, and "efficient" causation irrespective of ends and values. The result is that science speaks in a different language of "symbol-constellations that are radically unlike those familiar to common sense." In these constellations the experienced world of the craftsman and the poet is turned into something abstract, impersonal, and systematic. This is by design. As Dewey explains:

> Science or theory means a system of objects detached from any particular personal standpoint, and therefore available for any and every possible personal standpoint. Even the exigencies of ordinary social life require a slight amount of such detachment or abstraction. I must neglect my own peculiar ends enough to take some account of my neighbor if I am going to be intelligible to him. I must at least find common ground. Science systematizes and indefinitely extends this principle. It takes its stand, not with what is common and with some particular neighbor living at this especial date in this particular village, but with any possible neighbor in the wide stretches of time and space. And it does so by the mere fact that it is continually reshaping its peculiar objects with an eye single to availability in inference. The more abstract, the more impersonal, the more impartially objects are its objects, the greater the variety and scope of inference made possible. Every street of experience which is laid out by science has its tracks for transportation, and every line issues transfer checks to every other line. You and I may keep running in certain particular ruts, but conditions are provided for somebody else to foresee—or infer—new combinations and new results.[65]

Dewey's use of the train metaphor shows how science, while traveling far from its original departure point in common sense, nonetheless represents an extension of it. For him "scientific subject matter and procedures grow out of the direct problems and methods of common sense, of practical uses and enjoyments." As a social institution, science originates from a practical source—the desire of a society to expand their scope of practical knowledge about their environment through the methods of specialized inquiry. In this way science bears what Dewey calls a "genetic and functional relation to the subject-matter of common sense."[66] The need for better bridges, the demand to cure a disease, or the curiosity of what lies beyond our world all originate as the subject matter of common sense that are then taken up by science. The ultimate value of scientific abstraction, depersonalization, and systematization thus rests in its ability to encourage the exchange, connection, and free movement of ideas. In a diverse world, cooperative inquiry of this sort can only happen through a communicative structure designed for maximum access, utility, and stability.

The clear objection to this naturalistic perspective is that it denies the sort of "basic" research privileged by academic science and championed by the "Legend." As Ziman points out, however, the pressure for even academic science to serve public needs is not new. "Universities have long been active sites of research in engineering, medicine and agriculture, and in the applicable social science such as law and economics." This research, of course, was not necessarily intended not for direct technological or industrial application, but to more generally "illuminate the background to practical problems, and to provide active practitioners with the knowledge needed to solve them."[67] But even if there existed no conscious "problem" to which research was related, even the dedicated university researcher who honestly pursues her work for the sheer joy of discovery—exemplified in the persona of the pure mathematician—has a career only because the university deems her position important to the institutional mission. One should not conflate the personal motives of the researcher—who may, indeed, have no clear practical intent or naturalistic origin—with the motives of the institution which employs her, be that institution public or private.

Ironically, then, one of the greatest threats to the autonomy of "basic" scientific research is the denial of its own social utility. For the heyday of "pure" academic science has passed with the aristocratic notion of the university. Even the dualism between "pure" and "applied" science is no longer as applicable as it once was. Ziman, for instance, described a new era of "post-academic science" in which even the purest of academic disciplines are "under pressure to give more obvious value for money" and "being pressed into the serve of the nation as the driving force in a national R&D system, a wealth-creating technoscientific motor for the whole economy." In this new era the Mertonian norms of academic science are being invaded by the imperatives of industrial science. Thus whereas science had always been tied in some way to the illumination of issues that are of public concern and/or drive public curiosity, the "novel factor is the requirement that research should be explicitly targeted at *recognizably practical problems*." In postacademic science, evaluation of research must go beyond peer review to so-called merit review by nonspecialist "users."[68] On the one hand postacademic science has its benefits in encouraging multidisciplinary projects that serve (at least in the ideal) genuinely public interest. On the other hand it threatens to narrow the research focus to such short-term applications that it stifles the possibility for the long-term speculation and inquiry that can succeed only through more "playful" experimentation.

As a result the more that research scientists cling to the legend of the disinterested scholar, the more they will be marginalized in both institutional culture and the public at large. As Condit notes, those "who would deny this tether between science and the public needs to consider carefully why it is that we have a human genome project, but no superconducting supercollider."[69] The point is that neither a project of big science nor a department in a major university can be justified on the basis of seeking knowledge for its own sake. No aspect of science, including the humanities, can gain long-term institutional support without finding a way to anchor itself in the needs of common sense. The challenge is to do so while justifying the kind of inquiry whose promise comes not just in its capacity to build a better mousetrap but also in its ability to enrich our long-term existence in a common world, including our aesthetic and contemplative relationship with that world. This would be what Ziman calls "a stout intellectual and moral defence for science at the level of ordinary human affairs—the level at which nothing is absolute or eternal, but where we often forget that life is short, and feel passionately about pasts that we have not personally experienced, or plan conscientiously for the future welfare of people whom we shall never know."[70]

What Ziman calls for is a justification for science that satisfies the demands of the ontology of becoming that understands our world through the context of a changing history that we have inherited and which others will carry forward after our deaths. Science is neither a grasp of being nor a tool for profit; at its best it represents the possibility of humankind to collect their energies toward the enrichment of shared existence. Only by understanding its vital connection with common sense can we bring about a science that serves both public needs and public vision.

Contextualism and Warranted Assertions

What makes science so powerful is its logical structure. The power of logic is a result of its capacity for building abstract symbolic networks of understanding—for the building of "tracks," if you will—out of the sturdy material of propositions. A proposition differs from ordinary speech is that its meaning consists of "relation to other meanings in the system of which it is a member."[71] Most important, this relationship is formal. By "relation" Dewey does mean only that by being a word in the English language, the term "cat" or "love" or "hi" attains logical status by being a part of a culture's linguistic repertoire. The language of common sense, too, forms a system, but "the system is practical rather than intellectual. It is constituted by the traditions, occupations, techniques, interests, and established institutions of the group." By contrast, scientific "meanings are related to one another on the ground of the character *as* meanings, freedom from direct reference to the concerns of a limited group."[72]

The focus on universal applicability makes logical propositions have greater connectivity and coherence even as they allow for less flexibility and subtly. This characteristic sacrifices the aesthetic sensitivity of fine art for the ability to build ever-larger discursive structures with wider ranging applicability and scope.

What makes Dewey's conceptualization something much different than that of traditional realism is that he does not assume that greater universality, abstraction, or logical coherence of science equates with an intrinsic superiority over the practical beliefs and habits of common sense. Quite the opposite, Dewey values science insofar as its conclusions help enrich common experience by bringing equilibrium back to a disturbed situation. Put another way, as long as the resources of common sense effectively deal with the contingencies of one's social environment, there is no need for science. In an already stable situation, it is habit, most notably in the form of rituals and norms, which performs the role of judgment.

The cause and justification for science thus arises only in the context of experienced doubt. To experience doubt, one possesses uncomfortable feelings that are distinct from just the ordinary recognition of ignorance. Adapting the model of Charles Sanders Peirce, Dewey understands doubt and inquiry as being related as problem and solution: "Doubt is uneasy; it is a tension that finds expression and outlet in the processes of inquiry. Inquiry terminates in reaching that which is settled." Furthermore, Dewey differs again from realism by defining the "settling" of inquiry to be something more than the formation of a proposition. For him the settling of inquiry is the formation of new habits of thought and action that bring about a more balanced and "easy" experience. Just as germ theory demands that we wash our hands to avoid contagion, a settled inquiry signals a "readiness to act in a given way when, if, and as, that subject-matter is present in existence."[73]

Because of this practical and habitual reading of the goal of inquiry, Dewey prefers the term "warranted assertion" to the terms belief and knowledge.[74] By "warranted" Dewey means something justified on the basis of previous inquiry, and by "assertion" he means something which is a situated communicative act within an ongoing inquiry process. The goal of scientific inquiry is thus not the discovery of "truth," but the construction of "warranted assertions" that represent the best and most thorough judgment that can be made within a community of inquirers at a particular place and time in history. Warranted assertions take facts out of the "mind" and make the speech acts performed in contexts of shared judgment. As McGuire and Tuchanska argue, truth from this standpoint happens within particular "practices of referring" which occur "within the social world and among other cultural activities." That is why we can neither attach "truth" to the representational aspect of the warrant alone nor to an abstract state of "belief" that resides in a passive consciousness. Instead, "truth" must be viewed in terms of "disclosure" or an "ontological commitment . . . based on judgment relative to context and purpose."[75] The context of this judgment is larger than a laboratory. It occurs in its transaction with the cultural lifeworld of which science is a part.

Dewey's reading of science, based on his logical theory, shares with rhetorical theory an emphasis on the importance of context. It is the context in which warranted assertions are made, and not epistemological "truth" of propositions in isolation, that determines their pragmatic truth value. In this way scientific knowledge is as relative to *kairos* as rhetorical judgment. For Dewey logical forms neither exist in a realm of pure reason nor have a fixed or static meaning. From his contextualist theory of meaning, logical forms "accrue to matter in virtue of the adaptation of materials and operations to one another in the service of specified ends."[76] Put another way, the value and meaning of any logic form can only be determined in the concrete when it is used to provide order within problematic situations that demand reconstruction and modification to achieve an ideal resolution. In many ways this perspective agrees with aspects of the three dominant theories of meaning. It agrees with "the 'realistic' interpretation of generals in affirming that ways of acting are as existential as are singular events and objects"; it agrees with nominalism that "the logically general, whether generic or universal, has necessarily the character of a symbol"; and it agrees with conceptualism that "the general is conceptual or ideational in nature."[77] Where it departs from all of them is the rejection of the dualistic idea that the problem to be solved involves the correspondence between "idea" and "thing," the problem that in logical theory takes the form of the distinction between the "concept" and the "percept." Realism, nominalism, and conceptualism argue about where "general" or "universal" ideas are located and how well they match up to reality, but they all agree that these ideas are purely cognitive and exist in the realm of the mind. Even skepticism agrees on this point, choosing only to reject the validity of those cognitions. For Dewey's contextualism, by contrast, meaning does not refer to how words do or do not match up to things or ideas statically conceived; meaning exists insofar as symbols have helped bring order to and shared understanding about a particular problem that arises in a particular context.

Like rhetorical approaches to meaning, then, Dewey's radical contextualism views logic as a tool for reconstructing experience through temporal becoming, thereby making the determination of meaning fundamentally inseparable from situational context, both symbolic and experiential. What Dewey advances, in other words, is what Shook calls a "functionalist epistemology and pragmatic realism."[78] What this means is that Dewey, like Protagoras, accepted the "reality" of experienced objects as experienced while at the same time interpreting transcendent entities, expressed in terms of universal concepts, as general ways of acting that are instrumental in transforming the objects of experience.

This distinction is expressed in logic as the difference between what he calls "generic" and "universal" propositions. Corresponding to Dewey's pragmatic realism, a generic proposition is a "conception of a kind [that] is based upon a set of related traits or characteristics that are the necessary and sufficient conditions of describing a specified kind." Generic propositions thus rely on the actual existence of certain traits that appear consistently in some constellation—even if these appearances are simply in fictional representations, like pictures of centaurs. Hence the proposition "The sun is a yellow hot star that rises and sets" allows a diverse number of people to come to agreement about the nature of some set of common experienced stimuli and refer to it with a common name. By contrast, corresponding to Dewey's epistemological functionalism, a universal proposition is "a formulation of a way of acting or operating ... that functions as the ground for warranted inferential conclusions."[79] Hence the proposition "If you pull stare too long at the sun, you will go blind" informs people how to act in response to a particular "kind" of thing. This is a universal proposition because it involves an if/then statement that links together two ideas in some sequential relationship based on a logical system of meaning and understanding. Unlike generic propositions, however, universal propositions do not require existential status; they can exist purely in the realm of symbolic relationships. The statement "$2 + 2 = 4$" is thus a universal proposition; "Cats have four legs" is a generic one. A universal proposition represents a method of acting that might resolve some inferential difficulty; a generic proposition assists us in making sense of some actual experience by categorization and division.

What distinguishes the discourse of science from that of common sense is that its generic propositions appear to have little existential reference and its universal propositions no immediate practical significance. Generic propositions about dinosaurs, atoms, or gravitational forces often seem to exist in the realm of some fabulous fiction. And the universal propositions of quantum physics that call into question the universal propositions of Newtonian mechanics thus seem completely absurd to the practical-minded craftsman or engineer. Given this divide between the language of science and common sense, it is tempting to fall back into dualism that either affirms the truths of science on the basis of a higher rationality or rejects those truths on the basis on a practical and/or moral irrelevance. Once this dualistic position is taken, logic and rhetoric can thus part ways, with logic taking the side of reason and rhetoric of practice. The challenge, subsequent to drawing these battle lines, then amounts to one side proving the other to be full of hot air. And since this is, by now, a familiar fight, any victory is short lived, counterproductive, and intellectually regressive because it is based on the principles of the metaphysics of being which always forces upon us either/or alternatives.

Dewey's contextual theory of meaning attempts to break us from this negative spiral by insisting that the epistemological—meaning practical—value of any logical system of explanation is ultimately determined by how it transacts with a larger social and cultural environment over time. Even a discipline such as mathematics, which so often seems caught up its own symbol system, finds justification in this way. Dewey notes that historically "numerical determinations first arose as means of economic and effective adjustment of material means to material consequences in qualitative situations marked by deficiency and excess."[80] That mathematics has become liberated to such an extent that it often functions without conscious reference to any situation does mean that its discoveries may not be put to use in some unforeseen situation in the future. As an expression of possibility, scientific theories often exist purely as promissory notes that hope to pay off dividends in the future, even if that future is one simply of an enriched perceptual or creative experience. For Dewey, to talk about the "truth" of such a theory apart from experience is to spin one's wheels. For him verification is not a matter of simply matching up logical propositions with a set of empirical data; verification "is a matter of the systematic ordering of a complex set of data by means of the idea or theory *as an instrumentality.*"[81] What he means by "instrumentality" is simply that it helps bringing order to a problematic situation, much as looking at a map helps locate oneself in the forest so as to make one's way home. That people busy themselves making maps that lack immediate application does not make their work irrelevant or untrue; it simply means their work has yet to function as an instrumentality that makes them true.

It is important to point out that Dewey's contextualist theory of meaning applies not just to the logical forms of scientific theories but also to the logical forms that emerge from any social group, institution, or culture. The old schoolyard example that Eskimos have many words for "snow" is but a succinct expression of the theory that the meaning of words from a logical standpoint only makes sense in reference to the outstanding events and situations from which they emerged. Moreover, the cultural argument that learning a foreign language helps one understand their culture shows Dewey's theory in reverse— that one can work "back" to context by trying to discover the situational origin of the logical forms preserved in a culture's language. These ideas, so ordinary as to be mundane, take on a radical orientation only because of the entrenched vocabulary of epistemology that so often steers the conversation, even of its critics, into the same familiar tail-chasing exercise. The only way out of this cycle is to view meaning-creation in temporal context. For Dewey it is obvious that "there is not possible any such thing as a direct one-to-one correspondence of names with existential objects," but that does not mean that names are purely fictions with no existential reference. Rather, we should understand that "words mean what they mean in connection with conjoin activities that effect a common, or mutually participated in, consequence," even if that consequence is understood not in terms of weeks but in centuries.[82]

Recoupling Science and Common Sense

Science has the possibility of enriching the quality of these conjoint activities, but learning how to actualize this possibility requires looking more closely at the communicative relationship between science and common sense. As indicated by Dewey's complaint that the application of science is *to* human concerns rather than *in* them, the problem with the modern era is that in "the things of greatest import there is little intercommunication" so that the "paths of communication between common sense and science are as yet largely one-way lanes."[83] The route that was of most concern to Dewey was the path from science back to common sense. He took it for granted that "science takes its departure from common sense" but noted that "the return road into common sense is devious and blocked by existing social conditions."[84] As a result science grows out of organic activities only to become caught into a self-perpetuating logic no longer directed toward resolving any long-term problem. There are two results to this. First, it perpetuates a dualistic justification of knowledge that exists "for itself," a justification which culminates in dogmatic public assertions of "truth" that seek to enlighten the beliefs of common sense. Second, it licenses industrial "applied" science to dominate the sphere of practice. When combined, one thus has the metaphysics of realism appearing to license the wholesale exploitation of knowledge for specialized interests.

In short, in a decoupled science, the conclusions of research are co-opted by the needs of the system, which draws upon its technocratic ethos to force itself upon a reluctant lifeworld. In this situation a "class of experts is inevitably so removed from common interests as to become a class with private interests and private knowledge, which in social matters is not knowledge at all."[85] This situation manifests itself in what Charles Alan Taylor calls the rhetoric of demarcation in which practicing scientists seek to "exclude various non- or pseudo-sciences so as to sustain their (perhaps well-earned) position of epistemic authority and to maintain a variety of professional resources."[86] When successful, the rhetoric of demarcation results in what Steve Fuller calls "plebi-science," which is characterized by an elitist "distinction between the production (by experts) and the distribution (to nonexperts) of knowledge."[87] This demarcation, moreover, creates an "internalist" account of science that largely walls it off from public influence—the only interaction coming from "publicity agents" that purport to serve the public interest by flooding it with press releases from the citadel of knowledge.[88]

As most activists know, however, scientific authority in some form is vital to advance any cause. What is needed is more than a critique of realism; for as Ziman points out, those who activists who unmask the technocratic ideology of "objectivity" are actually "breaking their own swords in the struggle against their most feared opponents—the corporate and governmental enterprises that drive post-industrial society."[89] The issue is not science versus no science, but a worse science versus a better one. Therefore a form of expertise must be developed that has a kind of authority for the public beyond that of the magician or the monarch. For Dewey this means implementing methods of constructive transaction between scientists and the public concerning the relevance and application of their warranted assertions to matters of public interest. It requires, in other words, "recourse to methods of discussion, consultation and persuasion" which are intrinsic to democratic social life.[90] In place of both hostility and authority, Dewey calls for more critical engagement between scientists and citizens in a deliberative public sphere about matters of specialized research that intersect with public interests.

Fortunately, although the language of science and common sense are distinct in style and content, their boundaries are nonetheless permeable. This observation comes from philosopher of science Paul Feyerabend, who wrote it in reaction to the famous "debate" between Thomas Kuhn and Karl Popper concerning whether or not science should be a closed community or an open society. In his essay Feyerabend denies the periodicity of Kuhn's historical account that describes discrete periods of normal and revolutionary science that succeed one another. Instead, he suggests that there is simply a "normal *component* and the philosophical *component*" of science and that "the correct relation is one of *simultaneity* and *interaction*." The normal component represents the established rules of any field and is supported by "people who habitually resists change; who frown at any criticism of things dear to them; and whose highest aim is to solve puzzles on a basis that is neither known nor understood." They are, of course, the majority at any one time. But always accompanying the normal component are those philosophically minded scientists who exhibit a love of ideas. For Feyerabend, consequently, "changes in the *philosophical component* most likely *can* be explained as the result of clear and unambiguous *arguments*."[91] The only institutional support one needs to create such arguments is what Feyerabend calls the ethics of "proliferation," or the demand that we tolerate "even the most outlandish product of the human brain," and "tenacity," or the insistence that we encourage people "not just to follow one's inclinations, but to develop them further, to raise them, with the help of criticism . . . to a higher level of articulation and thereby to raise their defense to a higher level of consciousness." Then Feyerabend acknowledges something surprising for a philosopher of science—the role of journalism in legitimate scientific debate. Specifically he notes the importance of the relationship between journalism and the philosophical component of science:

> The normal component is large and well entrenched. Hence, a change of the normal component is very noticeable. So is the resistance of the normal component to change. This resistance becomes especially strong and noticeable in periods where a change seems to be imminent. It is directed against the philosophical component and brings it into public consciousness. The younger generation, always eager for new things, seizes upon the new material and studies it avidly. Journalists, always on the lookout for headlines—the more absurd, the better—publicize the new discoveries (which are those elements of the philosophical component which most radically disagree with the current views while still possessing some plausibility and perhaps even some factual support). These are some reasons for the differences which we perceive. I do not think that one should look for anything more profound.[92]

In Feyerabend's system, normal science occupies an institutional "center" based on an implicit paradigm that interacts with philosophical components along the margins. By necessity "the normal component almost always outweighs its philosophical part," but mass does not equate necessarily to power, as "a single man can revolutionize an epoch." Thus the general ignorance that most scientists exhibit toward philosophy is largely irrelevant for Feyerabend. He writes, "For it is not *they* who carry out fundamental improvement but those who further the *active interaction* of the normal and philosophical components, whose interaction consists almost always in the criticism of what is well entrenched and unphilosophical by what is peripheral and philosophical." In other words journalists and the media create a forum in which the active interaction of these components can happen.

Although effects of such an interaction are admittedly slow in coming, they do occur. Feyerabend notes that change may occur "because the younger generation cannot be bothered to follow their elders; or because some public figure has changed his mind; or because some influential member of the established has died and has failed (perhaps because of his suspicious nature) to leave behind a strong and influential school, or because of powerful and nonscientific institution pushes thought in a definite direction."[93] One sees in Feyerabend, then, a cyclical framework in which experimental philosophical ideas are tested out and promoted within the public sphere before gaining institutional support, either scientifically, politically, or educationally. This support then instigates new patterns and methods of inquiry that then become normalized over time before the cycle inevitably begins again. This more optimistic view, which acknowledges the permeability of scientific discourse, is echoed by

Ziman. "Looking at scientific paradigms from a naturalistic perspective, we often see them to be highly influential, but seldom absolutely dominant. There is ample empirical evidence that scientists do, at times, honour the norm of originality by thinking the unthinkable, seeing the invisible, and taking serious notice of the exceptional. Such 'heretics' often have difficulty in presenting their research claims formally to the scientific community; but the traditional institutions of academic science are usually too weak to silence them completely without the support of more powerful external institutions such as the Church or the State."[94]

What emerges is a cycle of inquiry bounded on one side by the commonsense discourse of uses and enjoyments and on the other side by the abstract, systematic, and logical discourse of science. The communicative aspects of this cycle can be broken into categories. The route from common sense to science can effectively be termed the "context of discovery" because within this route problems are identified and various solutions are proposed and deliberated. The route from science back to common sense can be termed the "context of justification" because within this route theories are advanced, justified, and tested. As a cycle, of course, these routes have considerable overlap. Discovery may begin at the level of paradigm, but it inevitably narrows its focus to the level of proof. Justification, meanwhile, may begin at the level of proof only to reveal previously unrecognized gaps and problems which demand further large-scale invention. Nonetheless, the distinction is important in order to recognize which direction a particular discourse is heading. If one takes global warming as an example, before it became widely accepted, shocking images of melting glaciers combined with the proposition that this phenomenon was caused by greenhouse gases functioned in the context of discovery. Subsequent to the development and general embrace of the theory, movies such as Al Gore's *An Inconvenient Truth* and the arguments over the Kyoto Protocol functioned within the context of justification.

Within both these contexts, communications takes one of two primary forms, either expressive or constitutive in terms of the rhetoric of inquiry. Expressive communication means the attempt to bring awareness that something is present and needs attention, while constitutive communication means the effort to confront or alter how objects within a logical theory are constituted. In the context of discovery the expressive function occurs as a kind of "signaling" that calls attention to events and objects within an unsettled and problematic situation, like warming polar temperatures and rising sea waters. The constitutive function manifests itself in the efforts by "philosophically" minded scientists and citizens to promote hypotheses and experimental ideas for more formal consideration, like the long efforts to attribute rising temperatures to greenhouse gases rather than normal temperature fluctuations. In the context of justification the expressive function takes the form of educationally oriented discourse, such as Gore's movie, that conveys the content of scientific theories to the public through the language of art, while the constitutive function represents the dialogue among scientists, engineers, politicians, and citizens, such as the Kyoto Protocol, concerning how scientific theories might be modified or applied in ways that help them contribute to the liberation and enrichment of the lifeworld of common sense. Again, all of these facets of communication occur within the larger communicative cycle between science and common sense and interpenetrate one another. But locating their primary emphasis enables a better understanding of their role within the broader and more complex universe of discourse, an understanding that is necessary to further the goal of furthering intelligent social judgment about complex issues.

The Stages of Inquiry

One of the most important functions of the rhetoric of science is to identify and trace the rhetorical situations that arise along the various points of the inquiry process. When discussing these stages, however, it is important to keep in mind that "science" here is being used much as "public"—not as a single monolithic institution or entity but as a legitimate authority of inquiry-based knowledge with respect to some public. The stages of inquiry are applicable not only to major government, university, or corporate funded research, but also to religious institutions, interest groups, think tanks, community organizations, or tribal authorities. The factors that matter in identifying a discrete inquiry process is a semi-autonomous organization dedicated to employing logical resources to bring order and balance to a situation through communicative transaction with the common sense of some public. In any democratic society, then, any number of "scientific" organizations will be supported by a diverse number of publics, each providing different warranted assertions that seek to transform common sense through rhetorical engagement. Again, it is the task for rhetoric not to define science per se but to identify the points of tension within and between institutions which perform the role of knowledge production.

Dewey assists in this endeavor by breaking down inquiry into six discrete stages that exist along the temporal continuity between science and common sense, beginning with problems in common sense that call for resolution through inquiry and ending with the warranted assertions of inquiry as they seek to alter the habits of common sense. These stages are signaling, defining, proposing, reasoning, warranting, and transacting.[95] Within each of these stages, rhetorical "devices" are undoubtedly employed at all levels as citizens and scientists communicate. Yet rhetoric exists only as a discrete discursive form in these stages, within certain contexts, that makes rhetorical discourse representative of something more than an assortment of devices. In these contexts rhetoric does what logic cannot—move people to collective practical judgment when they are face a rhetorical situation that confronts them with competing moral ends that can appeal to no unambiguous authority for its resolution.

In signaling, some habit of common sense has been obstructed without a discernable cause such that it brings about feelings of anxiety, confusion, disturbance, and discomfort. Hence there "is nothing intellectual or cognitive in the existence of such situations. . . . In themselves they are precognitive."[96] To say they are precognitive is not to say they are irrational. Dewey means that they are events that deal primarily with emotional intelligence, which is able to determine what is desirable and undesirable within a changed environment. For instance, a community suddenly beset by respiratory disease emotionally knows the symptoms of the problem, even if it cannot pinpoint the cause. What one needs in these situations is to gain a clearer understanding of the causes and conceptions of solutions. The signal is a call to inquiry which emerges from common sense and is directed toward science, requesting the cognitive resources of social inquiry to return some sense of balance to an unstable situation. As such, it arises at the expressive component of the context of discovery.

For privileged communities, of course, rhetoric is largely unnecessary in this stage, as their needs are immediately recognized and reacted upon by political authorities able to direct the resources of science. The rhetorical challenge typically focuses on the efforts by more marginalized communities who must work through indirect channels to call attention to their plight and warrant the expenditure of resources. Rhetoric must be employed to struggle against the institutional inertia of scientific bureaucracy to bring attention and recognition to the marginalized problems of common sense. Often relying on graphic portrayals of people's lives mysteriously transformed for the worse, rhetoric during this phase relies on the tragic power of spectacle in the mass media to direct public consciousness to some growing crisis. In his examination of the controversy over the health hazards that faced West Virginia coal workers, for instance, Gross concludes that it was "histrionics," which included an organized march on the capital, a mock funeral, and a display of diseased lungs to public officials, that "brought about whatever success the miners achieved."[97] This claim, of course, is overstated. The histrionics accomplished the goals of the signaling stage, but subsequent research and legislative action were required to bring about the changes in law.

Once recognized as a legitimate concern, the uneasiness that initiates signaling initiates the second stage of inquiry, defining. In this stage one seeks to define the nature of the problem that is to be solved, thereby transforming an indeterminate situation into a problematic one in which raw feelings and brute events begin to take on more coherent form as they are identified and located within a larger universe of meanings. This step is no small accomplishment. As Dewey explains, "A problem well put is half-solved," for without problem, "there is blind groping in the dark. The way in which the problem is conceived decides what specific suggestions are entertained and which dismissed; what data are selected and which rejected; it is the criterion for relevancy and irrelevancy of hypotheses and conceptual structures."[98] Rhetoric at this stage relates to the constitutive components of the context of discovery. One is not out simply to portray the graphic consequences of disequilibrium in common sense but to define the cause of this imbalance in such a way that it structures subsequent inquiry.

When the cause is universally and immediately agreed upon, no substantive rhetorical intervention is necessary at this stage. Where rhetorical intervention becomes necessary is when one must make a causal attribution with little popular appeal more known and accepted. To continue with the previous example, the whole controversy over the West Virginia coal workers was because the workers wanted to attribute their working conditions to their respiratory disease—an attribution that would have forced industry to alter work conditions and pay for medical costs. As Gross explains, until "phosphorous necrosis, asbestosis, or byssinosis is defined by a medical science driven by the cognitive technical interest, neither match workers, tile workers, nor cotton workers can sicken and die of it; therefore, their complaints are without an object."[99] Similar to the controversies over the health effects of smoking and the environmental effects of carbon dioxide emissions, the case of the coal workers was not just to define a problem but also to attribute institutional responsibility for its cause and its correction. In sum, to attribute the cause of evil to the devil is easy in a society of saints; to posit that an angel might be to blame takes considerable persuasive effort.

If defining establishes the starting point for inquiry, proposing defines its end. This stage seeks not necessarily to solve the problem, but to posit what a solution to the problem might look like. What makes this solution something more than utopian hope or personal wish is that it must be suggested with respect to the "factual conditions which are secured by observation." This suggestion takes the form of an idea, which "is first of all an anticipation of something that may happen; it marks a possibility." Thus ideas are universal propositions, "anticipated consequences (forecasts) of what will happen when certain operations are executed under and with respect to observed conditions."[100] By setting forth a clear goal, proposals structure the means and operations that are judged and modified by reference to how well they achieve that goal. They are not simply "ends" but "ends-in-view." For Dewey, the practical difference between an "end" and an "end-in-view" is the difference between a "remote and final goal" and a "contemporaneously operative" plan.[101] An end-in-view thus has a double meaning like the word "design": it "signifies purpose and it signifies arrangement, mode of composition."[102] As he further explains:

> An end-in-view arises when a particular consequence is foreseen and being foreseen is consciously adopted by desire and deliberately made the directive purpose of action. A purpose or aim represents a craving, an urge, translated into the idea of an object, as blind hunger is transformed into a purpose through the thought of a food which is wanted, say flour, which then develops into the thought of grain to be sown and land to be cultivated:—a whole series of activities to be intelligently carried on. An end-in-view thus differs on one side from a mere anticipation or prediction of an outcome, and on the other side from the propulsive force of mere habit and appetite.[103]

To say that science should cure cancer, develop zero-emission vehicles, map the universe, discover our human origins, or map the genome is to express various ends-in-view. Rhetorically this becomes a moral struggle over allocation of resources and hierarchy of ends. As with defining, rhetoric that proposes arises as a constitutive component of the context of discovery, only at the opposite end of the constitutive spectrum. Instead of locating a starting point, this stage articulates the kinds of conclusions we wish to produce to further a goal. Not surprisingly, forums for this rhetoric tend to be deliberative bodies responsible for making decisions that demand selection certain problems and goals over others, despite all being recognized *as* problems. Although still drawing on the appeals of pathos similar to the expressive component, they often make more rational and empirical arguments dealing with cost-benefit analysis and long-term projections. Accordingly the importance of rhetoric has an inverse relationship to institutional authority, such that persuasion must do the work that for others might be accomplished by money and power.

In her exploration of the shifting meanings of the "gene," Condit provides an excellent example of how science is constituted in large part by the utopian projections that guide research agendas. When Condit focuses on public rhetoric "which overtly defined the public motives behind legislation," she in effect focuses her attention on the changes in the proposing stage of inquiry over several decades. With respect to genetics, the first stage inaugurated the classical era of eugenics in which the "dominant metaphor was that of stock breeding." In this stage scientific research into genetics was guided by the ideal of a perfect racial "stock" that could be produced by the marriage of the "fit" and the weeding out of the "unfit." After World War II, of course, this metaphor quickly died out, and after a "century of turmoil, it promised to transcend the issue of heredity and become a mechanical part of the commercial process, subsumed in talk of genes as 'factories' and 'blueprints' and personal health options."[104] In other words the ends of scientific research shifted with the currents of common sense, moving from a utopian hope for a pure society to a more commercial and personal desire for a healthy body. In each case the ends-in-view for scientific research was guided by the rhetorical deliberations and debates that occurred in the proposing stage.

Once an end-in-view has been embraced by a community of inquirers, reasoning works to create the logical framework of an operative plan. Reasoning occurs when an idea, as a possibility, is placed within a larger universe of meanings in order to establish working relationships between propositions in order to develop a hypothesis. In other words reasoning is logical system building made possible only by abstracting the problem into the realm of formal logic, which follows this general line of thought, "If such and such a relation of meanings is accepted, then we are committed to such and such other relations of meanings because of their membership in the same system."[105] This is the stage of inquiry that lends itself most easily to traditional rhetorical hermeneutics—and for good reason. This stage of reasoning is the most linguistic and symbolic stage that comes closest to the realm of pure textualism. Detached as it is from situational constraints, scientific language here becomes speculative and metaphorical, relying heavily on the poetic and imaginative qualities of symbols to thread together a coherent explanatory and predictive system that appeals to our aesthetic and logical sensibilities.

It is important to emphasize, however, that this stage does not represent the establishment of a "paradigm." The rhetorical battles that occur during reasoning are ones over internal meanings and about public recognition. Hypotheses thus compete to become "theories" much as bills become laws—first by writing the text of the bill and then by promising results attractive enough that resources are committed to testing out its effectiveness in practice. In other words at the stage of hypothesis the argument is not about whether an idea is or is not true but whether an idea is worth enough to spend time and effort determining its truth based on how well it functions as a means to achieving the end-in-view. Only after this commitment is made can we "disclose precisely those conditions which have the maximum possible force in determining whether the hypothesis should be accepted or rejected."[106] Until this process of thorough experimentation occurs, however, the proponents of a hypothesis must rhetorically garner support from the institutional bodies able to initiate and sustain a systematic inquiry.

Clearly, then, those hypotheses suggested from within a dominant paradigm, scientific or political, will immediately acquire an authority that hypotheses from marginal paradigms will not. A hypothesis lacking such authority thus then seek recognition through a more vigorous advocacy and criticism performed in the mass media to gain attention that is denied within the institutional "gatekeeping" structures, such as peer review, that for good or ill tend to shut out alternatives that do not conform to the standards of the established paradigms. Hence we have the phenomena described by Feyerabend in which scientific hypotheses emerge from the periphery and use rhetorical methods to work their way toward the center, both in terms of scientific consensus and institutional support. Inversely we find efforts by dominant paradigms to intentionally suppress what Thomas M. Lessl calls "heretical" reasonings, like that of biological creationism and intelligent design, through strategies of "power-maintenance."[107]

The distinction between the stage of proposing and that of reasoning can be difficult to parse, but such parsing is necessary to understand the subtlety of institutional science. Following Condit's example, the metaphor of "stock breeding" represented the proposal stage whereas "genetics" represented the reasoning stage. This is because the metaphor of stock breeding as an end-in-view had existed in science at least since the era of Charles Darwin and drew from centuries-old racist assumptions that were current in many societies. What genetics had done was to provide a new, more technical way of achieving this end-in-view. With such an account, eugenicists were able to propose simple pairings and selections among chromosomes or hereditary factors that could sort out and eliminate the unwanted beads. Rather than discussing the manipulation of sacred human individuals with rights and dignity, such discourse was able to propose the manipulation of microscopic beads of collectively shared germ plasm.[108]

In other words the discourse of genetics represented a form of reasoning that seemed more capable of achieving the proposed end-in-view. Of course, by following this course of reasoning, the form of the proposal shifted and evolved. This only shows the importance of thinking of these "stages" as not only discrete temporal moments but also ongoing phases in any inquiry process that occurs over a spatial-temporal horizon.

Only when a hypothesis achieves some level of centrality, marked by general support both for its theoretical validity and practical utility, can it substantially pursue the stage of warranting. In this stage of inquiry, objective and ideational subject matter interact with one another for the purpose of producing warranted assertions directed toward the resolution of a problematic situation. It is during this stage that the shift is made from the context of discovery to the context of justification—of no longer seeking primarily to gain attention to a problem, solution, or hypothesis but seeking more to prove, and thus constitute, the validity and worth of a theoretical proposition.

One must avoid, however, falling not only into positivistic notions of "verification" in which discrete "facts" are matched up to a static "representations."

Verification, for Dewey, is a process that only makes sense within the context of some existential problem-situation whose resolution provides the final justification for any warranted assertions. That is why Dewey calls both nonexistential "ideas" and existential "facts" operational in this stage—because they operate to bring us closer to some end-in-view. On the one hand "ideas are operational in that they instigate and direct further operations of observation; they are proposals and plans for acting upon existing conditions to bring new facts to light and to organize all the selected facts into a coherent whole." Ideas, in other words, are guides for action, observation, and reflection, directing our attention and interest to specific aspects of our environment that otherwise might remain concealed from our view and then linking those aspects in a logical system of meanings. Facts, on other hand, are operational in the sense that they "are not self-sufficient and complete in themselves." One does not simply go around collecting facts. A fact become a fact when its serves a functional purpose in inquiry—when it "indicates a meaning relevant to resolution of the difficulty and serves to test its worth and validity."[109] The connection between ideas and facts is thus an operational one. Ideas provide the logical framework by which facts can interact with other another, just as facts may, through recalcitrance, obstruct the movement of certain ideas while raising the possibility of other alternatives. Their productive interaction represents the experimental method, summarized by Dewey: "When the problematic situation is such as to require extensive inquiries to effect its resolution, a series of interactions intervenes. Some observed facts point to an idea that stands for a possible solution. This idea evokes more observations. Some of the newly observed facts link up with those previously observed and are such as to rule out other observed things with respect to their evidential function. The new order of facts suggests a modified idea (or hypothesis) which occasions new observations whose result again determines a new order of facts, and so on until the existing order is both unified and complete. In the course of this serial process, the ideas that represent possible solutions are tested or 'proved.'"[110]

In contradistinction to neo-Sophistical approaches to science, the existential component of a "fact" does not evaporate in Dewey's perspective once it translates into the realm of the symbolic. Dewey firmly asserts "the necessity for symbols in inquiry," but he does not go so far as to render inquiry purely symbolic. The function of symbols, with regard to existential facts, is to formulate their significance within propositions that allow them to take on a provisional and logical character that liberates them from their qualitative immediacy. In other words the "carrying on of inquiry requires that the facts be taken as *rep*resentative and not just *pre*-sented." This "*rep*resentative" character allows brute or raw events to become a logical object that is part of a larger universe of meanings. Yet the existential component of the fact remains operational insofar as elements of its qualitativeness can be preserved (even if just in memory) or the totality of its existence reexperienced. The circular orbits of Copernicus may have existed largely as a symbolic idea, but there remained the fact of a pinpoint of light seen through the end of his telescope. The question was not whether the pinpoint of light was present, but under what system of meanings it served as a fact.

During the stage of warranting, specific relationships between facts and meanings within a theoretical perspective are largely determined by what Kuhn calls "normal" science. Rhetorical dispute thus arises when incompatible paradigms, both of which have enough plausibility to pass through the stage of reasoning, compete for recognition and resources as a more practical explanatory framework. Consistent with Kuhn's account, the necessity for rhetoric emerges because the choice between two logical systems of explanation cannot be decided by logic alone. To assume it can is, in effect, to post a purely objective logos by which to judge competing logoi. As Kuhn points out, however, the discourses of competing paradigms are usually "incommensurable," meaning they cannot be translated into the language of the other. Thus the "competition between paradigms is not the sort of battle that can be resolve by proofs."[111] For Kuhn this means that judgment must appeal to "more subjective and aesthetic considerations," "subjective" referring to things such as personal relationships, loyalties, and allegiances, and "aesthetic" meaning the ineffable sense that a "new theory is said to be 'neater,' 'more suitable,' or 'simpler' than the old."[112] Although Kuhn often falls back into a language which divides persuasion and logic along the rational/irrational divide, his account is useful insofar as he emphasizes situated conflict as the motivation for rhetorical action. Conversion from an established paradigm to a new one is thus always a gradual and cumulative process requiring the application of proliferation and tenacity to overcome institutional inertia. The rhetorical moment occurs in the context of that conversion, in the efforts to convert and to resist conversion.

In *Shaping Science with Rhetoric,* Ceccarelli provides three case studies that focus on the conflicts and controversies that arise within the stage of warranting. In her analysis of the "interdisciplinary inspirational" book-length writings by Theodosius Dobzhansky, Erwin Shrödinger, and E. O. Wilson, Ceccarelli explores the ways in which established scientists publish works written "to persuade their colleagues to undertake new research." These works are different from those in the reasoning stage because they are written from the standpoint of reflection rather than projection—they are efforts to take a "big picture" look at established research in order to concretely establish a whole institutional agenda based on a new organizational paradigm. In successfully warranting a new evolutionary synthesis, for instance, "Dobzhansky managed to negotiate a treaty between the two groups in a way that allowed naturalists to see a respectable merger of disciplines but that did not dissatisfy the geneticists who felt themselves to be in a position to call for an unconditional surrender of intellectual territory." By contrast E. O. Wilson's failure to achieve "consilience" through sociobiology failed to unite disciplines because it "employed a rhetoric of conquest, rather than the rhetoric of negotiation used by Dobzhansky and Schrödinger."[113] In short, Ceccarelli demonstrates how the rhetoric of warranting is closely associated with that of ideological discourse insofar as it attempts to create a representational of the world based on a systematic incorporation of facts and experiences, of means and ends. As such the scientific rhetoric of warranting often mirrors the political rhetoric of compromise and war.

Once warranting has been accomplished to a degree that has achieved an adequate level of consensus from a legitimating body of inquiry, the political project of transacting begins. It must be noted at this point that "political" is not used here as an epithet. The science during this stage is not "pure" only to be contaminated by being "applied" in common sense. Quite the opposite, the inquiry process only achieves the status of a science once it finds expression as a practical art that functions within the political realm of judgment. As Dewey warns, "Lest the man of science, the man of dominantly reflective habits, be puffed up with his own conceits, he must bear in mind that practical application—that is, experiment—is a condition of his own calling, that it is indispensable to the institution of knowledge or truth." By "experiment," Dewey does not mean the positivistic verification of propositional statements by isolated empirical data; he means an experiment that uses a proposition to guide action so as to intelligently deal with some situated problem. As he states, "Propositions exist relating to *agenda*—to things to do or be done, judgments of a situation demanding action." Consequently, verification in the positivistic sense is so narrowly construed as to be irrelevant. For Dewey the "widest possible range of application is the means of the deepest verification."[114] It is in the relationship between science and common sense that this kind of verification occurs.

Put another way, the return route from science to common sense is the social analogue to the biological act of tasting a food to see if it satisfies hunger. In this case of common sense, however, the "hunger" might be for energy independence, national security, progressive education, space exploration, or a more expansive view of the universe. To return to Dewey's naturalistic postulate, science addresses these needs and problems by detouring into the realm of conceptual abstraction which allows for the construction of a new system of symbols freed from its immediate qualitative context. As a result the "construction of purely relational objects has enormously liberated and expanded common sense uses and enjoyments by conferring control over production of qualities, by enabling new ends to be realistically instituted, and by providing competent means for achieving them."[115] Thus despite the great difference between the language of science and common sense, it is their cooperation within a shared problematic situation that gives them common ground. Detached from this context, science and common sense speak a different language that only serves to increase the divide between the system and the lifeworld that each employs a different discourse for different ends.

The democratic challenge during this stage of inquiry is to find a way to establish this common ground and create communicative forums to facilitate collaborative judgment. Occurring as it does within the context of justification, this stage has both expressive and constitutive components. The expressive component deals with the efforts of the scientific community to translate complex theories into ordinary language so as to facilitate the public understanding of science. The majority of such communication is largely of the educational genre, concerned with making the results of inquiry appear interesting and colorful so that people will take time out of their busy and distracted lives to learn about and apply them to their lives. In its basic form Dewey envisioned an educational discourse, propagated through nonprofit media outlets, which would address "the problem of an intelligent direction of social life" by presenting a product that embodied the "union of social science, access to facts, and the art of literary presentation."[116] In *The Public and Its Problems,* this idea is appears most visibly in Dewey's conclusion that democracy "will have its consummation when free social inquiry is indissolubly wedded to the art of full and moving communication." That is to say Dewey advanced a form of aesthetic communication that would transform complex subject matter into a powerful and persuasive message. This kind of message would "break through the crust of conventionalized and routine consciousness" in such a way that "the deeper levels of life are touched so that they spring up as desire and thought." Dewey's faith is expressed in his bold claim that "artists have always been the real purveyors of news, for it is not the outward happening in itself which is new, but the kindling by it of emotion, perception and appreciation."[117] In contradistinction to rationalistic social critics, Dewey thus looks to art as a solution to the problems of the public rather than one of the causes for them.

Such expressive communication becomes distinctly rhetorical when it faces ideological resistance by the public and/or the institutional bodies responsible to initiating science-based policy. The long and ongoing struggle of biologists to justify the teaching of evolution in schools, for example, has made almost any statement connection evolution and education implicitly rhetorical. Hence we have the phenomenon of scientists such as Richard Dawkins and Michael Behe writing polemical books against one another to rally public support for and against evolutionary theory and intelligent design.[118] The rhetorical challenge for both men is to successfully express to a public audience what a theory means, what value it has, and why its conclusions should be adopted over rival explanations. One sees this effort by scientists to transform public opinion most vividly in what John Brockman has called the development of the "Third Culture," a group of new, scientific "public intellectuals" such as Stephen Jay Gould or Daniel C. Dennett, who write directly for public audiences in order to render "the deeper meanings of our lives, redefinition who and what we are."[119] According to John Lyne, the interviews with such scientists in Brockman's book reveal a growing "rhetorical self-awareness among scientists."[120] In particular Lyne notes a passage by Dawkins, who praises himself for the development of the term "selfish gene," which identified the root cause of all motivational behavior in the biological fact that organisms wish to pass on their genes to their offspring. Dawkins notes: "The idea of the selfish gene is not mine, but I've done the most to sell it, and I've developed the rhetoric of it. . . . My contribution to the idea of the selfish gene was to put rhetoric into it and spell out its implications."[121] Lyne finds Dawkins's rhetorical confession provocative, concluding, "If his neo-Darwinist innovation can safely be called a rhetorical creation without fear of insulting him or of making rhetoricians feel that they have overplayed their hand, then we should be able to expand the rhetorical vocabulary for analyzing scientific controversy without its being simply a debunking tactic."[122]

Although Lyne aptly points out the rhetorical power of metaphor in public discourses of science, he still retains the definition of rhetoric as a series of devices, identifying the "selfish gene" as a metaphorical and thereby "rhetorical creation" designed for the purposes of persuasion. Yet this definition obscures the relationship between logic and rhetoric. Dawkins's selfish gene clearly functions rhetorically, but not because it is essentially a rhetorical creation any more than a logical or artistic one. Indeed Dawkins originated the term while doing postdoctoral work in 1966 and trying to find an "imaginative way of looking at evolution" in order to teach his students.[123] This artistic impulse then took on a logical function insofar as it began to alter our view of natural objects, such that we saw "animals as machines carrying their instructions around."[124] When Dawkins calls the selfish gene "rhetoric" he does not mean a discourse that encourages public judgment in contingent and uncertain situations. He means by "rhetoric" a different and creative way of looking at the world much in the way that Jeanne Fahnestock describes the function of a "figure": "The figure, then, is a verbal summary that epitomizes a line of reasoning. It is a condensed or even diagram-like rendering of the relationship among a set of terms, a relationship that constitutes the argument that could be expressed at greater length."[125]

Notable of Fahnestock's definition is its "logical" tenor. Thus "natural selection" operates as a metaphorical figure that alters the way we look at the world, and would be as logical a category as any once absorbed within a coherent system of meanings. In such a case a metaphor ceases to be simply "window dressing" and becomes formative of the theory itself. It becomes, in short, logical. Its origin as a metaphor has little to do with its eventual function and character. Dawkins, after all, *believes* in the selfishness of genes.

What makes Dawkins's "selfish gene" function rhetorically, then, is its power to capture the public attention and direct its judgment within political and moral controversies. Lyne and Howe capture this rhetorical character of the "selfish gene" in their analysis of how this phrase, originally discussed within an abstract, scientific context, drifts into the public discourse and becomes used rhetorically to justify, explain, or critique specific proposals for action within the political sphere. They offer one telling example of a British journalist who cites genetic selfishness as the cause of so much human misery but nonetheless sees hope that recent events, like the reforms of Gorbachev, show how we have within us the strength to overcome our biological impulses.[126] For Lyne and Howe this proves that metaphors have traveling powers that surpass the meager efforts of scientists to add disclaimers of qualifications. What "survives as rhetoric moves from one discourse frame to another is not the subtleties of disavowal, but the robustness of a language and imagery which have a life well beyond science."[127] One role of the rhetorical critic, then, is to trace how terms such as "selfish gene" drift across audiences and context, picking up different meanings and implications as they transact with new situations. Not its metaphorical nature but its moral and political significance makes it rhetorical.

Note how an effort to define the expressive component of scientific discourse at this stage of inquiry has turned into a discussion of its constitutive function, both in how theories themselves are constituted as well as in how they are practically applied in common sense. The ease by which this occurred gives the lie to the belief that one can clearly separate what goes on "inside" science from how it interacts with the "outside" world. As Lyne observes after reading *The Third Culture,* the interviews make "clear that linguistic and metaphorical choices are extremely important vehicles for transporting scientific arguments into various contexts *within the sciences* as well as into popular discourses," thus "throwing into disarray any attempts to sharply distinguish 'internalist' and 'externalist' accounts of scientific processes."[128] In other words when scientists, especially celebrity ones, go "public," the discourse they use to adapt to public audiences may then take on a life of their own, reacting back upon the very science to direct new inquiries that start the process of investigation anew.

The important point to remember is that in the ontology of becoming, science does not represent a series of atomic stages fated to reach a destination; it represents an overlapping sequence of events, actions, and interests that start and stop, regress and surge, overlap and break away. Some inquiries never get past the first stage, some die halfway through, some prematurely skip to ahead, and some on reaching the end only find themselves returning to square one. And at any point along the line, new events, undisclosed possibilities, or the revelation of contradictions may force one to return to earlier stages or to engage in two or more simultaneously. It is during these shifts that rhetoric tends to have the most constitutive impact on inquiry. For once an inquiry starts, inertia naturally builds to the extent that it becomes ever more difficult to complicate the assumptions with which it began or alter the goals and methods it adopted. Indeed some stages of inquiry may remain trapped in the stages of reasoning and warranting for centuries, as in the case of Scholasticism, or may be so obsessed with transacting that it pursues practical agendas which no longer have theoretical warrant, as with the majority of legislation surrounding the use of natural resources. This inertia functions as recalcitrance to change, necessitating the employment of rhetorical force to overcome constraint and establish new pathways of action. Because this change of course requires the advocacy of choice in the face of competing ends, it possesses a fundamentally moral activity that gives it uniquely rhetorical character. The only guarantee in this whole process is an experimental one—that where we began will not be the same as where we end up. But that, once again, is simply the ethics of the artist in action.

Science, Art, and Democracy

Scientific theories are more than dispassionate representations of the natural world; they are also works of art that transact with objective material by influencing practical policies and behaviors direction toward the resolution of some problematic situation over time. The results of this transaction function constitutively as a form of "verification" of the theory, in the sense that it performs what it promises. Without this practical transaction, a theory remains in the realm of abstract possibility. Only when a theory modifies objective material does it achieve some sense of consummation. The democratic problem is to establish forums in which citizens and scientists can communicate to one another how the conceptual material of science can best be utilized to resolve the shared problems of a community. Without such consultation, the result of scientific inquiry is inevitably a technocratic isolation in which the imperatives of the system overrule the needs of the lifeworld. Dewey returns to this theme in a later essay, "Democracy and Education in the World of Today":

> That asking other people what they would like, what they need, what their ideas are, is an essential part of the democratic idea. . . . Dr. Felix Adler expressed very much the same idea. . . . He said, that "no matter how ignorant any person is there is one thing that he knows better than

anybody else and that is where the shoes pinch on his own feet"; and because it is the individual that knows his own troubles, even if he is not literate or sophisticated in other respects, the idea of democracy as opposed to any conception of aristocracy is that every individual must be consulted in such a way, actively not passively, that he himself becomes a part of the process of authority, of the process of social control; that his needs and wants have a chance to be registered in a way where they count in determining social policy. Along with that goes, of course, the other feature which is necessary for the realization of democracy—mutual conference and mutual consultation and arriving ultimately at social control by pooling, by putting together all of these individual expressions of ideas and wants.[129]

The ideal cooperation envisioned by Dewey, and later universalized by Habermas, seems to have existed in his mind as a rhetoric-free zone, a zone dominated by what Dewey called "cooperation, goodwill, and mutual understanding."[130] In this ideal concerned citizens express their ideas and wants, experts clearly express how their specialized discourse may contribute to achieving certain ends, and through conversational dialectic the two groups constitute an intelligent plan of action designed with respect to a shared end-in-view. Of course, Dewey, writing in 1938, knew how far the world—including America—was from this ideal. For him, however, the burden of attaining this ideal fell heavily not on rhetoric but on education. For him, the rise of totalitarianism demonstrated that "we should take seriously, energetically and vigorously the use of democratic schools and democratic methods in the schools; that we should educate the young and the youth of the country in freedom for participation in a free society."[131] Consistent with Dewey's progressivism, these methods promoted instilling the habits of critical reflection and inquiry more than developing the arts of advocacy. For Dewey, it is the business of education to "cultivate deep-seated and effective habits of discriminating tested beliefs from mere assertions, guesses, and opinions; to develop a lively, sincere, and open-minded preference for conclusions that are properly grounded, and to ingrain into the individual's working habits methods of inquiry and reasoning appropriate to the various problems that present themselves."[132] When such habits are universally shared within a culture, blind obedience to authority—technocratic, religious, political, or otherwise—are rendered impossible. In the place of a bewildered and fickle mass he sought to constitute a discriminating and collaborative public.

What Dewey so often fails to acknowledge is that such a public, however necessary for genuine democracy, lacks the sufficient tools for public advocacy without equal training in rhetoric. The man who wears the shoe may know where it pinches, but if he cannot translate his pain into persuasion capable of influencing social action, the shoemaker remains deaf to his complaints. And the problem goes deeper still. Even if the shoeless man possesses rhetorical skill, adequate forums for rhetorical expression may not be available to him. As Goodnight and Farrell demonstrate in their classic analysis of Three Mile Island, the result of all these forces—dominance of technical reasoning over social reasoning, the absence of rhetorical deliberation, and the erosion of public participation and access within the mediated public sphere—is the all-too-frequent phenomenon that "the public finds its own role reduced to that of a passive receiver." Hence the crisis at Three Mile Island features not a thoughtful consultation between concerned scientists, citizens, and politicians, but a parade of specialists speaking in technical jargon and deceptive metaphors intended to bewilder and pacify a worried public. Farrell and Goodnight thus conclude that if "the public is to revitalized, then the language, the modes of decision-making, and procedures for establishing consensus must be discovered for both experts and generalists alike." This "language" of decision making is found in what they call the "once-esteemed art called rhetoric."[133]

The crisis at Three Mile Island reveals the inadequacy of a rhetorical understanding of science that busies itself with discovering hidden tropes that lie concealed beneath a veneer of realism. Such an inquiry does little to enable a citizen to know whether or not her child has been exposed to radiation poisoning, and does even less to provide that citizen the tools or the forums to make her fears, desires, and ideas known. What enables the very inquiry of Farrell and Goodnight is their acknowledgment that the domains of the social and the technical are "grounded in an historical dialectic, formed by social actors who must choose to regard some instances of knowledge as derived from science pertaining to facts in the natural world, and others as bounded instances of practical wisdom."[134] None of this posits an absolute distinction between truth and falsity or reality and appearance. It simply observes that discourses take on specific characteristics as determined by their subject matter, their goals, and their methods. Only by accepting a legitimate distinction between the language of logical reasoning and the language of common sense can one understand and react to the problems that occur then they clash within moments of crisis and judgment. For only with these moments of conflict, uncertainty, and urgency do we hear the demand for a "better" rhetoric.

Accordingly, we often find the most urgent rhetoric arises at the origin and the consummation of inquiry—that is to say, the expressive component of the context of discovery and the constitutive component of the context of justification. For it is at these points that scientific inquiry directly springs out of and then returns back to the world of uses and enjoyments of common sense. The spectacular media events that call attention to some problem in a community—a poisoned well, sick children, dying animals, rotting trash, a soot-filled sky—are matched in their dramatic portrayals only by the protests against scientifically informed policies that threaten that community, such as a quarantine, a sterilization program, a nuclear reactor, the dredging of a river, the harvesting of trees, or the denial of harm. Rhetoric at the origin of inquiry demands awareness and sympathy; rhetoric at its conclusion protests against ignorance and envisions utopia. In between, advocates employ rhetoric in a struggle over means and ends, endeavoring to form an inquiry that produces a warranted assertion capable to resolving the situation that most concerns their interests. The rhetoric of science studies how varied publics seek to direct and channel the energies of inquiry through persuasive discourse with the end of broadening and enriching the level of collaboration between science and common sense.

Summary

The radical democratic search for a "better" rhetoric necessitates the productive transaction between two often competing faiths—the faith in the potential for enlightenment characteristic of a rational society and faith in the wisdom of the community characteristic of a rhetorical democracy. A radical democracy blends these faiths together by creating a system of inquiry that pursues rational enlightenment through the logic of science but which acquires its direction and impulse from the needs and desires of the community which it serves. Within this framework, rhetoric functions as a communicative medium between the system and the lifeworld, consistently reminding the institutions of inquiry that the ultimate value of their warranted assertions, no matter how abstract, finds their consummation in the context of practical judgment. A radical rhetoric thus not only contributes to the process of current inquiry, but then absorbs the wisdom of past inquiry in order to better form and propel us toward shared but flexible ends-in-view. Only by contributing to and drawing on this source of potential enlightenment can society imagine possibilities beyond the bounds of tradition.

This radical framework did not originate with John Dewey; it originated with the Sophists. Protagoras, more than any other Sophist, attempted to navigate the tension between legitimizing the lived experiences of a community and praising the emancipatory potential of new ideas and methods. In one moment arguing that truth is defined by the *nomos* of a community, in the next he champions the wise man who can change those laws and conventions for the better. What allows Protagoras to make such contradictory-sounding claims is his progressive faith in the power of education. The claim of superior knowledge by a Sophist thus becomes an advertisement for a good teacher rather than a criticism of public ignorance; it is a promise to students that "they will be improved by this association."[135] Likewise, the rhetoric of the "wise man" relies on cultivating an ethos of a social educator who proposes new forms of thought and behavior within the context of preexisting values and beliefs. For Protagoras, not just the constitution of a shared culture was necessary for the advance of civilization. Rhetoric functions Sophistically not to "unmask" science but to direct it to help better serve public interests. The rhetoric that occurs within scientific inquiry culminates in the production of a scientifically informed rhetoric that liberates and enriches human experience even as it contributes to the further growth of knowledge in a world marked by both continuity and contingency.

Engaging this process seriously, however, means abandoning one of the core sociological and epistemological principles of the metaphysics of being—that our politics must conform to and grow out of our understanding of "nature" conceived as something apart from human life. In the ontology of becoming, human experience is not something *of* nature (fixed, rational, and comprehensible) but *in* a natural environment (temporal, interconnected, and transformable). No one has made this point stronger than Bruno Latour. For him, the contemporary fixation on "ecology" has only gotten it half right. Clearly contemporary politics must engage ecological thought that views events as parts of an interconnected whole; however, modern ecologists still cling to the metaphysics of being insofar as that "whole" is something that can be objectively discerned by dispassionate science and which guarantees a risk-free certainty. Politics must certainly take account of science, but so too must science take account of politics. In sum, Latour advocates for a new vision of "political ecology" in which both science and politics concern themselves with finding "the right way to compose a common world, the kind of world the Greeks called a *cosmos*." Political ecology "does not shift attention from the human pole to the pole of nature; it shifts from *certainty* about the production of risk-free objects (with their clear separation between things and people) to *uncertainty* about the relations whose unintended consequences threaten to disrupt all ordering, all plans, all impacts." Experience thus does not take nature as its "guide"; rather, experience and nature are equally guided and constituted by enlightened forms of art directed as collecting the resources of a common world. Latour continues:

> Politicians and scientists all work on the same propositions, the same chains of humans and nonhumans. All endeavor to represent them as faithfully as possible. Must we say that scientists do not adulterate what they say, unlike politicians, who supposedly practice the art of lying and dissimulation, as if the former had to convince and the latter persuade? No, because both callings delight in the art of transformations, the former to obtain reliable information on the basis of the continual work of instruments, and the latter to obtain the unheard-of metamorphosis of enraged or stifled voices into a single voice.... It was thought that political ecology

had to bring humans and nature together, whereas it actually has to bring together the scientific and the political ways of intermingling humans and nonhumans.[136]

In Latour's political framework, rhetoric clearly functions not as a form of dissimulation but as one of the arts of transformation that unites the scientific and the political in a common endeavor to bring about a shared environment that is both productively used and richly experienced. And if Ziman is correct about the rise of postacademic science, this move to political ecology may already be occurring. As he writes, the "essence of the new philosophy is in its open-minded, open-ended approach to a complex form of life where cognitive, social and material processes are inextricably commingled."[137] In postacademic science the barrier between "pure" and "applied" science has begun to break down, particularly as universities incorporate practical objectives into their research requirements, industry begins to recognize the long-term utility in funding basic research, and the government takes an ever-stronger role in the initiation of research projects. Contemporary science can no longer be examined as if it were a tower on a hill or a gentleman's club; as a social institution it has become fully networked in our education, our politics, our industry, and even our religion.

If the rhetoric of science is to contribute to the further democratizing of science as it grows toward political ecology, it must reveal the moments of transformations along the inquiry process in which citizens have the greatest capability for influence. At the same time, it must not conflate democracy with a populism that can have two deleterious effects. In the first case lurking behind many of the strong critiques of science are largely premodern partisan interests ready to exploit epistemological critiques by pushing forward fundamentalist agendas on the back of postmodern relativism, as on display most vividly in the recent rhetoric of Intelligent Design and the criticism of connection between HIV and AIDS. In the second case overpoliticization of science may serve to "damp down its creativity" by making it subservient to what Ziman calls bureaucratic modernism that "presumes that research can be directed by policy."[138] In other words part of the rhetoric of science is to show how even abstract and "useless" research can actually have long-term rhetorical influence in persuading us to see beyond our immediate self-interests in search of a longer-term horizon that is coming to be.

The transition to political ecology must therefore preserve the semiautonomy of scientific inquiry on wholly practical grounds even as it deconstructs the traditional bulwark of realism that has been used to isolate it from undue political influence. For, as Latour points out, "each ecological crisis has involved the scientific disciplines, researchers, and their uncertainties. Without specialists in atmospheric science, who would have felt global warming? . . . Without lung specialists and epidemiologists, who would have connected asbestos with lung cancer?"[139] If democracy is to be more than shortsighted majority rule based on short-term struggles for power, rhetoric must transcend its association with partisan interests and begin to serve the process of collective inquiry into the creation of a common world. It does so, in part, by critiquing the limitation of the metaphysics of being, but it also accomplishes its task through a serious and cooperative engagement with the arts and sciences that embody the collective wisdom of centuries and which hold out the promise of a better life.

3 Rhetoric and Aesthetics

IF THE PHILOSOPHICAL UNDERSTANDING of the relationship between logic and rhetoric has traditionally been seen as one of master and slave, the relationship between rhetoric and aesthetics has been more complex. For instance, from the rationalistic perspective of a metaphysical logic, rhetoric is a fundamentally aesthetic practice. Dealing as it does with the manipulation of the perceptions and emotions for the sake of producing pain, pleasure, and practice, rhetoric for a rationalist can be nothing other than a "mere" wallowing in the senses that embodies the antithesis of reason.

One finds such a view expressed in Enlightenment thinkers such as John Locke and David Hume. For Locke rhetoric involves the "artificial and figurative application of Words"[1] designed for nothing else but to "insinuate wrong *Ideas,* move the Passions, and thereby mislead the Judgment; and so indeed are perfect cheat."[2] Hume piles on even more condemnation, noting with scorn how "eloquence, when at its highest pitch, leaves little room for reason or reflection; but addressing itself entirely to the fancy or the affections, captivates willing hearers, and subdues their understanding."[3] To guard against these effects, Hume goes on to articulate a method that would effectively eliminate all rhetorical and aesthetic discourse that fails to address itself to unadorned understanding. "Let us ask," he writes, "*Does it contain any abstract reasoning concerning quantity or number?* No. *Does it contain any experimental reasoning concerning matter of fact and existence?* No. Commit it then to the flames: For it can contain nothing but sophistry and illusion."[4]

From this perspective aesthetics and rhetoric are not even loyal servants to logic; they are its sworn enemies. But few outside of the dying realm of positivism would today go so far as Hume to advocate for national speech-burning exercises. Most people accept the Platonic view that rhetoric is necessary to move the passions toward the good. They acknowledge a legitimate distinction between rhetoric that is "merely" aesthetic because it covers up a lack of substance and rhetoric that achieves eloquence because it gives beautiful expression to shared beliefs and values. This ideal of eloquence finds its greatest appeal in the idealistic tradition of religion. Bishop Berkeley, for instance, accuses Locke of misstating the ends of language when championing the ideal of "clarity." For Berkeley "the communicating of ideas marked by words is not the chief and only end of language, as is commonly supposed. There are other ends, as the raising of some passion, the exciting to or deterring from an action, the putting the mind in some particular disposition."[5] Pursuing these ends are thus justified for Berkeley insofar at they perform virtuous functions, such as bringing a soul to God or to realizing some moral truth in life. Yet this view simply returns us to the Weaver's interpretation of rhetoric as "truth plus its artful presentation."[6] This view does not so much rehabilitate the role of aesthetics in rhetoric as excuse its use when it is based on the outcome of dialectical inquiry. Rhetoric and aesthetics have simply moved from death row back to the slave's quarters. But at least they are still housed together.

Yet rhetoric and aesthetics split once again when viewed from the heights of the transcendental ideal of art. This perspective challenges the rationalist assumption that beauty should simply be the handmaiden to truth; it posits instead that truth *is* beauty. For the aesthetic idealist, there exists a nonpropositional kind of truth that comes to us only through intuitive revelation brought about through interaction with sensual forms. Ironically we find the roots of this perspective also in Plato. In the *Phaedrus*, for instance, he recognizes a kind of "madness" inspired by love of the gods which exists as a "divinely inspired release from normally accepted behavior."[7] In this aesthetic transformation, a new whole is born that generates a divine madness that transcends conventional logic. What Plato means by "divine madness," then, does not equate simply to a new passion for a preestablished rational truth. Madness represents an entirely new state of being that is partly self-generative. Neither material nor ideal, divine madness is the interaction of the sensual body with the spirited soul as it is touched by the hand of the gods. Great art brings forth this divine madness and gets us in touch with a higher beauty. In Dewey this Platonic view of art appears in his youthful *Psychology*, written in 1886, when he still was working within the confines of neo-Hegelianism:

> The great artists are, after all, only the interpreters of the common feelings of humanity; they but set before us, as in concrete forms of self-revealing clearness, the dim and vague feelings which surge for expression in every human being, finding no adequate outlet. Thus it is that we always find a great work of art natural; in its presence we do not feel ourselves before something strange, but taken deeper into ourselves, having revealed to us some of those mysterious of our own nature which we had always felt but could not express. The aesthetic judgment, in short, is implicit in all human beings. The artist helps it into light.[8]

As inspiring as this vision is, it comes at the expense of the partnership between rhetoric and aesthetics. When logic held the keys to the kingdom of truth, rhetoric and aesthetics could at least find common ground in their mutual concern with the world of appearance. But with the kingdom now open for colonization, idealist aesthetics shuns its former alliance with rhetoric in its effort wrest the keys from logical rationality. Once in power, however, the new boss is largely the same as the old boss. Romanticism might exchange reason with beauty, but it still reigns through the power of a beautiful truth. To uphold its duties to this truth, art must then remain equally untainted by concern with the ugly and contingent affairs of practice that holds the attention of rhetoric. Poulakos writes that "even though philosophers had acknowledged rhetoric's penchant for aesthetically pleasing discourse, they had denigrated it just the same for failing to adhere faithfully to the mimetically beautiful, conjuring up, instead, linguistic artificialities in the service of illusion and deception."[9] But to account for rhetorical successes, the field of aesthetics had to split itself in half the same way that logic had done. "Pure" aesthetics that seeks only to embody the truths of beauty was separated off from "applied" aesthetics that merely manipulates the world of appearances in order to move people to action. In the end, therefore, rhetoric is still a "perfect cheat" who beds with a lesser aesthetic and a lesser logic. The only difference is that they now have a higher aesthetic ideal to lord over them both.

Given this traditional hierarchy, it is tempting, as with logic, to simply kill the king and say that rhetoric and aesthetics are indistinguishable in their concern for the world of practice and appearance. Yet this leveling risks effacing important differences between the two spheres that may be useful in improving the practice of both. Logic, for instance, may equally be concerned with the world of practice and appearance, but that does not mean that logic, rhetoric, and aesthetics are equivalent. Weaver oversteps his reach when he envisions an ideal of logic as a conceptual pyramid that corresponds to the definitions of the universe; but he is right to say that the business of logic is to provide more complex frameworks of meaning that give one a relatively Olympian view of a situational landscape. His error comes primarily in ignoring the pragmatic function and experimental nature of such frameworks. One can thus take from Weaver's perspective what is valuable while rejecting those aspects which lead us back to metaphysical paralysis. Likewise one need not dismiss the "pure" aesthetic ideal as entirely a Platonic myth. There is a reason we read the dramas of Aeschylus differently than we do the speeches of Demosthenes. We rightly preserve a practical distinction between appreciation and persuasion. The challenge is to draw distinctions which do not harden into dualisms and reinscribe the familiar narratives of master and slave. What we need for a better rhetoric is not a debunked aesthetics but a richer one.

The search for a richer rhetorical aesthetics leads us toward a reconstruction of the idealistic tradition of art, a tradition represented in the United States by the work of Ralph Waldo Emerson. For Emerson democracy relies on the presence of eloquence to allow individuals to transcend the conventions of their social environment. The orator, Emerson writes, "possesses no information which his hearers have not, yet he teaches them to see the thing with his eyes. . . . By applying the habits of a higher style of thought to the common affairs of this world, he introduces beauty and magnificence wherever he goes."[10] The Emersonian tradition of eloquence fuses rhetoric and aesthetics within a democratic framework, crediting the power of beautiful discourse with producing the experiences of ecstasy necessary for progressive social change. Rather than retreat into the comforting lap of logic out of fear for the fires of passion, Emerson and his progeny suggest fighting fire with fire. If progressive artists cannot light the flame of hope for others to follow, that light will be switched on by the institutional machine and guided by the cold hands of instrumental reason.

Dewey situates himself in the Emersonian tradition in his youthful idealization of the "great artist." For Dewey the great artist produces a work of "self-revealing clearness" that makes an audience feel "taken deeper" into themselves only to emerge drenched in the "common feelings of humanity." It does not take a great inferential leap to realize how this kind of experience has rhetorical implications, nor were these implications lost on Dewey. In fact his most self-conscious critiques of rhetoric occur within his writing prior to 1890. In his *Psychology* Dewey points to oratory to exemplify, in Aristotelian fashion, how feeling and intellect cooperate in moving the will to action. "Many of the world's greatest orations, as well as deeds of valor," he notes, "are so many illustrations of controlled indignation. Feeling that merely expresses itself is uncontrolled; feeling that subserves the intellect or the will is controlled. Feeling does not cease to be feeling in becoming thus subservient; on the contrary, it becomes more susceptible, readier, and deeper." Oratory, in other words, moves the will by aesthetic feeling that transforms the divisions of mind and body into a sudden feeling of wholeness, unity, and purpose. What were before inchoate feelings of frustration and anger are thus transformed into "controlled indignation"—passionate emotion directed toward some constructive end. Dewey continues: "In *oratory,* indignation, enthusiasm, some passion, brings the whole resource of the mind to bear upon the point at issue. The intensity of feeling shuts out from the discourse all inharmonious images and irrelevant ideas far more effectually than any direct purpose of attention could bring about. The contingent and accidental detail that usually accompany the course of our ideas vanishes, and they follow each other in an original and vital unity, a unity which reflective thought may imitate, but only overmastering emotion produce."[11]

Again, Dewey here recalls Emerson's advice for the craftsmen of transcendental eloquence. As Emerson writes, "Put the argument into a concrete shape, into an image,—some hard phrase, round and solid as a ball, which they can see and handle and carry home with them,—and the cause is half won."[12] The aesthetics of rhetoric, for both Emerson and young Dewey, revolve around the artistic formation of a idea within visual and sensual form—a metaphor—that intensifies our attention onto an object, invests it with cognitive significance and emotional force, and through transaction with an audience transforms their experience into an original and vital unity. Unlike Emerson, however, who wrote to inspire future orators, Dewey used oratory simply to demonstrate some aspect of psychological theory and philosophical principle. Writing as an idealist, he saw oratory as providing the material proof that human psychology was best explained through the language of organic idealism in which "the true self-related must be the organic unity of the self and the world, of the ideal and the real, and this is what we know as God."[13] Oratory functioned in his early idealism to move the self toward its ideal, facilitating what he called the "progressive appropriation of that self in which real and ideal are one; in which truth, happiness, and rightness are united in one Personality."[14] Aesthetic experience thus resulted, in a Platonic sense, whenever the self reached a higher plateau of being, and art as eloquence was one of the vehicles for this journey toward the good and the beautiful. In sum, he was still tied to the philosophical tradition that distinguished between pure and applied aesthetics.

The challenge for a Sophistical interpretation of rhetorical aesthetics, grounded in Dewey's mature naturalism that rejects the metaphysics of being, is to account for this progressive hope without recourse to transcendental ideals. Mikhail Bakhtin describes this aesthetic ideal as embracing the "process of becoming," which features a "certain semantic openendedness, a living contact with unfinished, still-evolving contemporary reality (the openended present)." In this ontology, expressed for Bakhtin at its fullest in the spirit of the modern novel, the "present becomes the center of human orientation in time and in the world, time and world lose their completedness as a whole as well as in each of their parts. The temporal model of the world changes radically; it becomes a world where there is no first word (no ideal word), and the final word has not yet been spoken. [In the novel, for] the first time in artistic-ideological consciousness, time and the world become historical: they unfold, albeit at first still unclearly and confusedly, as becoming, as an uninterrupted movement into a real future, as a unified, all-embracing and unconcluded process." It is an important point that the modern novel is not simply a "vehicle" for expressing this world view as one might use propaganda to disseminate an ideology. For Bakhtin the novel embodies it in its very genre by its dialogical nature. By incorporating many voices permeated in part with "laughter, irony, humor, [and] elements of self-parody," the novel situates its reader within a shared universe in the making.[15] It thus resists the teleological pull toward certainty in favor of celebrating the open-ended present.

If democracy is to represent a rich and aesthetic form of social life, the kind of experiences described by Plato, Emerson, and young Dewey must be accounted for and constituted by methods consistent with the ontology of becoming that views our common world as a work of art. In his later work Dewey finds such an exemplar of this method in the Greek figure of Odysseus, a character who symbolized a new kind of citizen skilled in practical logic, creative art, and *kairotic* rhetoric who is able to persuasively advocate effective modes of action in response to problematic situations. Moreover, Odysseus represents the pragmatic dictum in action. Rather than obeying the dictates of some transcendental principles, Odysseus adapts his means to match his ends. Thus he acts on Dewey's pragmatic dictum that "that which guides us truly is true—demonstrated capacity for such guidance is precisely what is meant by truth."[16] Thus we find Dewey pointing to Odysseus as a paragon of the new kind of experimental rhetor who appears concurrent with the rise of democracy: "With the Greeks . . . we find a continuous and marked departure from positive declaration of custom. We have assemblies meeting to discuss and dispute, and finally, upon the basis of the considerations thus brought to view, to decide. The man of counsel is set side by side with the man of deed. Odysseus was much experienced, not only because he knew the customs and ways of old, but even more because from the richness of his experience he could make the pregnant suggestion to meet the new crisis."[17]

What does it mean to make a "pregnant suggestion" at the moment of "crisis"? When the declaration of custom can no longer bear the burden of collective judgment, when discussion and disputation call for a decision, when individuals rich in experience and learned in tradition must fuse word and deed within a new and unforeseen situation, what must be done? Clearly, the language of logic is not sufficient to carry the day. Calls for patient inquiry in a time of war, for instance, are akin to a boy reasoning with a tidal wave. Likewise, however, superficial aesthetic appeals cannot promise success beyond the moment. Propaganda may make the villagers happy until the waves crash down on their homes. A different discourse is needed for a pregnancy to be carried to term and a new possibility born. Logic has a vital role to play, but only aesthetics makes us passionately committed to a hope that is more than a dream but is a future that we struggle toward in greedy anticipation of beauty.

The Rhetorical and the Poetical

Before endeavoring to portray the aesthetic possibilities of rhetoric, it is important to gain a better understanding of the reason that rhetoric has been so frequently aligned with a degraded aesthetic practice. Common sense tells us, after all, rhetoric is "aesthetic" because it is superficial, dealing with decorative technique and stylistic pyrotechnics rather than structural analysis and logical coherence. Rhetoric, in short, is seen to appeal to our senses rather than our sensibilities, our body rather than our mind. As a result the aesthetics of rhetoric confine us to the world of appearance that distracts us with the ephemeral and the sensual. Are we to deny that such experiences with rhetoric are genuine? Or reject the possibility that rhetoric, as it is generally practiced, has a propensity to produce such experiences in an audience? For those who study rhetoric, the denigration of rhetoric to the realm of the superficial seems to warrant some kind of refutation. Yet this desire to bolster the ethos of rhetoric, while well intentioned, often fails to take seriously the criticisms of rhetoric from Plato onward. In exploring the nature of rhetoric, then, one should not fall into the opposite fallacy of insisting that all experience with rhetoric must be one of euphoric emancipation. The most basic method of improving an art is to diagnose its failures. This requires taking seriously the judgments of common sense in regard to what usually passes for rhetorical discourse.

Toward the end of improving the art of rhetoric first through critique, Dewey's aesthetic theory provides resources for understanding the causes of rhetoric's battered reputation. What makes Dewey's aesthetic theory so useful as a ground for a critique is his explicit rejection of any transcendental or metaphysical conceptions of art as existing somehow beyond experience. For him, all art, no matter how "fine" or "instrumental," functions *as* an art only insofar as functions as a medium of communication that serves to broaden and enrich some aspect of our experience. By this Dewey simply means that in art, as in language, there must be "the speaker, the thing said, and the one spoken to," and that the art product acts as "the connecting link between artist and audience."[18] This redefinition of art as communication rather than as a privileged class of objects with certain objective qualities embodies the core of Dewey's argument in *Art as Experience*. For him the work of art is not a purely independent and objective thing; "the actual work of art is what the product does with and in experience."[19] The challenge to any artist is to produce a product that can transact meaningfully with the experiences of the audience, just as the challenge to the audience is to invest enough energy to "perceive and enjoy the product that is executed."[20] Neither objectivist nor subjectivist critiques of art can thus fully explain how an art works. As Bakhtin emphasizes, the "work" exists only "in the totality of all its events, including the external material givenness of the work, and its text."[21] As communicative forms, art functions as art only with situated environments in which people with their own unique backgrounds of experience transact with objects whose meanings may change over place and time.

The interpretation of art as a form of communication mediates against the dualistic tendencies that mark the division between the literary criticism and rhetorical criticism. Traditionally art criticism has preferred to identify the work of art with the product in isolation, or with what Dewey calls "the building, book, painting, or statue in its existence apart from human experience."[22]

This idea presumes that art embodies, in objective form, universal qualities of "philosophical and aesthetic interest" that exist can be discerned by "judicious listeners or readers of any age."[23] Art, in other words, exists for a universal audience of ideal listeners. As a result, those who do not see the same things as that universal audience are said to have "misread" the work of art.[24] As Wichelns observed, much of the literary criticism of oratory as it was practiced around the turn of the twentieth century adopted this attitude, examining oratory as one would interpret a prose poem—as "musical, colorful, varied, and delicate, but, so far as the critic is concerned, formless and purposeless."[25] Rhetorical qualities did not exist in contextual performance but in a text preserved in glass.

Yet in his effort to distinguish rhetorical criticism of oratory from its literary counterpart, Wichelns does not question the validity of this interpretation when it comes to fine art; he simply insists that such an interpretation is inappropriate for a practical art like rhetoric. Rhetorical criticism for him is "not concerned with permanence, nor yet with beauty. It is concerned with effect. It regards a speech as a *communication* to a specific audience, and holds its business to be the analysis and appreciation of the orator's method of imparting his ideas to his hearers." For Wichelns the "line of cleavage between rhetoric and poetic" is the line at which uninhibited expression becomes situated communication: "For poetry always is free to fulfil its own law, but the writer of rhetorical discourse is, in a sense, perpetually in bondage to the occasion and the audience."[26] That bondage, for Wichelns, is the burden placed upon us when we must communicate, when we must say some*thing* to some*one* rather than to speak only to the Muses, whose response we never witness.

It was Wichelns's preservation of the dualism, rather than his emphasis on communication, that culminated in the decades-long reign of the neo-Aristotelian school of criticism that confined itself to what Black called "the evaluation of rhetorical discourse in terms of its effects on its immediate audience."[27] Not the attention to communication and audience, but the restriction of that attention to a narrow set of practical concerns *in contrast with* the broad scope and vision of literature, justified this methodology. The most revolutionary aspect of Black's *Rhetoric Criticism: A Study in Method* is simply its erasure of the sharp line of cleavage between rhetoric and poetics that inhibits and understanding of all discourse as potentially communicative and influential to a variety of audiences across time and situation. In his analysis of John Jay Chapman's Coatesville address, Black argues that its context "must be measured by a continent and whose time must be reckoned in centuries" and whose audience may include "all of those who are interested in a meaningful interpretation of the history and moral status of this country."[28] The boundary that had been maintained by Wichelns is erased by Black, meaning that neither rhetoric nor literature has a privileged position with respect to the analysis of a work of art.[29]

He appears to makes this effacement complete when he concludes that the Coatesville address, in functioning to actively shape perception of a moral crisis, "in conveying an experience that is unique for almost all its auditors and thus opening to them a new possibility for subsequent experience and creating in them a new potentiality for perceiving subsequent events, the speech shares, in its more modest way, a quality of the supreme works of our literature."[30]

Black does not conclude that rhetoric and literature are one in communicative intent; rather, he concludes that rhetoric has the potential to bring about an experience akin to the reading of great literature, an experience in which perceptions are shaped and possibilities opened. Ironically this idea that rhetoric and poetry may represent types of experiences with objects, and not the objects themselves, actually appears in Wichelns's essay. But it appears in the form of a quote from a Professor Baldwin, who writes, "Rhetoric meant to the ancient world the art of instructing and moving men in their affairs; poetic the art of sharpening and expanding their vision."[31] Wichelns, however, took Baldwin to mean that rhetoric and poetry represented two different *objects*. By contrast Black interprets rhetoric and poetry to represents two difference *tendencies*. For him they exist as relational qualities that occur within the transaction between artifact and individual. Nothing thereby prevents rhetoric originally designed to instruct and move to also sharpen and expand, and vice versa. Great rhetoric can incorporate the experience of the poetic within it, making a discourse both instructive and inspiring. For Black "the vision of the fullest rhetorical potentialities of the speech" comes to us when we "imagine an auditor who yields himself completely to its influence" and "who would be delivered from the conflict of niggling ideologies."[32] The possibilities inherent in the experience of literature thus appear to function rhetorically when those possibilities are fused with a sense of sudden commitment and clarity—when they are not just visions dancing in the imagination but destinations that call one's whole self to a new journey. In those experiences, rhetoric and poetics fuse.

Yet those experiences are hardly the norm. More often than not, instruction and inspiration part ways as soon as a rhetor opens his or her mouth. An auditor thus experiences with rhetoric a feeling of being "pushed" that contrasts with the more invitational and expressive method of poetics. In discussing Chapman, Black continues past the moment of the Coatesville address—a sermon condemning the vices of slavery, lynching, hate, and war—to the orator's later life after his son was killed in World War I. Black notes that Chapman later came to embody the very vices he had once condemned, giving "rabid expression to his agony in anti-German pamphlets," slipping into "parochialism" of Boston and Harvard and allowing "anti-Semitism and anti-Catholicism" to pour out of him. Although Black does not express explicit critical judgment of such actions beyond calling his life a "tragedy," clearly Black would consider Chapman's ideologically driven rants something other than literature, and his a discourse one which falls far short of the fullest rhetorical potentiality.[33] Yet clearly Chapman was practicing some kind of rhetoric here that made it distinguishable as such, even if largely distasteful. It is, strangely enough, these basic qualities of experience that exist even in the most crudely made artifact—only because they are the most visceral and identifiable—that gives us a clue as to what we mean by calling something "rhetorical."

In the long history of the critique of rhetoric, perhaps the most consistent is the accusation that rhetoric seeks to manipulate and exploit its hearers. However, when this issue is discussed in terms of the nature of the rhetor's intention or the status of certain truth claims, it goes only in circles. Only when such manipulation is discussed in terms of an audience's lived *reaction* to discourse do we begin to better understand what is at work in failed rhetoric. The key difference between successful and unsuccessful rhetoric is in whether an audience feels they have been treated, in Kantian terms, as a means to an end rather than an end-in-itself. Dewey describes this in terms of whether or not we an audience as "the *bearer* or *carrier* of an experience instead of a factor absorbed in what is produced."[34] In genuine aesthetic experience, the self feels a sense of natural and uncoerced movement toward some consummation; the self feels a creative and active participant in the making of something new. By contrast, rhetoric, being a more explicitly instrumental art, often seeks "control in a specified predetermined direction," it often treats the self as the "bearer" of some predetermined kind of experience.[35] With Chapman's later ideological rantings, for example, he aspires to make them function as willing vehicles to carry off and spread his hatred of Jews and Catholics. Unwitting auditors to such discourse would thus feel as if they had stepped onto an assembly line to have an ideology stamped on their foreheads.

In less dramatic terms, the feeling that one's self is being persuaded through discourse to act as a means to serve some specialized end characterizes the quality of experience we commonly associate with rhetoric. This precognitive association of events or objects with certain qualities marks our starting point for understanding the nature of rhetorical experience. This is similar to the method Dewey employs with the nature of aesthetic experience. He notes that in order to understand the nature of aesthetic, "one must begin with it in the raw; in the events and scenes that hold the attentive eye and the ear of man." As examples of esthetic events, he lists "the fire-engine rushing by; the machines excavating enormous holes in the earth; the human-fly climbing he steeple-side; the men perched high in air on girders, throwing and catching red-hot bolts."[36] Only by starting in the "raw," in the things that people naturally associate with some quality, can we begin with events that are not already predefined by some particular theory. Likewise, rhetoric must being in the raw, in the events and scenes that people feel to be rhetorical—the billboards on country roads calling us out of the fires of Hell; leaders standing with arms outspread before a roaring crowd; protesters displaying images of a dying world; a published letter appealing for sanity; a clash of raised voices in the town hall. These things, too, have aesthetic qualities, for they equally hold the attentive eye and ear; yet they also do more. They call upon us to play our role in a greater drama, to take on the burden of some responsibility, and to accept the wisdom of another. Thus when the human fly starts calling others to mount the stairway toward Heaven as he clings to the steeple side, something shifts in our attitude that announces that the situation has changed. Rhetoric has begun.

Enjoyment and Interest

What changes in experience to make it feel consciously rhetorical is the disclosure of the specialized end toward which a discourse is directed. The revelation of this specialized end thus transforms an aesthetic event—say, the men catching red-hot bolts—to a "stimulus to and means of an overt course of action," such as when catching those bolts demonstrates the lack of industry safeguards and the need for worker rights. This is not to say, however, that the two situations can be distinguished by the latter being an event plus an "interest." Both express some kind of interest, for interest is simply "an identification of a self with some material aspect of the objective world." The difference is between two kinds of interest. What makes the construction worker's actions so fascinating is the "fullness of participation" between the self and the work in which that self in engaged; although clearly there is an instrumental end of constructing a skyscraper, this is not a communicative intent of his action. One observes his movement of steel for its own sake, and his interest is tied up in the product itself. The union advocate, by contrast, performs the act with the interest of conveying some larger instrumental communicative meaning beyond the performative moment. The experience thus changes once the work of art functions to "subordinate an experience as it is directly had to something beyond itself."[37] The fascination of watching the man throwing and catching red-hot bolts thus becomes secondary to determining one's stance on labor laws and the rights of the working class.

The cleavage between the poetical and the rhetorical at the line between intrinsic enjoyment and specialized interest is also made by Kenneth Burke. Despite the fact that he defined the "essential function of language" in terms of its use as "a symbolic means of inducing cooperating in being that by nature respond to symbols," Burke did not conclude that this meant that all language was rhetorical. He only meant to say that rhetoric could only be understood on the basis of this function. What distinguishes rhetoric from poetics is the kind of cooperation being induced. In rhetoric language is used for purposes of both "cooperation and competition" and serves to "form appropriate attitudes that were designed to induce corresponding acts." In this case a rhetor seeks cooperation concerning acts that arise in conflict with other motivations, such as the choices between war and peace, solidarity or division, forgiveness or blame. In contradistinction, in poetics an artist could "still be concerned with symbolic action for its own sake, without reference to purposes in the practical, nonartistic realm."[38] In this case one can imagine a poet inducing cooperative endeavors to listen quietly to a performance, to gaze at a flower, to share space together for the sake of pleasure.

In dramatic literature, of course, characters often make rhetorical speeches and struggle toward specific ends. However, this does not make them rhetorical documents. "Where a rhetorician might conceivably argue the cause of Love rather than Duty, or the other way round," Burke explains, "in Poetics a profound dramatizing of the conflict itself would be enough; for in this field the imitation of great practical or moral problems is itself a source of gratification."[39] Indeed this dramatization of multiple voices for its own sake is what Bakhtin believes distinguishes the modern novel as a work of art from the novel as a form of propaganda. For in many works that feature multiple voices, they are not "fertilized by a deep-rooted connection with the forces of historical becoming that serve to stratify language, and therefore rhetorical genres are at best merely a distanced echo of this becoming, narrowed down to an individual polemic."[40] In other words simply because Shakespeare allowed Shylock a stage to voice his dissent does not make *The Merchant of Venice* a novelistic discourse, for at the end his voice is humiliated and crushed by Christian ideology. Bakhtin thus mirrors Burke in separating the rhetorical from the poetical based on the difference between practically interested monovocality and aesthetically interested multivocality.

The common *telos* of rhetoric, in other words, is to constitute in an audience a common interest and a common identification that extends beyond the immediate qualitative moment and results in action toward a specialized end. The desired outcome is the generation of what Dewey calls "purpose," which he defines as "identification in action." For Dewey purpose is not just a "hope" but an actual commitment: "Its operation in and through objective conditions is a test of its genuineness; the capacity of the purpose to overcome and utilize resistance, to administer materials, is a disclosure of the structure and quality of the purpose."[41] Yet rhetoric generates a specific kind of purpose distinct from fine art. In fine art, creation of the work of art within experience *is* the purpose, such that on seeing Michelangelo's *David* one might develop an interest in Renaissance sculpture so strong that one moves to Florence. In an experience of rhetoric, an audience does not generally develop identification with the rhetorical discourse itself but with something outside the discourse toward which it points. Thus when the *David* was first displayed in the Pallazzo Vecchio in Florence, it was read by some as a symbol of the Florentine republic as opposed to the reign of the exiled Medici family, causing some onlooking Medici supporters to pelt it with stones. For this audience the "intrinsic" beauty of the sculpture was merely a political symbol that, like David's distant look, pointed to an ideal that was separate from the object itself. Undoubtedly for supporters of the republic, however, it generated identification that solidified a common purpose—defense of the city's political structure against the "Goliaths" of the world.

Subject and Substance

Regardless of whether one agrees or disagrees with the rhetorical purpose perceived in an object, the effect of perceiving an end outside of the work itself directly contributes to the dualism of form and substance that distinguishes between the "real" subject matter of a discourse and its "merely" aesthetic presentation. For example, in a propagandistic campaign to reveal unsafe labor practices and advocate for social reform, a variety of different spectacles might be used to capture the attention of the media, but these would all be understood by an audience as having an identical message despite their differences in expression. Whether a construction worker throws red-hot bolts from a girder or a meat-packing employee reveals his severed right hand, their common persuasive intention makes the specific differences of their performances separate from the larger issue and thereby disposable in the long term. In a word, they become "decorative," for "in the degree in which decorative effect is achieved in isolation, it becomes empty embellishment, factitious ornamentation—like sugar figures on a cake—and external bedecking."[42] The perceived "disposability" of the aesthetic qualities of a discourse or performance then has the inverse effect with regards to its subject matter. With the qualitative immediacy of an aesthetic event deemed expendable, what remains is a logical proposition to which an audience's attention turns. Discussion then focuses not on what an artifact *is* but on what it *refers* to.

In criticism of fine art, this dualism occurs when what Dewey calls the "subject" of an artwork overshadows its "substance." Dewey defines the subject as what is outside an artwork, in terms of an external reference to an idea or thing, while its substance is the whole artwork itself as it interacts within a person's immediate experience. He paraphrases this distinction as between "the matter *for* and matter *in* artistic production. The subject or 'matter for' is capable of being indicated and described in other fashion than that of the art product itself. The 'matter in,' the actual substance, is the art object itself and hence cannot be expressed in any other way." To explain this difference, Dewey quotes Matisse's response to a woman who complained that she has never seen a woman who looked like the one in his painting: "Madam, that is not a woman; that is a picture."[43] The woman's attempt to see through and beyond the picture to its literal reference is no different in kind than a critic's effort to interpret some painting, poem, or dance purely as an expression or critique of some dominant ideology. In both the specific details of the artwork, its nuances and rhythms and shadings, are pushed aside as trivial decoration upon some larger purpose. The substance becomes merely an aesthetic vehicle for the subject.

The tyranny of the "subject" is not only the result of the biases of the critic. Poorly done art contributes to the trivialization of aesthetics by actually adopting this method in their creative process. The visceral response most people now have to Nazi and Stalinist propaganda, not to mention the worst of the jingoistic productions of the United States, derives from the fact that the production of art—especially in terms of the visual arts—was completely dominated by and subordinated to an instrumental political end. These works were created and viewed not for their own intrinsic beauty, but to realize some ideological end that existed as a set of intellectual and moral propositions, like the buying of war bonds or the eradication of a barbaric enemy. Propaganda exists as propaganda only insofar as feelings are rallied for some political end, and "adaptation to a particular end is often (always in the case of complicated affairs) something perceived by thought."[44] Thus the character of propaganda is not the domination of reason by feeling, but by the manipulation of immediate feeling for the purpose of some larger instrumental purpose.

Rhetoric, which generally lacks the systematic and institutional character of propaganda, nonetheless succumbs to a similar methodology which brings about the frequent epithet of "mere rhetoric." Unlike the paradigm of the expressive artist, who treats the creation of the art product as an end-in-itself, the paradigm of the rhetor is one who creates an object for some instrumental purpose outside of itself. Thus although both begin with what Dewey calls "antecedent subject-matter," which came about through some "original excitation and stir of some contact with the world," the expressive artist allows that subject matter to evolve as the art product evolves. Hence, a poet upon witnessing the horrors of Hiroshima might want to reveal the nature of man's inhumanity to man, but as the poem evolves, finds herself caught up in a new metaphor that journeys to new places. The rhetor, by contrast, tends to retain a commitment to the antecedent subject matter in order to ensure a clear and powerful message directed toward some exigence in her environment. She thus resists allowing metaphors to take on lives of their own, but constrains their function to be used as means to a specialized end. The result of this subordination of the appearance to the idea, more often than not, is an impression of insincerity. As Dewey remarks, "Insincerity in art has an esthetic not just a moral source; it is found wherever substance and form fall apart."[45] In other words rhetoric is often thought insincere for the very reason that form is taken to be simply the means of delivering the substance rather than being the substance itself. An audience leaves feeling the weariness one gets after shaking the hand of a quick-talking salesman—a sense that by being seduced by appearances, one has just been duped into swallowing a bad deal.

There is a reason, then, why rhetoric has traditionally been classified as a practical and instrumental art rather than a productive or fine art. Although rhetoric clearly involves the "making" of something—traditionally, a speech—the writing of that speech is akin to a cartographer drawing a map or a carpenter building a bridge rather than to a landscape painter giving expression to the feeling one gets on emerging from the mountain path and witnessing the golden color of the bridge at dusk; in sum, rhetoric seeks to motivate action about something else rather than inspire contemplation of itself. Of course, to the extent that a painting is used to reconstruct a lost environment or a speech is appreciated for its unique artistry, these categories are inverted. However, if one speaks in terms of the context of a thing's immediate and intended use, rhetoric usually is experienced as a tool for praxis rather than an object of poiesis. Rhetoric thus functions as an art in the sense of being concerned with "the act of production," but it tends to be less concerned than fine art with the qualities of the aesthetic, meaning a kind of receptive experience which is "appreciative, perceiving, and enjoying."[46]

Perception and Recognition

Capturing a deeper sense of the aesthetics of rhetoric requires a more sympathetic reading of idealists such as Plato and Emerson, who view beauty as something constitutive of truth and goodness. This need not entail becoming an idealist. Indeed one need only appeal to common sense to appreciate the idealistic distinction between an experience in which one feels a creative participant in a creative process and one in which one feels to be an outside observer of an instrumental act. Dewey explains the difference between these two experiences, the one of being pushed and flattered and the other of being liberated and inspired, as the difference between recognition and perception.

The experience of recognition comes about when some symbolic object is used primarily as a means to direct attention to something other than itself. In recognition, the natural development of experience is not only "arrested before it has a change to develop freely," as when a fire alarm interrupts the climactic scene in a movie theater, but is "arrested at the point where it will serve some *other* purpose," as when a viewer leaves the movie leaves not thinking about the plot and characters within the context of the drama but about, say, the how the film functions to critique the biases of some social group. What characterizes recognition, then, is the cognitive act of attaching "a proper tag or label" to something, meaning that most often "we fall back, as upon a stereotype, upon some previously formed scheme." Dewey gives examples of reception as when "a salesman identifies wares by a sample" or when "we recognize a man on the street in order to greet or to avoid him, not so as to see him for the sake of seeing what is there."[47] Recognition biases the categorical and the cognitive over the particular and the sensual; it makes us content to place a name upon an event and transform it into a familiar object to be treated in a familiar way.

The predilection of rhetoric toward "recognition" hardly needs a leap of imagination. The favored strategy of dictators, demagogues, and dissenters alike is to use discourse to simplify one's environment by portraying it as a chessboard with clearly identified friends and enemies, with each group then subdivided into pawns, bishops, knights, and kings. Receptive audiences venturing out into the world will then rely on a map of crude stereotypes to guide them; on encountering any particular person or event, then, some "detail or arrangement of details serves as a cure for bare identification," allowing them to "apply this bare outline as a stencil to the present object." She is a patriot, he is a traitor; that is a sin, this is a virtue; we inhabit a kingdom, they live in a wasteland, and so on. The advantage to this strategy, of course is that recognition makes it "easy to arouse vivid consciousnesses." By "vivid," Dewey means a particularly cognitive brand of consciousness that identifies a thing by its clearly defined stenciled outline. In recognition, there is "not enough resistance between new and old to secure consciousness of the experience that is had"; instead of appreciating the uniqueness and nuances of a thing in its immediacy that warrants concentrated attention, one is satisfied with judging it as the same old thing that can be treated in the same old way. Dewey concludes that even "a dog that barks and wags his tail joyously on seeing his master return is more fully alive in his reception of his friend than is a human being who is content with mere recognition."[48] For Dewey, when we allow out cognitive biases to obstruct our appreciation of our surroundings, we become something even less than animals. Still, all is not lost. Dewey observes: "What is distinctive in man makes it possible for him to sink below the level of the beasts. [But] it also makes it possible for him to carry to new and unprecedented heights that unity of sense and impulse, of brain and eye and ear, that is exemplified in animal life, saturating it with the conscious meanings derives from communication and deliberate expression."[49]

This "height" of experience, which for Dewey represents the aesthetic, is the final limit toward which one journeys the moment that recognition is replaced by perception. In contradistinction to recognition, perception does not rest content with a passive response to one's environment that confines itself to an act of labeling. In perception, "a beholder must *create* his own experience." This does not mean that perception is a purely "subjective" act of imagination. Rather, perception first requires an act of "surrender" to something within our environment, for to "steep ourselves in a subject-matter we have first to plunge into it." What surrender does for us is open up our whole field of awareness to the subtleties of a thing that we may have passed over in our haste to "recognize" it. A man we may have known for years thus might suddenly express a new quality of his character that so jars our preconceptions that we see him in a whole new light: "We realize that we never knew the person before; we had not seen him in any pregnant sense." The result is a "stir of the organism," an "inner commotion" in which the "perceived object or scene is emotionally pervaded throughout."[50] In the experience of surrender, then, we let go of dualisms not only between self and other but also between the parts of the self, such that our whole intellectual, emotional, and cognitive capacities cooperate in absorbing the full qualitative being of a thing.

Immediately following surrender in the act of perception is the act of "reconstructive doing." Rather than a "withholding of energy," as with recognition, perception is "an act of the going-out of energy in order to receive." In sum, we "now begin to study and to '*take* in.'" What drives this active reconstruction is our drive to bring some sequence of qualities and events into an ordered whole. Unlike logic, which detours into the realm of abstraction drained of its qualitative particularities, perception fuses the cognitive with the qualitative within the immediate moment. "*This* act of seeing involves the cooperation of motor element even though they remain implicit and do not become overt, as well as cooperation of all funded ideas that may serve to complete the new picture that is forming."[51] What he means by "implicit" motor elements are the acts of seeing, feeling, smelling, and hearing that do not involve overt movements but are nonetheless conscious and outgoing actions that consciously transact with the environment. In perception, our eyes might move across a landscape, taking in the shadings of trees and the misty hue of the distant mountains as we inhale the scent of pine and hear the faint whistle of a bird, all the while working to form these parts into a unified whole of experience that leaves us with a sense of breathless awe at the grandeur of natural beauty. How different, then, is viewing this same landscape with the assistance of the tourist sign that informs us of the many names given to it by Native Americans, European explorers, and American presidents. Perception challenges us to experience something with fresh eyes rather than accept the interpretation of others; it engages us with some part of the world in its uniqueness.

Given the openness, freedom, and individualization of perception, it is no wonder that rhetoric so often falls short of the expectations we have of an art that encourages genuine perception rather than one that offers only recognition. When subordinated to the demands of some external authority or end, rhetoric appeals to the senses only to channel them toward some instrumental goal that lies outside of what is being perceived. For instance, a revolutionary might address an audience on the grassy remains of an old battlefield, calling them to recall the sacrifices made for their freedom by some long-dead ancestors and rallying their support for the coming insurgency. Someone distracted by the sheer peace and grandeur of the landscape will thus be chastised for her lack of commitment to the cause; impatient to hurry his audience toward their destination, the revolutionary will stride across the field to point of where some hero died, where the flag was raised, and where victory was had, and woe to that person who pauses to appreciate the golden glow of the sun as it strikes the autumn leaves. The emotional excitement of the eager revolutionaries in the audience will thus be matched the resentment of those who feel their ability to freely perceive the world being suffocated under an ideological blanket. Whatever "aesthetics" of the revolutionary's discourse will thus be a purely "decorative" one that functions to attract an audience to its message as candy is used to tempt an unwilling child to do chores. The question, however, is whether the binary between rhetorical recognition and aesthetic perception can ever be bridged, and whether rhetoric will always be just a necessary evil that is both cruder than logic and less beautiful than art.

The Fine and the Useful

To envision a rhetorical aesthetics that is more than manipulative decoration, we must delve further into Dewey's aesthetic theory and the role he sees for art in a democracy. According to him the origin of art, like the origin of logic, is found within our naturalistic relationship between an organism and its environment. Within this relationship "life itself consists of phases in which the organism falls out of step with the march of surrounding things and then recovers unison with it—either through effort or by some happy chance." Art, understood broadly as *technē*, represents the human "effort" to recover unison with out environment through a deliberate doing and making rather than by instinct or by luck. Like the sciences, all arts share is a common origin in situations in which the "rhythm of loss of integration with environment and recovery of union not only persists in man but becomes conscious with him." In fine art, however, this "consciousness" of one's problematic situation does not give rise to a cognitive state of awareness that seeks expression in logical propositions. Quite the opposite, artistic consciousness is distinctively emotional, with "emotion" defined in terms of "the conscious sign of a break, actual or impending." Rejecting the definition of "emotion" as a name for some subjective feeling, Dewey claims that "an emotion is *to* or *from* or *about* something objective, whether in fact or in idea. An emotion is implicated in a situation, the issue of which is in suspense and in which the self that is moved in the emotion is vitally concerned." Emotion is the foundation of all deliberate art, for the "discord is the occasion that induces reflection" and "desire for restoration of the union converts mere emotion into interest in objects as conditions of realization of harmony."[52] As a result, many of the greatest accomplishments of art often follow the greatest tragedies and social disruptions, leading to a strange kind of craving in artists to experience the very moments when life is in turmoil: "Since the artist cares in a peculiar way for the phase of experience in which union is achieved, he does not shun moments of resistance and tension. He rather cultivates them, not for their own sake but because of their potentialities, bringing to living consciousness an experience that is unified and total."[53]

In the context of its initial creation, no distinction exists between "fine" and "useful" art. Indeed Dewey notes that in conditions of wholly collective social life that characterizes most of human history, art functions equally, and without distinction, in both capacities simultaneously. In classical Greece, for instance, the "collective life that was manifested in war, worship, the forum"—places we now associate with politics, religion, and law—"knew no division between what was characteristic of these places and operation, and the arts that brought color, grace, and dignity, into them." In Greece the instrumental and aesthetic functions of art were completely fused in any creative process, for social life had not yet been fully compartmentalized. Thus "athletic sports, as well as drama, celebrated and enforced traditions of race and group, instructing the people, commemorating glories, and strengthening their civic pride." To say to a Greek sculptor that his work was primarily self-expressive or to Presocratic philosopher that his theory would be a tool for technology would have been completely incomprehensible to him. For although their work clearly dealt with "imitation," it was not the imitation of the private thoughts of one's soul or the objective world of nature—imitation "reflected the emotions and ideas that are associated with the chief institutions of social life."[54] Although each artist dealt with a unique medium, they all saw themselves as reacting to a shared situation toward which the community had a largely common emotional response. The function of Greek artists was equally instrumental and aesthetic; they were to intelligently guide the community by helping interpret and express their emotions in a common language.

The modern separation of "art" from "science" is thus not intrinsic to the arts themselves but is based on historical shifts in economic and political conditions. In short, "compartmentalization of occupations and interests brings about separation of that mode of activity commonly called 'practice' from insight, of imagination from executive doing, of significant purpose from work, of emotion from thought and doing." With the separation and overspecialization of action, the alienation of the individual from shared community life brought about by modernity resulted in a detachment of the arts from their original function within the community. Thus "objects that were in the past valid and significant because of their place in the life of a community now function is isolation from the conditions of their origin." As a result of this isolation, the sphere of art becomes the mental and emotional life of the artist in his or her private studio while the sphere of science becomes the objective study of nature as it goes on in the laboratory. Science, instead of being a tool for social judgment, becomes the servant of technological reason, while art, instead of being a means communion and celebration, becomes largely a commodity for sale in the marketplace and used for personal ends of self-expression. The idea of "art for art's sake" thus functions alongside the implicit idea of "science for science's sake," with each speaking to its own circumscribed concerns that exist outside the common experience of the community.[55]

Recovering the continuity between and common origin of the "fine" and "useful" arts does not erase their differences; it only demonstrates that they are qualities of an art rather than objective and incommensurable categories. Put succinctly, art functions instrumentally insofar as it intelligently facilitates action toward something beyond itself in future situations; art functions aesthetically insofar as it enriches and expands experience by directing attention to itself within the present moment. Both begin with an emotional response so some situation but differ in what Dewey calls "tempo and emphasis." In the "art" of science, for example, the emphasis falls on problem solving, resulting in a far more regulated and even tempo that logically constructs a solution by building on and contributing to some body of logical knowledge. A scientist does not inhabit a particular moment but "passes on to another problem using an attained solution only as a stepping stone from which to set on foot further inquiries." By contrast the emphasis of the fine artist "is more immediately embodied in the object" and the tempo of production tends to vacillate between long periods of stagnation punctuated by bursts of inspiration.[56] The objective result of the artist is a concrete form in which meaning and experience in concentrated rather than, as with science, a logical object that contributes to some larger system of meaning or wider process of action.

The difference between the instrumental and the aesthetic can thus be compared with what Dewey calls the "gulf between the prosaic and the poetic as extreme limiting terms of tendencies in experience." The prosaic, he continues, "realizes the power of words to express what is in heaven and earth and under the seas by means of extension; the other by intension. The prosaic is an affair of description and narration, of detail accumulated and relations elaborated. It spreads as it goes like a legal document or catalogue. The poetic reverses the process. It condenses and abbreviates, thus giving words an energy of expansion that is almost explosive. A poem presents material so that it becomes a universe in itself, one, which, even when it is a miniature whole, is not embryonic any more than it is labored through argumentation."[57]

The instrumental arts tend toward the "prosaic" for the precise reason that description and narration of details and relations are necessary whenever one seeks to put a thing to use within a complex situation containing many variables. Just as engineering is prosaic because it must take into account so many factors in order to build a bridge, the instructions of how to operate a power tool, a household appliance, or child's new toy function similarly, although with less jargon.

Dewey's implicit characterization of the prosaic as embryonic and argumentative helps to clarify this instrumental function. By "argumentation" in this passage, he means logical rationality rather than rhetorical persuasion. For him argument functions to place some object within a universe of discourse and thereby demonstrate its relationship between propositions and consequences. The term "embryonic" refers to the process by which the miniature evolves over time within some larger environment toward its maturation as a whole. Both a seed and an idea are embryonic to the extent that they are instrumental in bringing that whole into existence in cooperation with other environmental factors. These two qualities have a reciprocal relationship to one another. Argumentativeness helps develop something "small" into something "big" by tracing out its associations without other meanings, objects, and events. Without the potential for growth and application, argumentativeness is mere belligerence; without cultivation and care, an embryo dies in utero. The instrumental arts bring our potential ideas and actions to term by facilitating behavior and judgment within a problematic situation.

The poetic condensation and abbreviation of energy differs from the prosaic in that it is a "miniature whole," a "universe in itself." This does not, as in idealistic aesthetics, mean that the poetic somehow embodies the universal spirit; rather, it means that an object contains within itself a relative sense of completeness, of internal unity and coherence that is lacking in the prosaic. As a work of art, of course, the interaction of an audience is necessary for this "universe" to be realized in experience, and by its transactional nature, whatever universe that is realized will be unique for each individual. As Dewey makes clear, a work of art is "recreated every time it is esthetically experienced," meaning that a "new poem is created by every one who reads poetically."[58] Yet a poetic object nonetheless facilitates aesthetic feelings of wholeness by inviting people to linger and dwell within the limits of that experienced object rather than using it as a springboard to some other experience. Although no guarantee can ever be made that any particular individual will feel themselves drawn into a miniature universe by any art product, one certainly has a right to anticipate those feelings on viewing the Parthenon rather than on reading a guidebook for Athens. Whereas the former is a destination to be had, the latter is a means to approach that destination.

Instrumental arts such as science thus provide a "signboard" function of directing one's course to an experience by pointing the way and setting "forth some of the conditions that must be fulfilled in order to procure that experience." In this sense "'science' signifies just that mode of statement that is most helpful as direction."[59] Poetry stands at the opposite extreme: "The poetic as distinct from the prosaic, esthetic art as distinct from scientific, expression as distinct from statement, does something different from leading to an experience. It constitutes one. A traveler who follows the statement or direction of a signboard finds himself in the city that has been pointed toward. He then may have in his own experience some of the meaning which the city possesses. We may have it to such an extent that the city has expressed itself to him—as Tintern Abbey expressed itself to Wordsworth in and through his poem."

Dewey goes on to explain that Wordsworth's poem about Tintern Abbey does not, as would the "statements of a gazetteer" or the account of an "antiquarian," simply enhance the experience of something else by pointing to it with much enthusiasm; for the "poem, or painting, does not operate in the dimension of correct descriptive statement but in that of experience itself." Thus whereas "prose is set forth in propositions," the "logic of poetry is superpropositional."[60] To go to Tintern Abbey and read Wordsworth's poem for inspiration misses the point, for it treats the poem as a proposition rather than as something which transcends the propositional. The work of art constituted by one's transaction with Tintern Abbey and the one constituted by Wordsworth's poem are two distinct experiences, neither of which can be reduced to a mere means to the other. What Dewey wishes to show, then, is that by following the signboard instruction to the Abbey, one might be struck with the grandeur of the destination such that one is then inspired to new artistic production to capture the essence of that experience. The result is a new art product, the poem, which might then equally represent a destination for one who craves the beauty of words over that of stone.

Form

All this is to say that what characterizes the quality of the aesthetic is the presence of form. At its most elemental, form exists whenever there is a "sense of qualitative unity." Form thus is "arrived at whenever a stable, even though moving, equilibrium is reached," when changes "interlock and sustain one another," resulting in "coherence," "endurance," and ordered "relations of harmonious interactions that energies bear to one another." These adjectives Dewey uses make one think that he is proposing a "classical" view of art that insists upon stability, balance, and order to be the external qualities that lie on the surface of some object. However, this interpretation confuses the form with the formalistic, thus making form the counterpart of substance, which then is defined only as "matter." In this dualistic view the material substance comes first "ready-made" and the artist then searches "for a discovery of form in which to embody it." Read formalistically, form is a kind of mold into which matter is poured and thereby can exist independently of matter as a might a collection of pastry cutters displayed on a shelf. For Dewey, however, the distinction between substance and form understood in terms of the difference between "*what* is said and *how* it is said" is legitimate only as a method of analytical reflection that occurs subsequent to actually experience a work of art. In the actual production and experience of art, "there is no distinction, but perfect integration of manner and content, form and substance." In other words the "work itself *is* matter formed into esthetic substance."[61] In speaking of "form," then, Dewey refers to the totality of the work of art as it functions in experience over time.

Whereas the formalistic tends toward the categorical and generic, form functions as an event brought about when diverse forces, movements, conflicts, and energies resolve into a working whole that is more than the sum of its parts. Form thus is the consummation of movement that occurs through the continuous processes of transaction within the ontology of becoming. Even the chaotic and the turbulent thus obtain form whenever they reach a state of qualitative unity. "The experience, like that of watching a storm reach its height and gradually subside," Dewey explains, "is one of continuous movement of subject-matters. Like the ocean in the storm, there are a series of waves; suggestions reaching out and being broken in a clash, or being carried onwards by a cooperative wave. If a conclusion is reached, it is that of a movement of anticipation and cumulation, one that finally comes to completion. A 'conclusion' is no separate and independent thing; it is the consummation of a movement."

The use of a "storm" to represent aesthetic form is not simply metaphorical; for Dewey aesthetic experience is not something limited to our exposure to great works of fine art. Aesthetic form is a quality of all experience that achieves some level of consummation and participation that follows a "phase of disruption and conflict." Activities as diverse as the development of a scientific theory, the running of a race, the cooking of a meal, the give and take of a conversation, the planting of a flower, the fighting of a battle, or the balancing of a checkbook all thus achieve form when they achieve some degree of qualitative unity that makes its completion also a pleasure and satisfaction. Dewey thus defines form as "*the operation of forces that carry the experience of an event, object, scene, and situation to its own integral fulfillment.*"[62] These forces are at work equally in a natural event, like a storm, as in an artistic product, like a poem. As long as transaction with some aspect of one's environment brings about a sense of qualitative unity, then it contains within it the germ of the aesthetic that marks the greatest works of art.

What lacks form, and are thus "nonaesthetic," are those things which inhibit the natural development of experience. Contrary to popular assumptions, therefore, the opposite of the aesthetic is not the rational, the scientific, the logical, or the empirical. Although each of these things may lack intrinsic aesthetic quality, in any situation they may contribute to a movement toward some qualitative end. To get to Tintern Abbey, after all, one must be able to read the signboards and traverse the landscape. Thus, for Dewey, the "enemies of the esthetic are neither the practical nor the intellectual. They are the humdrum; slackness of loose ends; submission to convention in practice and intellectual procedure." What marks the nonaesthetic thus lies within two limits. At the one pole there is "the loose succession that does not begin at any particular place and that ends—in the sense of ceasing—at no particular place," and at the other pole there is "arrest, constriction, proceeding from parts having only a mechanical connection with each other."[63] In other words events lack aesthetic quality whenever form is *absent*, as when a crowded room of children results in completely disordered outbursts of energy, or when form is artificially and coercively *imposed* upon an event, as when children are forced into rigid classroom exercises for the sake of grafting some systematic data onto their brain. No wonder, then, that schools so often are the most nonaesthetic institutions in any society, as their efforts at "balance" amount to vacillating between two unproductive spectrums of experience.

One thus gets a sense of the meaning of aesthetic form by examining more closely its development in the child. A frequent misunderstanding of the aesthetics of a child's "play" is the assumption that playfulness is the complete lack of purpose or constraint. Anyone who has actually played with a child knows the complete opposite is true. As Dewey observes, "No one has ever watched a child intent in his play without being made aware of the complete merging of playfulness with seriousness." Play occurs not in the absence of order (for that is simply chaotic impulses running amok) but rather the "ordering of activities toward an end," as when with "playing with blocks the child builds a house or a tower." The play of a child thus differs from the play of kitten in that the child works consciously toward some goal whereas the kitten plays purely instinctually for an end which exists outside of their conscious intent. Thus the "first manifestations of play by a child do not differ much from those of a kitten. But as experience matures, activities are more and more regulated by an end to be attained; purpose becomes a thread that runs through a succession of acts; it converts them into a true series, a course of activity having a definite inception and steady movement toward a goal."[64] One readily sees the difference in the level of aesthetic pleasure experienced in a child who is independently able to build a tower of blocks in his or her own vision from both a child who lacks the self-discipline to sustain attention and effort because of parental neglect and a child who simply follows the firm instructions of a parent who is well meaning but overly authoritarian. Aesthetic form begins to develop within in the transaction between the child and the tower and consummated in the moment of construction. Once the project is concluded, the child generally tears it down to begin again. In short, the child is not instrumentally interested in constructing a building; she is engaged in the cumulative process of bringing her experience of play to fulfillment. This consummation is form.

Rhythm

The emphasis on movement toward some end explains the significance Dewey places upon rhythm as one of the necessary conditions of form. The importance of rhythm, however, can only be fully appreciated from a naturalistic perspective. "Apart from the relation of processes of rhythmic conflict and fulfillment in animal life, experience would be without design and pattern." Rhythm, in other words, is the aesthetic manifestation of continuity through experience. In animal life rhythms are "beats of want and fulfillment, pulses of doing and being withheld from doing" in which energy "gathers, is released, dammed up, frustrated and victorious." Rhythm thus differs from the merely repetitive or sequential. A clock may have a "beat," but music has "rhythm." What marks rhythm is an accumulation over time as forces and energies interact and build. Thus "whenever each step forward is at the same time a summing up and fulfillment of what precedes, and every consummation carries expectation tensely forward, there is rhythm."[65] In nature there is a kind of rhythm to the hunt, the sun rising and setting, the seasons changing, the wind blowing a leaf across the water, the storm clouds approaching over the horizon, and the cycle of birth and death that mark a family, a herd, a tribe, or a nation. The presence of these rhythms in experience makes possible the constitution of form because of their temporal and continuous nature.

Uniquely aesthetic form appears when rhythm passes through several stages before consummating in a sense of qualitative unity. Dewey defines these stages as possessing the characteristics of continuity, accumulation, tension, conservation, anticipation, and fulfillment. What links together these characteristics is that they embody some working dynamic relation between parts within a developing whole. Each term thus "fixes attention upon the way things bear upon one another, their clashes and unitings, the way they fulfill and frustrate, promote and retard, excite and inhibit one another." Relations thus are "modes of interaction," and as such, they have an intrinsic relationship to factors of resistance. The relation of fulfillment is most contingent upon resistance. For without resistance "there would be a fluid rush to a straightaway mark; there would be nothing that could be *called* development and fulfillment."⁶⁶ The craving for resistance so characteristic of the competitive spirit is thus misread when interpreted simply as a desire for trophies and awards; the desire that drives competition is not for the victory itself but from the struggle toward victory, a process which has a decidedly aesthetic quality.

The word that fully captures the rhythmic stages of aesthetic form is the one which so inspired Kenneth Burke: drama. For Dewey a drama encompasses the rhythmic flow of relations as they move toward fulfillment; it presents "balance and counterbalance," describes objects with "avail and counteravail," and portrays "power that is intense because measured through overcoming resistance." Dramas capture attention because they tell a story in vivid detail such that one's whole consciousness—intellectual, emotional, perceptual—are caught up into the developing plot. Thus "contrast of lack and fullness, of struggle and achievement, of adjustment after consummated irregularity, form the drama in which action, feeling, and meaning are one." Yet despite the clear presence of cognitive and logical meanings in a drama, the dominant unity conveyed by a drama is nonetheless dominantly emotional. Caught up with the people, events, objects, and situations in a drama, our emotions attract and repel us from certain things and give each a unique and subtle emotional hue. Thus one can even say that emotions are themselves intrinsically dramatic in their being as they deal with our relations to the things in our environment within some developing situation. As Dewey notes, all "emotions are qualifications of a drama and they change as the drama develops."⁶⁷ Much of the most powerful works of art, therefore, regardless of their medium of expression, often engage the viewer in some dramatic scene, even if the explicit components of that drama must be supplied from past experiences of the audience. The important aspect is not that a drama takes on the formalistic qualities of literary drama but whether an object facilitates an experience of being pulled into a dynamic and rhythmic narrative. The *Mona Lisa* is thus no less dramatic than *Oedipus Rex* because it is a painting, and John Coltrane's album *A Love Supreme* tells no less a story than the song "America the Beautiful" because it has only three words in it. The quality of drama is determined by the work of art, not just by the art product examined in isolation.

Finally, one feels oneself in the midst of aesthetic experience as one feels at the conclusion of a drama—of being emotionally "transfigured." This moment is akin to an epiphany in which turbid emotions are suddenly transformed and channeled into new patterns through rhythmic organization, leading to an experience characterized by "clarification, intensification, and concentration."

Again one must remember that these qualities are not simply "there" in any object or experience understood in isolation from a continuous temporal development. To repeat, the "real work of art is the building up of an integral experience out of the interaction of organic and environmental conditions and energies," meaning that the "act of expression that constitutes a work of art is a construction in *time.*" The emotional transfiguration requires a building up of energies—an accumulation that anticipates some fulfillment—that passes through turmoil on its way to consummation. During this period of development in which an individual feels drawn into some drama, one stirs up "a store of attitudes and meanings derived from prior experience," and as "they are aroused into activity they become conscious thoughts and emotions, *emotionalized images.*" The moment of "inspiration" comes about when someone is "set on fire by a thought or scene," when "elements that issue from prior experience are stirred into action in fresh desires, impulsions and images."[68] During these moments the dualisms and divisions one carries about in conscious experience are dissolved as the whole resources of the self, including all elements of rationality and passion, become absorbed into the qualitative moment. When experience is clarified, intensified, and concentrated in this way, an experience results that clearly demonstrates what Plato meant by "divine madness." Dewey writes: "In art as an experience, actuality and possibility or ideality, the new and the old, objective material and personal response, the individual and the universal, surface and depth, sense and meaning, are integrated in an experience in which they are all transfigured from the significance that belongs to them when isolated in reflection. 'Nature,' said Goethe, 'has neither kernel nor shell.' Only in esthetic experience is this statement completely true. Of art as experience it is also true that nature has neither subjective nor objective being; is neither individual nor universal, sensuous nor rational. The significance of art as experience is, therefore, incomparable for the adventure of philosophical thought."[69]

Aesthetic experience challenges traditional philosophy because it stands in refutation of the many dualisms that philosophy constructs to separate us from ourselves and our world. In the aesthetic moment the concepts we isolate in conscious reflection are rendered speechless, thereby creating a single totality that alters one's vision of the world and unifies our body and intellect. No wonder, then, that aesthetic experience is often associated with the "animal" side of our being. Dewey notes that "the poetical, in whatever medium, is always a close kin of the animistic." Indeed the animistic quality of the aesthetic is what has always made it a threat to the established conventions that seek to order human experience into a systematic hierarchy. And this social anxiety about and fear toward the aesthetic is real, for its animistic quality is thoroughly amoral. Aesthetic experience "may be one that is harmful to the world and its consummation undesirable," but its aesthetic quality nonetheless provides it with a motivating force.[70] Aesthetic experience journeys into the unknown and finds pleasure in the consummation of that journey. In that journey contains the fruits of the novel and the experimental. It remains for civilization to judge the fruits of aesthetic experience to be worth consuming or worthy of condemnation. But that is a question not of aesthetics but of judgment.

Imagination and Morality

With respect to public morality, art has always been caught between two views, the "art for art's sake" attitude that eschews public advocacy and the "moralistic" view that sees art as a means of reforming culture. Dewey's intervention within this debate surrounding the public responsibility of the artist and the moral function of aesthetics straddles both perspectives in a way that contributes to a richer understanding of the relationship between rhetoric and aesthetics. On the one hand Dewey sympathizes with the proponents of "art for art's sake," asserting that art should be "wholly innocent of ideas derived from praise and blame." By this claim Dewey does not mean that art should be irresponsible, but that it should not be beholden to any fixed moralistic code of ethics that enforces the classification of the universe into categories of good and evil. On the other hand Dewey appears to give art an important moral function, agreeing with Shelley that "art is more moral than moralities," in which "moralities" refers to "consecrations of the status quo, reflections of custom, reenforcements of the established order."[71] For Dewey, then, art can only liberate personality when it is itself liberated from the moralities of convention—when it steps outside of the established order and expresses a social vision that may seem, by the consecrations of the status quo, wholly *im*moral. By doing so, art achieves freedom from social constraint while still seeking to communicate with an audience as it is coming to be.

As with so much of Dewey's writing, this position on the social function of art can only be understood within the context of his naturalistic ontology of becoming. This perspective can be determined by seeing the relationship between two propositions: that the "moral office and human function of art can be intelligently discussed only in the context of culture" and that "imagination is the chief instrument of the good."[72] By interpreting the arts in the context of culture, Dewey means to distance himself from the individualistic tenor of much aesthetic criticism that "suggests to the reader a moral intent on the part of the poet and a moral judgment on the part of a reader." For Dewey an individual work of art must be understood as something that emerges from and reacts upon "the total environment that is created by the collective art of the time." Rather than isolate an aesthetic text and then speculate how its "intrinsic" moral message might affect some hypothetical and thoroughly generic individual, one situates a text within the dynamic relations of cultural experience that draws from the past and anticipates the future in varied and diverse ways. Moreover, the cultural approach to art views its work as a continuous transaction with culture that occurs in historical time. Whatever moral quality of art is thus the result of this collective transaction, not anything inherent in the product itself. In this way, even "technological arts" have moral significance, for they "shape collective occupations and thus determine direction of interest and attention, and hence affect desire and purpose."[73] One need only consider the invention of television to appreciate how even something that we usually consider just a "medium" in fact can justifiably be read as having a moral message—insofar as morals are understood as issues of shared practice and not simply a list of abstract principles.

Situating the moral function of art within the entire social and historical milieu of culture explains Dewey's emphasis on the imaginative quality of art over any explicit or implicit moral "message" an object may be read to have in isolation. By "imagination," Dewey means our capacity to vicariously inhabit possibilities that extend beyond the limits of the old and the familiar. Thus "an imaginative experience is what happens when varied materials of sense quality, emotion, and meaning come together in a union that marks a new birth in the world." What makes this "new birth" possible is not simply the rejection of the known paired with unconstrained revelry in fantasy. The results of such experiences, characterized by hallucinations brought about by disease or drugs, may produce something "new," but they hardly produce a "birth" capable of living on its own. What marks genuine imagination is the blending of the new and the old such that it produces "a way of seeing and feeling things as they compose an integral whole," the effect of which is "the large and generous blending of interests at the point where the mind comes in contact with the world."[74] The "new births" that result from imaginative vision reorient us to some aspect of the world as it is coming to be, thus marking the adventure of possibility.

Read through the lens of imagination, the moral function of art begins to take on a rhetorical character insofar as it opens possibilities that can be taken up experimentally by a culture as it progresses into the future. Moreover, this imaginative function is not confined to the fine arts. Science, too, embodies imaginative experience when it posits a world beyond the one we know. For as Dewey points out, the "most realistic presentation of a scene by words puts before us, after all, things that, for direct contact, are but possibilities. . . . The meaning it conveys may be actual at some time and place. But as entertained in idea, the meaning is for that experience a possibility." What distinguishes the imaginative possibilities inherent in art from those in other forms of communication is that art "is an *intensification* of the idealizing office performed by words in ordinary speech" and that the "possibilities are embodied in works of art that are not elsewhere actualized."⁷⁵ Art intensifies our idealizing capacity by generating real possibilities that inspired action, experimentation, and effort that changes culture over time.

Dewey's larger point is that we can never determine the moral impact of any object—artistic, scientific, or rhetorical—by isolating it from its environment in the hopes of deciphering its moral message. To assume that we can inextricably binds us to the moral codes of the past. It is a truism that any public, over time, becomes "inured to certain ways of seeing and thinking" and hence "likes to be reminded of what is familiar." When this occurs, "unexpected turns then arouse irritation instead of adding poignancy to experience," and this irritation quickly becomes the justification for claims of immorality. This situation impacts more than the arts: "The history of science and philosophy as well as of the fine arts is a record of the fact that the imaginative product receives at first the condemnation of the public, and in proportion to its range and depth. It is not merely in religion that the prophet is at first stoned."⁷⁶ What makes art such a threat to convention, more than science or philosophy, is that it suggests possibilities in such a way that are more than factual propositions or descriptions; art actually embodies a kind of experience such that people actually feel taken outside of themselves. Rather than simply proposing an idea, art invites people to inhabit an new world—to experience for themselves how it feels, if but for a fleeting moment. But in this moment, a door opens upon a possible future whose consequences are unknown. Dewey writes:

> Only imagination vision elicits the possibilities that are interwoven within the texture of the actual. The first stirrings of dissatisfaction and the first intimations of a better future are always found in works of art. The impregnation of the characteristically new art of a period with a sense of different values than those that prevail is the reason why the conservative finds such art to be immoral and sordid, and is the reason why he resorts to the products of the past for esthetic satisfaction. Factual science may collect statistics and make charts. But its predictions are, as has been well said, but past history reversed. Change in the climate of the imagination is the precursor of the changes that affect more than the details of life. The theories that attribute direct moral effect and intent to art fail because they do not take account of the collective civilization that is the context in which works of art are produced and enjoyed."⁷⁷

For Dewey art makes the advance of civilization possible because it ever remains dissatisfied with the present and eager for a novel future. More than any other human invention, "art has been the means of keeping alive the sense of purposes that outrun evidence and of meanings that transcend indurated habit."⁷⁸ What Dewey highlights here is art's intrinsically imaginative and emotional quality that does not exclude cognition or rationality but functions as the substrate in which they operate. "This is what is meant when we say that art is universal—more universal than is the other intangible, science, since the arts speak a language which is closer to the emotions and imaginations of every man."[79] Art positions us with respect to our environment, pushing away that which dissatisfies and drawing us toward that which beckons. That is why art functions as what Matthew Arnold called "criticism of life." But this is a criticism different than that which appears in popular media or academic journals. Art is a criticism of life "not directly, but by disclosure, though imaginative vision addressed to imaginative experience (not to set judgment) of possibilities that contrast with actual conditions." Thus we criticize our surroundings not by direct argument; it "is by a sense of possibilities opening before us that we become aware of constrictions that hem us in and of burdens that oppress."[80] Even a child's innocent drawing of a world of sunshine, flowers, and a happy family thus might, in certain contexts, be a more powerful condemnation of the state of society than all the published academic criticism combined.

The Universality of Art

The example of the child's drawing brings us back to Dewey's assertion of the relative "universality" of the language of art. By "universality," he does not mean a kind of Platonic idea or representational truth common to all people. Dewey took it as a given that human cultures are incredibly diverse and are not simply differing manifestation of some structural absolute. However, he also observed that communion somehow remains possible in a world fraught with division and difference. Dewey notes that the "power of music in particular to merge different individualities in a common surrender, loyalty and inspiration, a power utilized in religion and in warfare alike, testifies to the relative universality of the language of art."[81] In music one is able venture out into the world and inhabit the diverse rhythms of other cultures and feel as if one has genuinely experienced part of their universes. The reason for music's universality gets to the heart of Dewey's notion of art. He observes:

> What has been said in general about the power of an art to take a natural, raw material and convert it, through selection and organization, into an intensified and concentrated medium of building up an experience, applies with particular force to music. Through use of instruments, sound is freed from the definiteness it has acquired through association with speech. It thus reverts to its primitive passional quality.... It is the peculiarity of music, and indeed its glory, that it can take the quality of sense that is the most immediately and intensely practical of all the bodily organs [the ear] (since it incites most strongly to impulsive action) and by use of formal relationships transform the material into the art that is most remote

from practical preoccupations. It retains the primitive power of sound to denote the clash of attaching and resisting forces and all accompanying phases of emotional movement. But by the use of harmony and melody of tone, it introduces incredibly varied complexities of question, uncertainty, and suspense wherein every tone is ordered in reference to others so that each is a summation of what precedes and a forecast of what is to come.[82]

It is often observed that music, like mathematics, comes as close to pure "form" as the human imagination can manage. This observation is based in fact. There is a reason why music, more than any other art, sets the "tone" or "mood" for any social occasion. Nobody would play free jazz to rally the troops, and few couples would request a drum march to serenade them during a romantic dinner. Likewise, viewers of an opera often prefer performances sung in a language not their own; the specific meanings of the words, in fact, often get in the way of one's ability to become carried by the musical form. In opera, then, more than perhaps any other musical form, we see how the "differences between English, French and German speech create barriers that are submerged when art speaks." Unlike idealistic interpretations, however, what "speaks" in art is not a universal idea or spirit, even if artists often interpret their work as functioning in this capacity. Usually what art communicates in the moment is not a cognitive meaning at all but simply a feeling of being connected with others in a shared world, of being part of a "community of experience that issues only when language in its full import breaks down physical isolation and external contact." In a world fraught with division, then, it is "not surprising that supernatural force has been ascribed to language and that communion has been given sacramental value."[83] This religious interpretation, however, itself suffocates the universality of the message by imposing upon it specific cognitive and moral meaning. It is one thing to view Michelangelo's *Pietà* as a universal expression of human love, tenderness, and sacrifice; it is quite another to view it as a demand that we accept Christ as our martyred savior.

The universality of art, in other words, speaks in a language that draws from what is common in human experience—the natural rhythms that characterize our relationship to our environment. These rhythms are not simply the rhythms of "nature" in the sense of the cycle of the seasons or the rising and setting of the sun; they are the rhythms of expectation and loss, of tension and fulfillment, of struggle and death, of birth and hope. The creation of a community of experience is made possible when we witness in the art of others the rhythms we have experienced in ourselves. What follows are moments of integration that produce "an organic blending of attitudes" that expands people's "sympathies, imagination and sense." For instance, Dewey notes that "barriers are dissolved, limiting prejudices melt away, when we enter into the spirit of

Negro or Polynesian art," and this "insensible melting is far more efficacious than the change effected by reasoning, because it enters directly into an attitude."[84] It is not uncommon for a person who has lived for years with an entrenched bias against another people, and who may have even argued extensively about the subject with critical interlocutors, to suddenly have all those biases melt away when finally exposed to simple things like school children drawing pictures, a family sharing a meal, or a community celebrating through dance and song. Art thus can accomplish through a single expressive act what years of public argument often cannot do—constitute a genuine feeling of communion.

Solidarity and Self-creation

The problem with moralistic criticisms of art is that they interpret communion to be an experience that has essential causes and consequences. Put another way, they assume an almost religious interpretation of communion as an act that must sanctify some moral code. For them, when a reader consents to enter the world of the novelist, she acts as when a parishioner open her mouth for a wafer in church—as a promise also to swallow the larger ethical system of which it represents. Wayne Booth, for instance, argues that most novelists have an artistic vision that consists "of a judgment on what they see, and they would ask us to share that judgment as part of the vision."[85] Booth's issue is not those who produce novels that explicitly advance a distasteful morality, but those that would deny their moral responsibility and retreat into an ironic tone that leaves a reader without a clear grasp of the subject at issue. Dewey would superficially appear to agree with Booth in his statement that authors cannot help communicating no matter how much they try not to. Like Booth, Dewey observes that "is not necessary that communication should be part of the deliberate intent of an artist," for "its function and consequence are to effect communication."[86] Yet for Dewey communication need not always have a moralistic basis or effect. The universal component of artistic communication does not rely on sharing some ideal of the "good." Quite the opposite, it communicates by a kind of empathetic understanding by an expression of some common emotional experience that often amounts to nothing more than a statement that everyone feels degrees of pleasure and pain at some point in their lives, regardless of the ethical context in which those feelings occur. Moral systems might be built around this claim, but in itself it is simply an acknowledgment of our common human condition.

Lastly, the diverse historical uses and interpretations of art works of all mediums undermine Booth's assertion that authorial voice or intent necessarily constrains the "moral" lesson one takes away from them. If one looks to film for characters who give voice to modern moral condemnation, one could do worse than identify characters like *Scarface*'s Tony Montana and *Wall Street*'s

Gorgon Gekko, yet these characters have become cult heroes for certain publics despite the fact that their actions were quite explicitly condemned by the filmmakers. One need not waste time multiplying these examples. The larger point is that moral judgments are made by people, not objects. Richard Rorty is thus correct to note that "ecstasy and tenderness not only are separable but tend to preclude each other," meaning that our ecstatic reaction within any work of art usually occurs suddenly and instinctively and without conscious judgment or moral quality.[87] These may occur subsequently, but then they are not parts of the aesthetic experience itself, but a reflection upon its meaning. In other words, often we identity with villains because the rhythms of their lives speak to us in ways that one-dimensional heroes do not. We might publicly say we admire the virtues of Starbuck while secretly admiring those of Ahab.

On this point, then, Rorty shares with Dewey an appreciation for the intrinsic value of aesthetic experience when it makes us aware of some previously hidden part of ourselves or others that we had not fully recognized. Sympathizing with lecherous users like Vladimir Nabokov's Humbert or frightening tyrants like George Orwell's O'Brian does not necessarily turn us into these men; our sympathy may very well "help us become less cruel" by revealing to us the nature of cruelty and the cruel parts of ourselves.[88] Put another way, only Puritans of various stripes believe that one can become good simply by denying exposure to evil. Usually quite the opposite is true, and that ignorance of the nature of evil—even within ourselves—makes us unwitting participants in evil. The most detrimental doctrine, in terms of ethical practice, that ever appears in the New Testament is the idea that to consider an evil deed in the mind is as sinful as to perform the deed in act. This doctrine actually inhibits our ability to resist "sin"—however defined—by inhibiting our ability to understand the nature of that sin and how it might be resisted or changed. The irony of Christians who, after a life of sensualism, are "born again" to preach such ideas is that the strength of their own faith is a product of a full life of experience. Art helps us reach the "saintly" insights of St. Augustine without having to actually live his life. Without art, the only way to become St. Augustine is, in fact, to be a sensualist.

For solidarity to genuinely increase, which in Dewey's vocabulary equates to "civilization," one needs to explore the nature of every experiences that can possibly bring about a sense of communion. Only by fully striving to be beyond good and evil can art ever truly bring about an authentic sense of the good, for only by that method can we ever imaginatively explore the regions beyond convention. Which brings us back to music. What makes music such a civilizing art is its ability to invite the widest spectrum of individuals to share in formal rhythms that speak deeply to their lived experience. Music has this capacity because of how it functions as a work of art—as something produced within the transaction between an art product and a person's experience. It is common sense that music, of all the arts, tends to recall vivid memories of the past by providing a rhythmic framework that binds together a series of events in memory, regardless of whether they are parts of a formal ceremony, like a graduation or wedding, or simply a series of significant happenings that happen to coincide with a musical score, like that song that was playing on the radio when a teenager first leaves home for college. These examples represent the unique fusion of the universal and the particular that occurs in aesthetic experience, in which the universal forms embodied in a work of art are "filled in," as it were, by the matter and substance of experience such that a new meaning—whether an emotion, an attitude, or a cognition—is created for the individual. Music, at its purest, pushes these limits to the extreme, such that the forms are so broad that they create spaces for diverse meaningful participation that produces unlimited variation on a common theme.

Democracy is to civilization what jazz is to music—a celebration of diversity within a common rhythm and shared community. "Civilization is uncivil because human beings are divided into non-communicating sects, races, rations, classes and cliques," Dewey observes.[89] Political "art," as propaganda, fuels these divisions, subordinating its freedom to explore the universal forms of aesthetic experience to some cognitive principle and moral code that interrupts the natural rhythms of development. No wonder, then, the propagandistic music almost always results in something akin to a march that lacks rhythm of any kind, demanding rather that people participate in an artificial beat as vicariously as do the gears of a metronome. The music of a democracy flourishes in the rhythms that allow experience to reach its full consummation, trusting that the varied results of those fulfillments—no matter their immediate consequences—will ultimately contribute to the larger cultural development of social wisdom and judgment. Jazz, in its original inception, was thus condemned, as all new music tends to be, as contributing to the moral decay of a society insofar as it allowed people to have aesthetic experience in its rawness and fullness. Now it is consistently heralded as America's "classical" music. This is what it means to understand the moral and civilizing consequences of art in its total sociohistorical context. Only from this perspective can we fully appreciate the function of imaginative vision over time as we seek communion with our fellow humans.

Categories of Rhetorical Experience

Defining a particularly rhetorical experience can thus only be determined by comparing it qualitatively with other types of experiences. For Dewey, these types represent the intellectual, the aesthetic, and the practical. When the work performed in experience is primarily cognitive, reflective, and abstract, an experience has characteristically *intellectual* quality. In an intellectual experience, one "steps back" and analyzes a thing by isolating its parts, identifying their relations to each other and to its surroundings for the purposes of understanding. The discourses of logic, particularly as represented by the sciences, tend to produce intellectual works because it focuses almost exclusively on making explicit the relationships between objects at the expense of aesthetic form. By contrast, aesthetic experience does not "distance" oneself from the immediate qualitative force of something in order to attain greater cognitive understanding; it immerses an individual in the experience of a thing in its here-ness and now-ness, allowing oneself to be captured by its rhythms and carried along toward consummation. The purely aesthetic thus freely inhabits the moment without allowing "outside" concerns to guide perception and attention—whether those concerns are instrumental or emotional. Lastly practical experience represents "an action undertaken for a particular and specialized end outside the perception, or for some external consequence."[90] If by intellectual experience we understand a thing while by aesthetic experience we *appreciate* it, by practical experience we treat a thing as a means to an end. In practical experience, we look beyond the thing to a future experience in which it can be used rather than dwelling on its qualitative or logical character.

Any single communicative object might thus bring about any one of the three experiences, depending on context. For example, many scientific theories in their original articulation have uniquely aesthetic qualities that facilitate appreciation as works of art. One cannot observe the Copernican sketches of a solar system of perfect spheres and not be struck at their formal beauty and elegance. Yet these sketches were done to posit an intellectual framework that could explain the physical movements of celestial bodies. When seen for this purpose, the sketches were done to illustrate some larger cognitive theory rather than to invite aesthetic lingering. The issue is not their beauty but their accuracy as warranted assertions. Lastly one might also see these sketches, in their original context, as practical demonstrations useful in conveying an idea to others in a visual medium. Copernicus himself, in drawing his perfect concentric orbits of the planets around sun, might have judged it not by its intellectual accuracy or aesthetic balance but simply its effectiveness as a way of clarifying his idea to others for professional or political ends.

Based on this example alone, the kind of experience brought about by rhetoric clearly has the most affinity with the practical. This is why Aristotle defined rhetoric as primarily a "practical" rather than a "productive" art, because although it clearly creates a discursive product consistent with an act of poeisis, its *telos* is primarily one of action, of praxis, not of appreciation. Yet Aristotle also recognized that rhetoric was not *purely* practical as, say, an instruction booklet is practical. Because rhetoric arises in contingent situations that demand collective action, it also must facilitate intellectual experience of thoughtful reflection to produce intelligent judgments in the manner of the experimental logician; and because rhetoric competes against other discourses for audiences' the attention and interest, it must be capable of producing aesthetic pleasure in the manner of the creative artist. The synthesis of the intellectual and the aesthetic within a practical framework has been the reason rhetoric has been both hard to define and frequently criticized. To the extent that scientific and artistic discourses move into the sphere of the practical, they seem to take on rhetorical qualities; but to the extent that the rhetoric treats intellectual and aesthetic objects as mere means to a practical end, it risks debasing and distorting those discourses on which it relies to make its case. The syllogism becomes the enthymeme while the poem becomes the trope. Intellectual thought becomes streamlined, aesthetic experience becomes truncated, and the oration closes on a call to action that points an audience to some action, idea, or object beyond itself. When successful, an audience feels as if the sails have been filled and the course has been set; when unsuccessful, and audience feels buffeted by banal imagery and crude reasoning that leave their ships lurching in unfriendly waters.

The dramatic differences between the experiences brought about by successful and unsuccessful rhetorical acts are wide enough to justify using different names to roughly classify them. Let us take the terms "manipulation," "persuasion," "argument," and "eloquence" to refer not to a set of objects but to a spectrum of experiences. What has often gone by the derogatory use of the name "rhetoric" has actually meant to designate the experience of manipulation. In manipulation, expressive form and intended effect are not only separate but also stand in contradiction to one other. Form thus represents a superficial "surface" that hides an underlying "substance" and seems to point in a completely different direction than what is actually intended by the discourse. The experience of manipulation comes about whenever the expectations created by a communicative act are subsequently violated by the terms of that same act, as when one signs a contract without reading the fine print. The tendency for organized propaganda campaigns to employ such "bait and switch" tactics accounts for the equation in most people's minds between propaganda and manipulation.

By contrast, in the experience of persuasion, the subject matter of a discourse is stated openly. As in advertising, flirting, politics, or "parlor-room" discussions, practical purposes are freely acknowledged such that what remains of the communicative transaction is a strategic employment of cognitive, emotional, and aesthetic appeals designed to produce voluntary consent. Persuasion thus is closest to a kind of game playing, where means are openly subordinated to ends such that playfulness, experimentation, and even a certain degree of sloppiness are expected. To fail in persuasion is thus not to offend or betray, but simply to lose. The audience for persuasion invites the other to make a case and remains open to suggestion, but it still retains the right to freely walk away at any time. Like paying for a ticket to a show, an audience for persuasion must have its needs met or else it will refund its money.

When the stakes are higher and the standards more formal, persuasion gives way to the experience of argument. In argument the game turns into a more vigorous competition in which there are clear winners and losers based on a more rigid set of rules. As in the sphere of science and law, one feels they have to "prove" a case or act as a judge on the reasoning of others. As a result, logical reasoning becomes the primary method of proof and logical coherence and validity its standard. The presence of rules and standards that constrain the methods of persuasion accounts for why argument is so often heralded as the privileged form of rhetoric, but the artificiality of such formalistic criteria also explains why the experience of argument rarely produces genuine conviction. Being a part of an argument usually leaves one with the feeling of performing a duty rather than being part of a game, and those who feel no obligation to such duty quickly opt out.

Despite their differences, each of these three experiences of rhetoric share a common quality—the separation of form and subject. In manipulation, the form contradicts and masks the subject, as a wolf dressed in the skin of a sheep. In persuasion, form and subject stand in relationship as means and ends. The relationship is not antagonistic, as with manipulation, but the form nonetheless is a flexible and disposable vehicle to deliver a fixed subject to an audience. Argument is like persuasion except with a fixed form. Instead of being able to experiment with new methods of persuasion, arguers must employ logical reasoning to support their stance on an external subject matter. As a result, all three result in an experience that lacks the qualities of unity characteristic of aesthetic form. Audiences experience things like style, evidence, arrangement, delivery, and purpose as discrete "elements" that can be dissected on their own account and judged as parts of a whole that is little more than an aggregate. Given that these three types of experiences represent the great majority of what people experience as rhetoric, no wonder that even when rhetoric satiates partial needs it often leaves people unfulfilled as a whole. Rhetoric, more often than not, resides in the sphere of the almost, the patchwork, the rundown, the guess, the sketch, and the promise. In this sphere, such discourse performs the crucial function of facilitating collective judgment when certainty in not possible, thereby helping us grope through the dark passages of crisis and contingency. Yet these efforts typically lack the sense of wholeness and rhythm that characterizes aesthetic form.

The Experience of Eloquence

In stark contrast to the preceding experiences of half-ness stand the testimonies of eloquence. Like Plato's divine madness, the experience of eloquence constitutes a whole that is larger than the sum of its parts, which consummates in a transformative moment in which individuals feel taken beyond themselves to find themselves. There is too much evidence in the history of rhetoric to deny that such an experience is "authentic" in the sense of being sincerely felt by a person to be real. Young Dewey's idealistic interpretations of such experiences may read like transcendental notions in a purely qualitative moment, but only a person who has never actually felt moments of ecstasy and passion in the world fraught with banality and strife could deny that the root emotions of such experiences are thoroughly genuine. The reason great oratory has transcended the label "rhetoric" to be placed within the category "eloquence" is because it brings about experiences that feel more aesthetic than practical. Indeed the practical effects of eloquence seem almost an accidental effect of a larger and deeper shift in perspective. One emerges from eloquence as if waking from a long dream that has clouded one's eyes, and with new vision comes new paths, new destinations, new obstacles, and new passions. Most rhetoric focuses on directing our actions with a familiar world. Eloquence alters our world view by changing not only the landscape on which we stand, but transforming the very people who stand upon that ground.

One realizes in the experience of eloquence a similar meaning to what Aristotle said about the difference between poetry and history. As young Dewey writes approvingly in his *Psychology*, "It is thus that Aristotle said that poetry is truer than history, meaning by history the mere record of succession of fact. The latter only tells us that certain things happened; poetry presents to us the permanent passions, aspirations, and deeds of men which are behind all history, and which make it." Whereas history speaks to the intellect, poetry speaks to the creative imagination, whose function "is to seize upon the permanent meaning of facts, and embody them in such congruous, sensuous forms as shall enkindle feeling."[91] The fact that modern philosophy, including Dewey's own, looks askance at idealistic assertions of "permanence" concerning human nature does not mean that the experiences of permanence as they occur in rare moment in our lives are any less real when understood as events. We may ultimately find transient what we thought permanent. Yet the effect of eloquence in the moment, more often than not, is to make us feel as if we have suddenly realized something sublime, transcendent, or universal—something which is larger than ourselves that will outlive our deaths. In his early "Poetry and Philosophy," Dewey writes that when poetry "flashes home to us some of the gold which is at the very heart and core of our every-day existence, that poetry has its power to sustain us, its sympathy to enhearten us."[92] Eloquence not only discloses the hidden gold that lies within and without us but also sets us upon a journey of discovery.

All this is to say that eloquence achieves a synthesis of *poiesis* and praxis that is lacking in most rhetorical discourse. When Aristotle defined rhetoric as a practical art, he was not ignorant of the obvious fact that orators made speeches just as poets made poems. He simply emphasized that, in rhetoric, the thing made was primarily a means to a practical end that would largely be thrown away once that end was achieved. Just as the act of building ceases once the house was made, speeches understood as acts were ephemeral things that died once the applause died. Whereas poems were made to express the permanent ideals and problems of humanity, rhetoric came into being to apply those ideals to solving some of those problems. Precisely for this reason, then, the typical experience of rhetoric is one of division. The thing made calls attention not to itself but to actions beyond itself. An audience thus faces a choice between, on the one hand, appreciating the qualities of the made object at the risk of missing its practical purpose and, on the other, concentrating so hard on matters of practical judgment that whatever artistry went into the making is lost on the air.

One way to unite *poiesis* and praxis is to understand both making and acting within the context of transactional experience. The power of eloquence that so attracted the Ancients can only be understood in terms of rhetoric's ability—however rarely exhibited—to channel passionate action by thoroughly remaking the relationship between human beings and their environment so as to produce the experience of being different people acting in a different world. This, then, is the "work" characteristic of the art of rhetoric when it constitutes the experience of eloquence—the making of a "home." What distinguishes the idea of a "home" is that it signals an abode, a living space, which becomes a part of the self that inhabits that space. To create a home is to create a codependent relationship between organism and environment such that each cares for and supports the other. There is concern and attachment as well as ownership and duty. Dewey observes that through "habits formed in intercourse with the world, we also in-habit the world. It becomes a home and the home is part of our experience."[93] When this relationship is established, something powerful happens. To fight for a hole in the ground would seem to most an act of meaningless futility, particularly for soldiers on the trenches in a war they do not understand. But to observe the sacrifice that is made time and again by people of few means against overwhelming odds, all in defense of home, is to witness something sublime. That is why exile, of all punishments, may be the cruelest, for it makes a person an alien to himself or herself.

For the human organism, then, "home" encompasses more than just an animal's instinctual need for shelter. A home exists only in relationship to what Dewey calls "that indefinite expanse beyond which imagination calls the universe." For human beings with the capacity for imaginative projection, every situated act is performed on a stage that extends our horizons of both space and time. We live as historical beings within an infinite universe whose bounds only exist to be exceeded. The possession of a home within that indefinite expands gives us a sense of proportion, control, and sanity. Even if our imaginations might wander into distant galaxies or long-dead civilizations, we always can return to our home in which we are surrounded by the familiar, the loving, and the habitual. We might even see our home as a microcosm of that universe, such that the "part" encompasses the "whole," much like ancient mythologies that make a nearby land mass the cradle of life and the habitation of the gods. Modern religions follow much the same pattern, only replacing specific land masses with the Earth as a whole. In both cases, we acknowledge a world beyond the limits of our own, but somehow manage to make our familiar surroundings the space in which the universe chooses to direct its attention and expend its energy. With every reconceptualization of the meaning of the universe, human beings find a way to create a sense of home. This creation is one of the great triumphs of religious art. "A work of art elicits and accentuates this quality of being a whole and of belonging to the larger, all-inclusive, whole which is the universe in which we live," Dewey writes. "This fact, I think, is the explanation of that feeling of exquisite intelligibility and clarity we have in the presence of an object that is experienced with esthetic intensity. It explains also the religious feeling that accompanies intense esthetic perception. We are, as it were, introduced into a world beyond this world which is nevertheless the deeper reality of the world in which we live in our ordinary experiences. We are carried out beyond ourselves to find ourselves."[94]

The fact that such experiences have been traditionally associated with religion does not necessitate accepting all the metaphysical baggage that religions throughout history have loaded upon them. The assertion that certain religious experiences are "proofs" of some doctrine is a logical interpretation that exists outside the qualitative immediacy of the experience itself. The feeling that one has been carried out beyond oneself to find oneself exists independently from any formal religion. Indeed this kind of experience is identical with the aesthetic experiences enjoyed by secular humanists who may even view religion as an obstacle to their creation. Yet religions have historically had a vested interest in producing such experiences in order to create a passionate attachment to a community, an ideal, and a shared sense of home. Dewey observes that "by sacraments, by song and pictures, by rite and ceremony, all having an esthetic strand . . . religious teachers were the more readily conveyed and their effect was the more lasting. By the art in them, they were changed from doctrines into living experiences."[95] Worshippers who had aesthetic experiences within the church felt the universe come home to them in a way unparalleled in ordinary experience usually marked by the feeling of separation and oppression. In church, they felt a sense of being a meaningful part of a unified whole, such that they even felt the universe to be an expansion of their own selves. To adapt a pregnant phrase from the New Testament, they not only felt the kingdom of God within them but also felt their own soul to *be* the kingdom of God.

Remaking the Self

Such ecstatic feelings can only be explained by a process of making that uses experience as its raw material. In genuine works of art, the individual does not feel as an *observer* of a separate and discrete object; the individual feels a participant within the making of the object itself. Expressions that one feels "taken over" or "sucked in" or "overwhelmed by" or "immersed in" are easily dismissed if taken to be metaphysical explanations; they are something else when interpreted as metaphorical expressions. In the presence of the work of art, something new is created within the self. But this creation is not immediate and without resistance, for then the experience would not be perception but recognition. Resistance is necessary to generate the tension and accumulation that is consummated in the aesthetic moment. This resistance is within the organism itself, represented by things like "embarrassment, fear, awkwardness, self-consciousness, [and] lack of vitality." In the presence of a work of art, these resistances are overcome and transformed into something expressive and whole. Most important, the effects of these consummations are not ephemeral—"eloquent utterance," as Dewey explains, "is not writ in water. The organisms, the persons concerned are in some measure remade." The lasting effects of powerful aesthetic experiences leave lasting traces in the way we relate to our environment. Often "there is a direct lowering of tension between man and the world" as we see our surroundings with new eyes. As a result "man finds himself more at home, since he is in a world that he has participated in making. He becomes habituated and relatively at ease."[96] Thus even if the obstacles that face people still exist in the same form afterward, one approaches them with a new confidence, a new understanding, or a new method that makes them seem less threatening.

Just as art is a *poiesis* of objects, then, aesthetic experience is a *poiesis* of self in transaction with objects of art. Dewey writes: "Not only is art itself an operation of doing and making—a *poiesis* expressed in the very word poetry—but esthetic perception demands, as we have seen, an organized body of activities, including the motor elements necessary for full perception."[97] In other words aesthetic experience requires one to become partly an artist oneself—indeed, an artist *of* the self. Poiesis blends with praxis when the self that is produced achieves a different and more practical orientation to the environment such that new habits are born while others suppressed. This is an effect Scott Stroud calls "*orientational meliorism*," which improves the "quality of actual, lived experience through the changing of a subject's orientation."[98] What is important is that such orientations be intrinsic to the experience of making and not added on as some recognition direction toward a specialized and external end. For as soon as one feels some expressive object to be pushing them toward a direction outside of the work, then the generative feeling of *poiesis* ends and experience of manipulation or persuasion begins. When this shift occurs within a developing transaction, the feeling is vivid and jarring—like being rudely dropped to the ground after a passionate sermon ends with the appeal to "pass the hat." The sometimes overwhelming need for rhetors to ask an audience to "pass the hat" has been the single greatest cause for the dearth of eloquence throughout history.

The relative incommensurability between the experience of eloquence and explicit appeals for practical judgment explains why eloquence has traditionally been aligned with the genre of the epideictic. Aristotle describes epideictic speech as dealing with matters of praise and blame related to concerns of the present detached from any practical judgment. Clearly, however, Aristotle's classificatory system cannot be taken as an absolute. Epideictic speech, like Pericles's *Funeral Oration*, very often arises in reflection of past events and makes value judgments that potentially alter our future behaviors. Aristotle would have known this as part of the common sense of Greek culture. Unless we are to take Aristotle to be a fool, something else must be at work in this designation. We approach a richer interpretation of Aristotle when we take his description not to refer to the "objective" qualities of a discourse interpreted in isolation, but to the kind of experience brought about by epideictic speaking. Both forensic and deliberative speech, for example, tends to produce experiences of detachment from the qualitative immediacy of one's surroundings. Forensic speaking reconstructs past events using argumentative proofs constrained by epistemological standards, and deliberative speaking projects people into future environments that have come into being to address the practical judgments about to be made. In both, therefore, an audience must rely on the highly cognitive ability to visualize events that exist beyond the horizons of their perceptual field. This cognitive feeling thus creates a sense of detachment that tends toward the experience of the intellectual and practical rather than the aesthetic.

In stark opposition, what marks the experience of epideictic speaking is the aesthetic transformation of the relationship between an organism and its immediate qualitative environment. The "present" for Aristotle thus does not refer to "this year" or "today," it refers to *here, now, together, forever*. It is for this reason that epideictic speaking so heavily emphasizes the social and natural environment in which the speech takes place. Memorial commemorations of great battles and the men and women who fought them require one to be present on the battlefield together with veterans, just as celebrations of the founding of nations or communities must call people together into shared communal spaces that represent the heart of those social groups. The fact that a speaker on the Fourth of July mentions the War of 1812 and predicts a future of liberty and freedom thus is irrelevant to whether the experience ultimately impacts the present. The question is whether, at the conclusion of the speech when the fireworks explore overhead, one feels more at home in the small section of the universe one shares with others. The subsequent effects of such an experience—remembering the past in a new, more patriotic way, or using our newfound attachment to our home as justification for war—are clearly significant and often predictable consequences, but it is important to distinguish these effects as products of reflection that are distinct from the emotional and aesthetic consummation had in eventful time. In forensic and deliberative speaking, these judgments are reflectively recognized and understood by an audience as they listen; in epideictic speaking, any explicit judgments are deferred and left to develop on their own. Consequently, when partisans begin advocating political actions during commemorative events, the speeches cease to be experienced as epideictic. Neither the text nor the context determine the genre of a speech; it is the nature of the transaction between art and audience within some bounded situation.

Eloquence relates to epideictic speech—just as argumentation relates to the forensic and persuasion to the deliberative—not in terms of its subject matter or context but in terms of the qualities of its experience. For example, the Declaration of Independence, in its original rhetorical context, has no "essential" interpretation in terms of its Aristotelian genre. Loyalists and revolutionaries would certainly interpret the declaration deliberatively, as a persuasive intervention into an explosive political debate over the decision of America to break from the British Empire. Historians and lawyers might interpret the list of grievances forensically, as an argumentative series of proofs defending an empirical claim based on past fact. Yet for the great number of people, the power of the declaration lies not in its factual laundry list but in its Preamble. Indeed most people now deliberately ignore the second part of the declaration because it so disrupts the eloquence of the first. Jefferson accomplished a level of eloquence unparalleled in political prose for the very reason that he had found a way to make a nation feel like a home. No wonder, then, that Jefferson's words continue to inspire people around the globe. Despite the fact that they were written for a specific context, Jefferson managed to give universal expression to the desire of human beings to feel at home within a political system. The Preamble deals neither with what has been or what will be, nor with philosophical principles stated in the abstract. It deals with what exists within the common world we inhabit together through time, which includes infinity.

Room, Volume, Spacing, Position

The experience of eloquence brings about a transformed experience of how we understand our position within an environment understood through the spatial and temporal characteristics of becoming. But Dewey does not see space and time as existing as discrete categories but as two facets of a process of unfolding and development. For Dewey, what "exists are things acting and changing," and a constant quality of their behavior is both temporal and spatial. The interaction of space and time are thus better understood through three general themes—room, volume, and spacing. By "room," Dewey means "roominess, a chance to be, live and move." Room thus stands for "breathing-space" understood not only physically but also emotionally, imaginatively, and intellectually. Room is the freedom to experiment and explore possibilities in contrast to being constricted, choked, overcrowded, pressured, and pushed. Yet mere room without "occupancy" or "filling" would be "blank and empty." To be fulfilling, room must also possess volume, which is room with mass and density. Room expands and volume fills. Spacing, then, provides the rhythmic quality to room and volume such that it consummates a form. Spacing establishes relations between the parts that make up the whole of a room; it thus is indicative of "energy of position as well as of motion."[99] The disorganized jumble of a bachelor's apartment thus lacks spacing as much as an undifferentiated sequence of folding chairs in a corporate conference room. Both may have a certain degree of room and volume, but the components within that space are not conducive of rich and productive habitation based on possibilities.

Despite the physical examples just employed, these categories should be understood as general qualities of an experience with something, not geometric measurements of an object. Speaking of volume, Dewey notes, for instance, that "novels, poems, dramas, statues, buildings, characters, social movements, arguments, as well as pictures and sonatas, are marked by solidity, massiveness, and the reverse." By association, then, they are equally marked by room and spacing. On viewing the *David,* for instance, one feels space and time expand even though the sculpture is housed in a small rotunda. David gazes into an imaginative horizon (room), populated with his adversaries (volume), and stands prepared against his foes, his body at ease and ready to advance or withdraw, parry or strike (spacing). As indicated by Dewey's reference to "arguments" and "social movements," even rhetoric, then, might possess room, volume, and spacing—not understood in terms of how words might relate to one another on a page but to how the symbolic rhythm and form of a discourse works to create an experience rooominess, massiveness, and motion. Martin

Luther King Jr.'s "I Have a Dream" speech thus achieves the heights of eloquence not by telling people what to do, but by so thoroughly transforming the rhetorical landscape in which one struggles and prevails. It is not by accident that King begins by referencing the Gettysburg Address and ends by quoting the Declaration of Independence. These three artifacts are linked in a common endeavor to constitute the meaning of it means to be at home in America.

For rhetoric, the most important spatial and temporal characteristic is spacing—what Dewey also refers to as "position." Although Dewey implies the terms are synonymous, I believe there is rhetorical warrant for making a distinction. Spacing indicates the relationships among components or parts of a whole scene as it develops and shifts over time. In drama, for example, room and volume would describe scenes and agents whereas spacing would represent plot—the shifting of relations. Position is spacing as viewed from the perspective of an agent. In drama, position represents the agency and purpose of that agent with respect to the spacing of other elements in the scene. Accordingly Dewey writes that "position expresses the poised readiness of the live creature to meet the impact of surrounding forces, to meet so as to endure and to persist, to extend or expand through undergoing the very forces that, apart from its response, are indifferent and hostile." This interpretation of position has a far more individualistic and motivational tenor than his more "objective" account of spacing. That is because Dewey uses this term when speaking of the effects of art on the organism rather than the qualities of the art product. Thus Dewey continues: "Through going out into the environment, position unfolds into volume: through the pressure of environment, mass is retracted into energy of position, and space remains, when matter is contracted, as an opportunity for further action."[100] Here Dewey speaks not of room, volume, and spacing as components of a work of art; he speaks of position as a component of behavior within an environment marked by resistance, tension, and possibility. The clear relationship between these two ideas is that the effects of works of art positions organisms in new ways and with greater confidence. When these works produce positions able to overcome constraints direct energies toward some common goal, then those works of art also function as works of rhetoric.

The Art of the Possible

The reason the experience of eloquence has been associated with the work of "fine art" than with "practical art" derives not from the fact that one has practical effects while the other deals only with beautiful speech. What is "fine" about eloquence is the manner in which practical transformations occur. Dewey observes that "poetry teaches as friends and life teach, by being, and not be express intent." Eloquence teaches in the manner of poetry, by speaking directly to one's being in the world with others and allowing instruction to happen on its own. One might even assert that art, like science, predicts and controls what an event might come to be—only differently: "Art is a mode of prediction not found in charts and statistics, and it insinuates possibilities of human relations not to be found in rule and precept, admonition and administration." This insinuation occurs, then, not by shouting but by whispering. To exemplify his point, Dewey quotes Keats, who says that "man should not dispute or assert, but whisper results to his neighbor," and then follows with a quote by Shelley, who writes that "art may tell a truth / Obliquely, do the deed shall breed the thought." By whispering obliquely a truth that speaks of our shared being, one addresses the imagination rather than the cognitive judgment. One insinuates a possibility that might grow within an individual's experience—but not as an "ideology" grows, as by a predetermined course toward a specialized end. Imagination, to function as imagination, necessarily involves the active participation and contribution of the individual. That is why, according to Dewey, the "first intimations of wide and large redirections of desire and purpose are of necessity imaginative."[101] Imagination liberates us from the familiar and the conventional precisely because it invests old substance with new vitality and form drawn from the material of one's lived experience. Even long-dead ideologies might then find sudden vibrancy when reworked in imagination. Thus we have the irony of conservative aristocrats like Plato consistently giving inspiration to the most radical and revolutionary movements.

With respect to the growth of civilization, the imaginative transformations that occur in the presence of eloquence have the most lasting effects on the future. What they lack in immediate spectacle they make up in long-term potency. Black's recovery of the Coatesville address speaks precisely to the importance of eloquence even when addressed to an audience of three, one of whom included a dog. Chapman was eloquent not because he argued for a cause beautifully; his eloquence spoke to the nature of our being, our home, and our common identity. Even more important, he spoke to an audience of history. What Chapman said in the nineteenth century speaks to the human condition in such a way that still matters today, and will matter any time we stand aside meekly in the face of atrocity. Great eloquence, like great art, proves itself as such not by any qualities that can be identified in the moment of its performance, but by its ability to powerfully move diverse audiences across the varied contexts of space and of time. There is an element of truth, then, to the notion that artists must ignore the audience. Although Booth rightly observes that no act of communication is ever is absent an audience, genuine eloquence requires one to still speak imaginatively to an audience that is not an actuality but a possibility. To allow one's immediate audience to constrain expression limits one to a reworking of platitudes and proofs. Dewey observes that whenever the "artist desires to communicate a *special* message, he thereby tends to limit the expressiveness of his work to others—whether he wishes to communicate a moral lesson or a sense of his own cleverness."[102] What goes by the epithet "popular" is a result of this overconcern with audience adaptation and was the cause of Plato's accusation of "flattery." Plato advocated an impossibility when he suggested that the artist should be completely free of social awareness. Yet the importance of detachment is real. One must simply expand the notion of communicability to include an audience coming to be in time. Dewey writes:

> Indifference to response of the immediate audience is a necessary trait of all artists that have something new to say. But they are animated by a deep conviction that since they can only say what they have to say, the trouble is not with their work but those who, having eyes, see now, and having ears, hear not. Communicability has nothing to do with popularity.... But if the time span be extended, it is true that no man is eloquent save when some one is moved as he listens. Those who are moved feel, as Tolstoi says, that what the work expresses is as if it were something one had oneself been longing to express. Meantime, the artist works to create an audience to which he does communicate. In the end works of art are the only media of complete and unhindered communication between man and man that can occur in a world full of gulfs and walls that limit community of experience.[103]

The experience of eloquence has such power because it makes one feel part of the movements of history—of being part of a community that is only now unfolding itself into the world and molding some part of the universe into its home, even when that feeling of community exists in the few or in the one. In this experience rests the hope of democracy. It is the reason Dewey places art above praise and blame and why he makes art more moral than moralities. The possibility that a new vision of community might be born in a lone soul on encountering a work of art, and that this vision might then take root in the souls of others through the whispers of what might be, is the only way that human society can advance beyond what has already been. Dewey notes that one of the frequent consequences of powerful aesthetic experiences is a yearning to hold onto them so tightly that one ceases moving forward. Great works of art become mere idols: "Art becomes stereotyped, and contented with playing minor variations upon old themes in styles and manners that are agreeable because they are the channels of pleasant reminiscence. The environment is, in so far, exhausted, worn out."[104] What made the Dark Ages so "dark" was simply that art became used as a means of constraining, rather than liberating, the imagination. Democracy reverses this process; it places its faith in the creative possibilities to which art gives birth. Eloquence, then, is the aesthetic disclosure of the possibilities of being to the imagination. Democracy is the process in which a community intelligently discriminates between and experimentally pursues the possibilities disclosed by eloquence over historical time.

Criticism and Construction

When the contexts that give birth to eloquence eventually pass into contexts of discrimination, experimentation, and judgment, the more instrumental manifestations of rhetoric become significant. What the experiences of persuasion and argumentation lack in aesthetic form they thus make up for in logical function. In Dewey's aesthetic theory, these aspects of rhetoric are best explained in terms of aesthetic criticism, which for Dewey equates with judgment. In judgment, one performs the logical functions of analysis and synthesis, of taking apart and putting together; its purpose is "to evoke a clearer consciousness of constituent parts and to discovery how consistently these parts are related to form a whole." Like the process of scientific inquiry, criticism functions as a kind of cartography that "surveys" an environment and designates relations, obstacles, destinations, causes, consequences, and pathways. When performed well, a critic's "surveys may be of assistance in the direct experience of others, as a survey of a country is of help to the one who travels through it." When good criticism then culminates in insight, then "criticism becomes itself an art."[105] Yet it is an art more as logic is an art, not as a unification of poiesis and praxis but as a *technē*. It is explicitly instrumental and used for something beyond itself. In art criticism, it functions as a "guide" to enhance a subsequent work of art. In rhetorical criticism, it facilitates our judgment and appreciation of a work of rhetoric. To understand the relationship between criticism and practice, one need only replace the "object" of criticism with our natural and social environment. The practical arts of science and rhetoric thus function, in effect, as criticism of life, showing how objects and events relate to one another within some situational whole.[106] As Kenneth Burke has long emphasized, rhetoric criticizes the drama of social life just as the literary critic judges the drama of the novel or the stage.

It is important to emphasize that even the most critical, analytical, and intellectual work has the capacity to constitute aesthetic form. To repeat, any discourse that accumulates tensions which are eventually consummated within a moment of unified understanding has elements of the aesthetic. Consequently even the most abstract philosophical discourse, such as Kant's *Critique of Pure Reason*, possesses its own aesthetic quality because of the fact that logical tensions are progressively overcome as one approaches a unified vision of human rationality. What blinds us to the aesthetic qualities of such discourse is that most of the process leading up to the consummation requires the labor of intelligence rather than of feeling, and most people view intelligence to be the enemy of the aesthetic. Yet Dewey notes that intelligence is an intrinsic component of the aesthetic feeling, for it is intelligence which allows one to overcome resistance and move forward toward unity. Indeed the "existence of resistance defines the place of intelligence in the production of an object of fine art," for intelligence assists in "bringing about the proper reciprocal adaptation of parts."[107] For those unable to overcome resistance, intimidating work like that of Kant remains firmly situated in the realm of the nonaesthetic. Yet for those able to hold many contradictory ideas within their imagination at once, the progressive resolution of tensions leads to moments of genuine aesthetic pleasure. That is why, despite assumptions to the contrary, scientists, philosophers, and mathematicians often have richer aesthetic experiences than those who spent their lives in surrounded by "great" art that functions for them as expensive wallpaper.[108]

The difference between the aesthetic form characteristic of intellectual or practical experience and that of a dominantly aesthetic experience turns on what kind of substance is being formed through the overcoming of resistance. In intellectual experience, the substance consists primarily of propositions and the resistance occurs in the recalcitrance that exists in the relationships between propositions. Certain ideas are hard to break apart while others are difficult to put together. Newtonian physics and Euclidean geometry, for example, represented a set of propositions that requires the hard labor of Einstein to finally shatter and re-form, resulting in the highly aesthetic proposition of $E = mc^2$. This revolution in physics then lead to new practical experiences in which the substance resisting and being formed represented tangible "things" of the natural world. The production of the atomic bomb, for instance, was inspired by Einstein's intellectual work but was finally brought into material existence only through the hard work of engineers who experimented with causes and effects. The actual "bomb" thus has an aesthetic form of its own when seen as a functional object, just as a car seems more beautiful when its engine runs. The interlocking of parts into a functional system mirrors the logical interlocking of propositions to create a functional idea. Both senses of form thus derive from their relationship to some situational problem to which they can be applied as a solution. Their beauty is in their use, in terms of external application.

The substance of a dominantly aesthetic experience, by contrast, comes from the self. What resists are parts of ourselves, the products of past experiences, and it is these experience which must, then, be rearranged and transformed in order to aesthetic experience to come about. Dewey writes that in order to perceive esthetically, an individual "must remake his past experiences so that they can enter integrally into a new pattern. He cannot dismiss his past experiences nor can he dwell among them as they have been in the past." In the aesthetic moment the material of the self undergoes transformation. It is only in this sense that art is "instrumental"—aesthetic experience produces a refreshed attitude toward the circumstances and exigencies of ordinary experience by bringing about feelings of "enduring serenity, refreshment, or re-education of vision."[109] In this way, even witnessing of an atomic explosion might produce an aesthetic experience of this sort when it brings about new patterns of experience. A purely engineering mind would look upon an atomic test as the consummation of a successful technological challenge. An aesthetic consciousness, like that of Oppenheimer, might make him realize that he has become Death, destroyer of worlds. For Oppenheimer this experience then altered his attitude toward science and society, culminating in his lifelong campaign for peace and disarmament that gave him serenity of conscience even though it posed great risk to his reputation and career.

In contradistinction to such moments of private revelation, rhetoric brings about the experience of manipulation when it consciously attempts to bring about specific intellectual or practical effects in the guise of aesthetic experience. Particularly within strategies of identification and division, in which notions of "us" and "them" are employed as justification for action, one feels oneself being used as means to an end. Aesthetic experience is almost demanded of an audience, such that one feels obliged to give signs that one has "seen the light." One thinks of the rhetoric of religious revivals that define the clear boundaries between the saved and the damned and then "invite" people who have been overwhelmed by the Holy Spirit to approach. Worse still are televangelists who then follow these sessions by posting the number one can call to give a donation. The spectacles of display superficially directed toward the "self" are thus actually intended to instill some intellectual doctrine of belief and practical habits of giving that support some institutional structure. The fact that political parties largely adopt this model demonstrates both the short term efficacy of the persuasive strategy and the level of ethical depravity characteristic of most political discourse. This says nothing about the "nature" of rhetoric other than that, like all art, it can be done poorly.

Kairos *and Decorum*

Rhetoric finds a more "authentic" voice when it simultaneously embraces its habitation in the particular, as in its most instrumental form, even as it speaks the language of the universal, as when it achieves a degree of eloquence. This is the great insight of Leff's attempt to recover "decorum" as a term that means something more than adaptation to conventional norms; for Leff, decorum is "the process of mediation and balance connected with qualitative judgment."[110] This aesthetic reading of decorum is consistent with Dewey's own. What makes an act lovely for Dewey, and hence in possession of decorum, is when there exists, as in the Greek ideal, a "feeling of grace and proportion in right conduct, a perception of fusion of means and ends." An act possesses decorum not because it satisfies the dictates of etiquette; it possesses decorum when universal ideas, values, or qualities achieve a local habitation in such a way that thoroughly fuses means and ends so as to constitute an aesthetic whole. For example, he says that the "spiritual" gets a "local habitation and achieves the solidity of form required for esthetic quality only when it is embodied in a sense of actual things. Even angels have to be provided in imagination with bodies and wings." Decorum occurs when these embodied forms transact with experience and bring about a unity of method and purpose that seeks a higher end through cumulative practices that contribute toward that end and are consistent with its values. And this effect does not require the moral sanction of angels. Dewey goes on to say, as an example, that the "adventures of a pirate have at least a romantic attraction lacking in the painful acquisitions of him who stays within the law merely because he thinks it pays better in the end to do so."[111] Our traditional fascination with the actions of great villains occurs precisely because they seem to possess a sense of decorum that we rarely have the strength of character to perform. Decorum has nothing to do with moral virtue and everything to do with achieving a formal unity of relations in a particular act.[112]

This aesthetic and amoral definition of decorum represents an understanding that departs from its traditional interpretation as conformity to conventional protocols and values. For most people decorum is directly associated with living up to social expectations of behavior even at the expense of practical effectiveness. The conservative demands of decorum are then said to stand in tension with the experimental impulses of *kairos*. A decorous speaker, in this view, treats a rhetorical situation as a disciplined space in which performers must obey certain tradition-bound rules to produce virtuous and beautiful discourse. By contrast, a *kairotic* speaker would view a rhetorical situation as a timely opportunity to break with those rules in order to make a practical difference in an exceptional moment. In situations which lack a sense of urgency, then, decorum becomes dominant; in the context of crisis, *kairos* carries the day. Hence, in the traditional interpretation, decorum becomes dominant in hierarchical societies such as the Roman Empire, whereas progressive and dynamic societies like classical Greece tend to promote a *kairotic* consciousness. From a conventional understanding, the perennial tension in any rhetorical situation is how to abide by decorum while still meeting the needs of *kairos*.

Although this conventional reading of decorum, which has dominated rhetorical theory ever since Roman times, highlights a necessary tension between decorum and *kairos*, it errs in reading an unwarranted moralism into decorum. Subordinating decorum to the dictates of conventional morality makes it little more than an expression of social control; as a result decorum read this way produces not beautiful speech but ugly speech. Dewey notes that "'decorum' and 'propriety' which once had a favorable, because esthetic, meaning are taking on a disparaging signification because they are understood to denote a primness or smugness assumed because of desire for an external end."[113] The "external end" in the case of rhetoric is the pleasing and flattering of an audience such that one gains consent by parroting what people already value and believe. This kind of performance tends toward the ugly because it produces the very experience of manipulation so typical of base rhetoric. Decorum, when read as a kind of social command, requires speakers to persuade audiences only by first putting on a "show" of identification and respect even if the speaker cares nothing for the audience or its values. This aura of falsity then encourages *kairotic* speakers to dismiss adaptation and appropriateness altogether in an effort to shatter all tradition and convention that would constrain their actions. In both cases, rhetorical artistry is largely absent, the one because of obsequiousness and the other out of insolence.

One recovers a more aesthetic understanding of both decorum and *kairos* by recalling the rhetorical practices of the Sophists and Plato. Given the opportunities presented by the new democracy, the impulse of the Sophists was to violate the speaking norms of the old aristocratic order in order to achieve timely and effective short-term victories in law, politics, and war. The "anything goes" atmosphere that reigned, particularly in the law courts, made playfulness of paramount significance as the fate of one's property and life might be decided by a single vote. For philosophically minded critics such as Plato, however, the Sophists suffered from tunnel vision. Their rhetoric saw history as a series of discrete and particular moments that had no essential connection to the other. Yet Plato did not, like members of the old aristocracy, argue for a return to the old ways of going things. What he desired was more revolutionary—a rhetoric that looked beyond the needs of the moment to the needs of the eternal as determined by the ideals of the good, even if such acts would result in one's own physical suffering and death. For the Sophists, timeliness was paramount because they viewed the immediate future as contingent upon the actions in the present; for Plato, place dominated in the broad sense of inhabiting the shadowy world of the senses that masked a deeper and more enduring reality that was unfolding in historical time. Yet both shared an understanding of the appropriate (*to prepon*) that did not subordinate the manner and content of expression to social convention. Both equally rejected the conventional definitions of decorum.

What made Plato a more decorous speaker than the Sophists was thus not that he obeyed speech conventions while the other violated them. Indeed Plato was as willing as Socrates to stick his finger in the eye of popular fashion when he thought it justified. But Plato only justified such acts when they met the standards of transcendental aesthetics. The creation of a beautiful object that embodied the spirit of the good and the true was self-justifying for Plato. The meaning of decorum, for him, is the expression of universal forms within a particular discourse that used ideal means to point toward an ideal end. To accomplish this task requires a great deal of knowledge, foresight, and artistry, acquired over years of disciplined training; moreover, it is important to note that this observation remains true even after Plato's metaphysics have dropped away. Regardless of whether or not one believes that such entities as the good, beautiful, and true actually exist, Plato's dialogues remain the expression of universal ideas in dramatic form that achieve a level of aesthetic unity unmatched in the history of Western philosophy.[114] Decorum is the ability to produce lasting works of aesthetic beauty even in moments that press one toward the quick and easy way out.

By contrast the Sophists approached rhetorical situations through the lens of *kairos* because they viewed rhetoric primarily as an instrument for encouraging action within moments of contingency and uncertainty. This instrumental perspective emphasizes the status of rhetoric as a means within a particular situation that is recalcitrant to universal understanding. The goal in *kairotic* situations is not to produce an object that inspires contemplative lingering for the sake of aesthetic pleasure but to move us from here to there as efficiently as possible. Sophists such as Gorgias, therefore, praise the power of rhetoric to manipulate emotions in such a way as to produce the desired actions as does a drug. For Gorgias the aesthetic is a primarily instrumental matter of manipulating style for practical effect; hence his fame for producing Gorgianic "figures" such as antithesis and parrallelism. Yet Gorgias can avoid producing the experience of manipulation by being completely transparent about his intentions. In sharp contrast to the preacher who unexpectedly asks the congregation to "pass the hat," the Sophists were more like street performers who produce spectacles with the hat already placed conspicuously on the sidewalk. An audience thus watches such performances knowing that their reason for being lies in the action subsequent to the performance itself, and they make their judgments accordingly.

Despite their differences, decorum and *kairos* really represent two ends of a single spectrum of practice understood in different magnitudes of space and time. The "spaciousness" of decorum derives from the fact that it speaks to a sense of stability and continuity across time, as if the place in which one stands will always exist, even if just in memory. When one speaks with decorum, one honors history and posterity by creating an object whose particular beauty endures because it speaks to a more universal audience. Timeliness ceases to be a consideration, not because time is not important but because it is a constant. In contradistinction *kairos* sees time and space as always in flux and impossible to predict. The platform on which one stands might tomorrow be embers, and what is said in done in the present will determine the character of the environment on which the sun shines in the morning. That *kairos* interprets as "timeliness" should not thus be read as neglecting the details of place; timeliness simply indicates that the characteristics of place are changing rapidly. In other words decorous action is appropriate for a situation experienced as being part of a universal and continuous whole; *kairotic* action is appropriate for a situation experienced as being a momentary exception to the rule.[115]

The ugliness characteristic of so much rhetoric comes about primarily because the distinction between decorum and *kairos* is taken to be a dualism. In this case *kairos* necessitates an immediately practical rhetoric that attends to matters of contextual judgment while decorum presses one to produce an intellectually and aesthetically rich discourse that ignores matters of practice in order to express the grandiose thoughts of the eternal mind. To be decorous when one should be *kairotic* is thus read to be irresponsible, while being *kairotic* in a decorous moment is to be impudent. Yet what both sides of the dualism have in common is lack of aesthetic form. One the one side, a narrowly interpreted *kairos* becomes merely a tool for some practical end that is hastily produced and easily discarded. On the other side a rigidly defined decorum becomes a mere vehicle for the expression of some ideal subject matter. Both thus point to something beyond themselves that renders literal the adjective "mere," for something is mere when it serves only as a disposable tool for some more significant purpose. The rhetoric of a Sophist employing pathos to sway a jury is thus as mere as the rhetoric of a Platonic poet using *poiesis* to educate the masses about the nature of the good. This classification does not make such discourses shameful or ineffective, but it does render their form something less than whole.

Rhetoric achieves a sense of aesthetic unity only when decorum and *kairos* are viewed as two ends of a continuous spectrum along which most rhetorical practice lies. Thus even at the extremes of each side—say, the general shouting orders in the midst of a battle on the one and the minister ritually reflecting on the nature of God on the other—there is a some combination of the universal and the particular that must be understood in terms of compression or expansion of space-time as experienced in the moment. The general must react to the immediate feints and thrusts of the enemy in order to win the battle, but even the battle must be seen in the context of a larger war that may extend over months, years, and even centuries. Gettysburg, for instance, may be retold as a series of individual decisions that occurred in the heat of battle, but it may also be interpreted as a timely victory that turned the tide of the Civil War and possibly led to the preservation of the United States as a unified nation. And a minister may adopt a humble position as, quite literally, a mere vehicle for the divine and everlasting Word, and yet his words might function in the situated moment to resolve doubt of a conflict-ridden parishioner and commit them to timely action. The letters of the Apostle Paul thus seem to span both spectrums equally; written as *kairotic* epistles to specific audiences that faced specific problems in the first century, they are now read as decorous reflections upon the universal meanings of Christian doctrine that impose duties on all believers.

Summary

It is in this fusion of the decorous and the *kairotic* within a single discourse that we find the aesthetic form characteristic of great rhetoric. What this fusion requires is the ability to dialectically travel between extremes and in doing so construct a discourse that facilitates similar movement in audiences both immediate and coming to be. If decorum allows us to embody universal forms in particular artifacts and actions in a deductive spirit, *kairos* encourages us to attend to the particular in order to inductively posit new universals. The relationship between the two processes in time is experimentalism. As an experimental discourse, rhetoric achieves aesthetic form only in relationship to the environment in which it is produced—in terms of its origins and consequences. Yet this environment is not a dualistic one that exists in two realms of the practical moment and the transcendent ideal; experimentalism assumes an environment that is continuous and always in process of growth and decline, of expansion and retraction, of permanence and change. The origins and consequences of rhetoric extend potentially into an infinity whose boundaries are marked off only by the situated needs of one's hermeneutic perspective. This includes not only the critic but also the audience itself. Nothing necessitates that an individual auditor experience a speech through any fixed boundary of time. One individual might see only into the next minute while the other's imagination is sent spinning into eternity. Great rhetoric has the potential to inspire both experiences simultaneously—that in realizing one's place in the universe as it is, we act more effectively in the timely moment, and that by acting in the moment, we come to realize new forms of possibility inherent in the universe that is coming to be.

Plato calls this realization of possibility a "divine madness" precisely because it seems to transcend the limits of logical rationality. The aesthetic component of rhetoric speaks to this feeling of transcendence, allowing people the freedom to imagine themselves, others, and the world as greater and more beautiful than perhaps it is and ever will be. Yet only by projecting such hope can we ever hope to become greater and more beautiful than we are. Weaver is correct to point out that rhetoric at its truest "seeks to perfect men by showing them better versions of themselves, links in that chain extending up toward the ideal, which only the intellect can apprehend and only the soul have affection for."[116] In Dewey's vocabulary logic takes on the burden of apprehension and aesthetics the task for affection, while rhetoric embodies the spirit of movement that throws into the future world of contingency with a new understanding and a shared hope. Yet rhetoric embarks on this project of perfection experimentally, pragmatically, and in the tragicomic spirit which, in Condit's words, "recognizes that human beings are powerful and flawed symbol-using animals. We invent symbolic and nonsymbolic tools that are always capable of carrying us over the edge of the abyss. If there is to be salvation from our own combined power and imperfection, it lies in our ability to recognize what havoc our symbol systems urge us to create, to understand that those potentials are always with us, and, through shared understanding of our comic position, to dampen our more virulent tendencies with the varied tools of laughter, awe, disgust, and insight."[117]

Thus even if we truly believe, at any one time, that there genuinely exists a sturdy chain that we can ascend toward a fixed ideal, the contingencies of the world will shatter that ideal and break that chain. But our responsibility is not to curse the world and bemoan our fate; our responsibility is to acknowledge our fallibility and press onward with renewed humility, sympathy, courage, intelligence, imagination, and faith. This faith is not in some higher force to come and save us, however; our faith is a radical one. Our faith is in the liberating power of the human spirit when harnessed through the collective forms of democratic communication, including that form we call rhetoric.

Conclusion

THE GREAT LESSON OF DEWEY'S MATURE PHILOSOPHY is that the constitution of civilization is intrinsically an accomplishment of art—the intelligent and sympathetic process of doing and making that makes our shared world a richer place to inhabit. As he writes, "It is by creation of the intangibles of science and philosophy, and especially by those of the arts, that countries and communities have won immortality for themselves after material wealth has crumbled into dust."[1] Democracy, as a form of civilization, thus only exists insofar as it learns from and encourages the development of the arts, sciences, and philosophies that make existence something more than the instinctual struggle for survival. For Dewey "a democracy is more than a form of government; it is primarily a mode of associated living, of conjoint communicated experience."[2] What makes democracy different from other forms of associated living is that it places its faith in the ability for the arts of communication to draw from, direct, and give form to human experience without recourse to something "beyond" or "above" our existence. Democracy, in Dewey's words, "is belief in the ability of human experience to generate the aims and methods by which further experience will grow in ordered richness."[3] Putting this belief to work requires more than simply the release from formal constraints to free expression. It requires a shared commitment to communication, to sharing experience, that has been the exception rather than the rule in human history.

A radical democracy thus commits itself to the universal development of a radical rhetoric. This rhetoric draws from the resources of experimental logic for practical judgment while constituting new relationships between the self, society, and environment through the aesthetic form. In radical rhetoric, an audience thus progresses through the stages of aesthetic form—continuity, accumulation, tension, conservation, and anticipation—using the more intellectual and practical experiences of persuasion and argumentation to build up layers of energy that eventually find fulfillment and consummation in the aesthetic experience of eloquence. Radical rhetoric is thus not a discrete act that happens in a synchronic moment. Even in its performance, it is a development in time. Walker, for instance, demonstrates that "in a large and complex argument," there is "a progression from enthymeme to enthymeme to enthymeme, building up an accumulated fund of value-laden, emotively significant ideas . . . that are variously brought to bear, forcefully and memorably, in the rhetor's final enthymematic turns."[4] What Walker points out in what is already implicit in Dewey's aesthetic theory; that logical form is a subset of aesthetic form, and that enthymemes work to build logical proofs only to find them wholly transformed through one's final aesthetic turns.

Dewey's social and aesthetic theory leads us to the controversial conclusion that neither rhetoric nor democracy can afford to mock the Platonic goals of consummating truth, beauty, and goodness within a singular work of art. For all his metaphysical bluster, Plato established ideals that remain inspiring and necessary for social progress. Yet the achievement of these ideals can only be attained through a Sophistical understanding of art and a naturalistic ontology of becoming. Truth, beauty, and goodness are not metaphysical forms that look down upon the world as gods. They are experimental ends-in-view that we continually revise even as we strive after them.[5] Rhetoric emerges at those points at which our struggle to ascend meets obstruction, when our habits are frustrated, our goals unclear, and our methods opaque. In that moment of crisis, our fate is decided on whether we turn this way or that, with each step moving us ever more distant from an alternative reality that might have been and toward a reality that is coming to be in time. The responsibility of rhetoric at these moments may be so great as to make us abandon our responsibility to the art and give ourselves up to forces beyond our control. Yet this is not the path to civilization, but to barbarism. The common faith of humanity may be ideal, but it is not idealistic. They are ideals of our own creation, made by us to further the enrichment of human experience. Dewey writes:

> The ideal ends to which we attach our faith are not shadowy and wavering. They assume concrete form in our understanding of our relations to one another and the values contained in these relations. We who now live are parts of a humanity that extends into the remote past, a humanity that has interacted with nature. The things in civilization we most prize are not of ourselves. They exist by grace of the doings and sufferings of the continuous human community in which we are a link. Ours is the responsibility of conserving, transmitting, rectifying and expanding the heritage of values we have received that those who come after us may receive it more solid and secure, more widely accessible and more generously shared than we have received it.[6]

Giving concrete form to ideal ends means more than waving ideographs about in a speech in order to hear the sound of acclaim. More often than not this ideographic interpretation of "ends" culminates in the eventual experience of manipulation in which the postulated ends contradict the actual ones. In other words ideographs such as "justice" or "freedom" or "democracy" are, more often than not, merely deceptive fantasies used to mask brutal realities. They do not function as ends-in-view, as operative plans which guide the determination of means in order to reconstruct a problematic situation. As Dewey frequently emphasizes, the meaning of "democracy" is not found in its ends alone, but in the relationship between the means and the ends. This was particularly evident in 1937, when "democracy" was being used to justify the worst of atrocities:

> For democracy means not only the ends which even dictatorships now assert are their ends, security for individuals and opportunity for their development as personalities. It signifies also primary emphasis upon the means by which these ends are to be fulfilled. The means to which it is devoted are the voluntary activities of individuals in opposition to coercion; they are assent and consent in opposition to violence; they are the force of intelligent organization versus that of organization imposed from outside and above. The fundamental principle of democracy is that the ends of freedom and individuality for all can be attained only by means that accord with those ends. The value of upholding the banner of liberalism in this country, no matter what it has come to mean in Europe, is its insistence upon freedom of belief, of inquiry, of discussion, of assembly, of education: upon the method of public intelligence in opposition to even a coercion that claims to be exercised in behalf of the ultimate freedom of all individuals. There is intellectual hypocrisy and moral contradiction in the creed of those who uphold the need for at least a temporary dictatorship of a class as well as in the position of those who assert that the present economic system is one of freedom of initiative and of opportunity for all. There is no opposition in standing for liberal democratic means combined with ends that are socially radical. There is not only no contradiction, but neither history nor human nature gives any reason for supposing that socially radical ends can be attained by any other than liberal democratic means.[7]

A radical democracy thus represents a commitment to the communicative and productive arts, particularly as developed through the free association of individuals concerned with contextual matters of judgment, as the means by which we cooperatively advance the progress of civilization. Rhetoric stands alongside science, philosophy, and the "fine" arts in their dedication to furthering the progressive vision of a democratic society.

This book is being published at a time of great anxiety, strife, instability, transition, and hope. The collapse of financial markets has undermined the laissez-faire ideology that has guided global economic policy for decades; lingering nationalistic and ethnic tensions have erupted into new forms of terroristic violence and genocide; the grinding poverty of the developing world and in the pockets of the wealthiest nations humiliates the grand ideals of the "civilized" world; AIDS continues to ravage the most helpless of us; archaic reproductive policies and political instability fuel population growth that overwhelms the capacities of the natural environment to sustain it; new forms of slavery condemn millions of women and children to a life of servitude; unbridled industrial expansion corrodes the very health of the planet's atmosphere; and the trends of global capitalism threaten to undermine some of the very foundations of democratic social life. Yet this is also a time of great hope. Whatever one's politics, the inauguration of the first African American president of the United States is proof that progress in the capacity for human understanding is real and that disruptions in the social order often necessitate the emergence of new possibilities.

It speaks to Dewey's underlying rhetorical sensibility that he would see the rhetorical possibilities in an analogous time during his own life, the Great Depression. Speaking to the National Association for the Advancement of Colored People in 1932, an association he helped found, Dewey observes that the organization's time of crisis is also one of opportunity. But this opportunity comes not from the naïve faith that one has nowhere to go but up; rather, opportunity comes from the fact that to begin something new one must put an end to what has come before and has refused to go. For Dewey the "depression marks the end of the period of illusions and hallucinations," the end of the "paradise of folly" which believes that progress is free and misery a product of accident or vice. There was, then, at least some gain: "It is something to become aware of the need for new ideas, new measure, new policies, new leaders, to bring about a great social reconstruction. More specifically, I think our depression has compelled us to think more fundamentally on social matters, economic matters, political matters, than we have been thinking for some years."

The Depression was a rhetorical situation writ large; it was an exigent circumstance in which old habits ceased to function, impulses rose to a peak, publics came together in anxious deliberation, and the need for far-reaching vision was dire. Most important, however, it was a situation in which thinking was made possible. Dewey continues: "I met an engineer, a leader in his profession, a few weeks ago and he said, 'Do you know I have only begun to think since 1932.' I would not take his remark too literally because I knew he had thought very effectively; but I knew that he had not had to consider the relation of his work, that of the engineering profession, to the whole social and economic construction before that collapse of 1929 in the way that he has to do now." What Dewey highlights is the kind of thinking that is distinctively rhetorical, a thinking in which a person situates oneself within an interconnected public to whom one has responsibilities. In these cases even a "scientist" takes on the role of the citizen and bears the burden of facilitating collective judgment.

Even more notable about Dewey's address to the NAACP is its palpable rhetorical spirit. For Dewey knew that the Depression hit the African American community more than any other. "Doubtless the group which you represent has suffered more than any other, more keenly, more intensely," he states. "Doubtless you are the first, on the whole, to lose employment and the last to be taken on." At the same time, the Depression brought about a productive change in the relationships between publics: "The depression has also disclosed a community of interest among all the minority, repressed and oppressed groups of the country." This community of interest, according to Dewey, needed to be strengthened and find public expression: "Now, this compulsion to think more fundamentally has also the advantage of bringing with it a greater freedom not merely of thought but of expression. In that way it gives the minority, the oppressed, groups of this country a better opportunity to express themselves, their needs, their wrongs, their demands for greater freedom, a larger opportunity and a wider field than they have done in the past."

The Sophistical spirit of the passage is striking. Dewey specifically refers to the *kairotic* moment as one that makes it possible to make the weaker argument the stronger. Moreover, the end toward which Dewey points also resonates with the classical Greek goal: "self-management of their own affairs in industry." Lastly, Dewey signals that this goal can only be achieved outside the conventional political system designed to marginalize their voices. What they need is to use "their energy and influence to find a new political outlet, a different one, which would give them some kind of actual representation." Instead of being subsumed by party machines, Dewey, in effect, suggests a development of a new rhetorically inspired social movement.[8]

We see in this example the centrality of ethics, inquiry, and aesthetics to a radical rhetoric in a radical democracy. Ethically rhetoric is responsible for the bridging of differences and the development of common interest within and across publics. Yet this formation requires inquiry into the situational needs and constraints of those publics as they exist within a civil, political, and industrial environment. To cry, "Solidarity!" without the comprehending the forces which foster division and the narrowing of interest is to shout into the wind. Better, says Dewey, that publics have the capacity to cry, "Bunk!" when they are able to use the resources of intelligence to see through the efforts by those in authority to create "suspicion, dislike and division among the mass of the people." Finally, one requires aesthetic vision to be able to create new orientation of the self to its environment such that one brings about a sense of home. Thus, Dewey concludes, it is only in "the degree in which all the minority groups cut loose complete from both of the old parties and join in some new part, which will help bring about a social and economic reconstruction in the interest of a society which is cooperative and human, in that degree the day of economic slavery for the masses in this country will come to an end." This challenge is most certainly a rhetorical one, but it is reserved for a radical rhetoric that eschews easy binaries and slogans in favor of a rich and eloquent discourse which draws from the available resources of public wisdom, science, and arts in order to contribute to the development of a common world.[9]

This basic principle of the ontology of becoming is that this common world is one always in the making. It is a collective work of art that we build together in a shared environment. Hannah Arendt eloquently sums it up this way: "The common world is what we enter when we are born and what we leave behind when we die. It transcends our lifespan into past and future alike; it was there before we came and will outlast our brief sojourn in it. It is what we have in common not only with those who live with us, but also with those who were here before and with those who will come after us. But such a common world can survive the coming and going of the generations only to the extent that it appears in public. It is the publicity of the public realm which can absorb and make shine through the centuries whatever men may want to save from the natural ruin of time."

In this common world of becoming, the present moment always stands somewhere between death and birth, between mortality and natality. Philosophy has always concerned itself with mortality, with the things that came before and leave their eternal presence in the world as it is and always will be. Rhetoric, however, always functions in the sphere of natality, of bringing into being within those creative moments of rupture when our endings signal new beginnings. It is thus a form of action as Arendt defines action. For her "the new beginning inherent in birth can make itself felt in the world only because the newcomer possesses the capacity of beginning something anew, that is, of acting." Yet an action does not live only in a moment; it is not a stillbirth. Action leaves its traces in conditions of power, a potentiality which for Arendt is "actualized only where word and deed have not parted company, where words are not empty and deeds not brutal, where words are not used to veil intentions but to disclose realities, and deeds are not used to violate and destroy but to establish relations and create new realities. Power is what keeps the public realm, the potential space of appearance between acting and speaking men, in existence."[10]

A radical rhetoric for a radical democracy is an ethical, intelligent, and aesthetic action in the world of becoming that collects individuals together voluntarily for the common purpose of channeling shared power to transform their common world. This does not deny the existence of base rhetoric or systematic propaganda which seeks to sow division or impose an artificial unity on human thought and labor. Nor does it slide into the tragic idealism of those who would seek the Promised Land by taking vengeance upon evil. Our faith in ideals must, as Kenneth Burke urged, be accompanied by a comic humility. As Arendt argues, the freedom embodied in the doctrine of "forgiveness is the freedom from vengeance."[11] This was the enduring wisdom of Martin Luther King Jr., whose teachings John Peters calls "one of the best options for coping with abuse in this world. He taught people how to bear witness with their presence."[12] King's action gives the lie to those who would call "radical" only the actions of brutish ignorance that align stupidity with force in the name of an unattainable ideal. A genuinely radical act is often one of refusal—of refusal to act as others have called you to act, of refusal to cease moving forward, of refusal to get out of the way.

A radical rhetoric thus calls forth the desire to seek out a wisdom greater than oneself, the love to join arms with those who are your strangers, the courage to stand one's ground in the face of violence, the passion to articulate a beauty that can be found only in this world, the intelligence to map out a path toward a distant horizon, and the imagination to weave the many strands of this interconnnected universe into a home. We are fated to struggle together toward an open-ended future even as we build the road underneath our feet. To plunge headlong into time is thus as futile as refreshing to take a step for fear of what might come. We must choose our fate if it is not to be chosen for us. It is thus the responsibility of a radical rhetoric to contribute to this process by which we travel down that "ever-present new road upon which we can walk together."[13]

NOTES

Introduction

1. Dewey, "Democracy Is Radical," 298–99.
2. For Dewey's attitude toward art, see Alexander.
3. Ellul, *Propaganda*, xviii.
4. Foucault, *Essential Foucault*, 317.
5. Wichelns, "The Literary Criticism of Oratory," 26–27.
6. Jaeger, *Paideia* 1:286.
7. Ibid. 2:151.
8. Farrell, *Norms of Rhetorical Culture*, 267.
9. Greene, "John Dewey's Eloquent Citizen," 189–200, 190.
10. Foucault, *Essential Foucault*, 26–34.
11. Danish, "Power and the Celebration of the Self," 291–307, 305.
12. Guthrie, *Sophists*, 115.
13. Translated by Eric Havelock as quoted in Havelock, *Liberal Temper in Greek Politics*, 58.
14. Isocrates, *Antidosis*, §253–56.
15. Specifically Greene responds not to Dewey but to Christopher Lyle Johnstone's reading of Dewey.
16. Dewey, *Experience and Nature*, 104.
17. Dewey, "Ethics of Democracy," 246.
18. Dewey, "Creative Democracy," 227.
19. Schudson, "Why Conversation Is Not the Soul of Democracy," 300.
20. Dewey, "Basic Values and Loyalties," 277.
21. Peters, *Courting the Abyss*, 275.
22. Crick, "Composition as Experience," 254–75.
23. Foucault, *Essential Foucault*, 248.
24. Ibid., 354, 179.
25. Crick, *John Dewey*, 7.
26. Ibid., 10.
27. Dewey, *Experience and Nature*, 132.
28. Burks, "John Dewey and Rhetorical Theory," 126. Three examples of attempts to reveal the rhetorical implications of Dewey are Johnstone, "Dewey, Ethics, and Rhetoric," 185–207; Mackin, "Rhetoric, Pragmatism, and Practical Wisdom"; and Bitzer, "Rhetoric and Public Knowledge," 67–93.
29. Dykhuizen, *Life and Mind of John Dewey*, 64.

30. For the evolving relationship between aesthetics and communication in Dewey's thought, see Crick, "John Dewey's Aesthetics of Communication," 303–19.
31. Dewey, "Fred Newton Scott," 120–21.
32. Stewart and Stewart, *Life and Legacy of Fred Newton Scott*, 19.
33. Ibid., 3.
34. Kitzhaber, *Rhetoric in American Colleges*, 223.
35. Ibid.
36. Stewart and Stewart, *Life and Legacy of Fred Newton Scott*, 3.
37. Dewey, "Fred Newton Scott," 121.
38. Danish, *Pragmatism*, 64.
39. Peters, *Courting the Abyss*, 275.
40. Boydston, *Poems of John Dewey*. This particular poem was the first half of number 75 and appeared on pages 54–55 in Boydston's book.
41. Dewey, *Quest for Certainty*, 111.
42. Poulakos, *Sophistical Rhetoric*, 53, 65, 64.
43. Dewey, *Public and Its Problems*, 208.
44. Ibid.
45. Dewey and Tufts, *Ethics* 7:362.
46. Ibid., 362–63.
47. Farrell, *Norms of Rhetorical Culture*, 282, 194, 1, 199, 83, 229.
48. Charland, "Norms and Laughter," 339.

CHAPTER 1: *Rhetoric and the Ethics of Democracy*

1. Weaver, *Ethics of Rhetoric*, 232.
2. Wichelns, "Literary Criticism of Oratory," 22.
3. Dewey and Tufts, *Ethics* 7:175, 166–67.
4. Ibid., 175.
5. Nor it is sufficient to argue that democratic ethics celebrate individuality whereas communistic ethics celebrate universality. For democracy "is not mere assertion of the individual will as individual; it is not disregard of law, of the universal; it is complete realization of the law, namely the unified spirit of the community." Dewey, "Ethics of Democracy," 242–43.
6. Ibid., 243.
7. Dewey, *Human Nature and Conduct*, 280.
8. Dewey, "Ethics of Democracy," 244.
9. Dewey and Tufts, *Ethics* 7:285.
10. Ibid., 306, 231.
11. Foucault, *Essential Foucault*, 23.
12. Poulakos, "*Kairos* in Gorgias' Rhetorical Compositions," 89.
13. Miller, "Foreword," xiii.
14. White, *Kaironomia*, 14.
15. Poulakos, *Sophistical Rhetoric*, 61.
16. Fragment DK 85B1 quoted in Waterfield, *First Philosophers*.
17. Wichelns, "Literary Criticism of Oratory," 21.
18. Wander, "Ideological Turn in Modern Criticism," 111.

19. Dewey, *Logic*, 88.
20. Plato, *Theaetetus*, 167a–168b.
21. Dewey, "Postulate of Immediate Empiricism," 163.
22. Ibid., 167b.
23. Hauser, "Rhetorical Democracy and Civic Engagement," 1.
24. Plato, *Statesman*, 404a.
25. James Madison, Federalist Number 10, Constitution Society, http://www.constitution.org/fed/federa10.htm/.
26. Ellul, *Propaganda*, 8–9.
27. Hamilton, *Greek Way*, 154.
28. Dewey, "From Absolutism to Experimentalism," 155.
29. Plato, *Theaetetus*, 167c.
30. Ibid.
31. Poulakos, "Toward a Sophistic Definition," 43–44.
32. Dewey, *Quest for Certainty*, 195.
33. Bitzer had written his master's thesis on Dewey and had acknowledged the influence of Dewey's ideas in a personal conversation with the author.
34. Quoted in Bitzer, "Functional Communication," 26.
35. Bitzer, "Rhetorical Situation," 13–14.
36. Vatz, "Myth of the Rhetorical Situation," 155.
37. Commentaries of Bitzer's essay are twelve and counting. See Benoit, "Genesis of Rhetorical Action," 342–55; Biesecker, "Rethinking the Rhetorical Situation," 110–30; Brinton, "Situation in the Theory of Rhetoric," 234–48; Consigny, "Rhetoric and Its Situations," 175–86; Garret and Xiao, "Rhetorical Situation Revisited," 30–40; Hunsaker and Smith, "Nature of Issues," 144–56; Jamieson, "Generic Constraints," 162–70; Larson, "Lloyd Bitzer's 'Rhetorical Situation,'" 165–68; Patton, "Causation and Creativity," 36–55; Lybarger and Smith, "Bitzer's Model Reconstructed," 197–213; Vatz, "Myth of the Rhetorical Situation," 154–61; and Wilkerson, "On Evaluating Theories of Rhetoric," 82–96.
38. Vatz, "Myth of the Rhetorical Situation," 158, 154.
39. Biesecker, "Rethinking the Rhetorical Situation," 242, 243.
40. Bitzer, "Rhetorical Situation," 4.
41. Bitzer, "Functional Communication," 24.
42. Lybarger and Smith, "Bitzer's Model Reconstructed," 200.
43. Hunsaker and Smith, "Nature of Issues," 156.
44. Dewey and Tufts, *Ethics* 7:163.
45. Dewey, *Human Nature and Conduct*, 134.
46. Darsey, "Joe McCarthy's Fantastic Moment," 429.
47. Ibid., 433.
48. Lybarger and Smith, "Bitzer's Model Reconstructed," 201.
49. Dewey, *Experience and Nature*, 10, 13.
50. Dewey, *Art as Experience*, 251.
51. Dewey, "Conduct and Experience," 228; emphasis added.
52. Dewey, *Experience and Nature*, 5.
53. Rorty, *Consequences of Pragmatism*, 87, 85.

54. Dewey, *Experience and Nature*, 10.

55. This perspective appears in the work of Michael Calvin McGee, who writes that the "people," even though "made 'real' by their own belief and behavior, are still *essentially* a mass illusion," a collection of discrete individuals "infused with an artificial identity." See McGee, "Ideograph," 345.

56. Dewey, *Art as Experience*, 261.

57. Bentley and Dewey, *Knowing and the Known*, 4.

58. Dewey, *Experience and Nature*, 28; emphasis added.

59. Bentley and Dewey, *Knowing and the Known*, 101f.

60. Dewey, "Conduct and Experience," 220.

61. Bentley and Dewey, *Knowing and the Known*, 125, 4, 101.

62. Dewey, "Half-Hearted Naturalism," 76.

63. Dewey, *Experience and Nature*, 293.

64. Ibid., 148.

65. Ibid., 34.

66. Dewey, "Context and Thought," 5.

67. Dewey, *Experience and Nature*, 39.

68. Latour, *Reassembling the Social*.

69. Dewey, "Postulate of Immediate Empiricism," 158, 160.

70. Dewey, *Experience and Nature*, 245, 147.

71. Ibid., 132.

72. Ibid., 331.

73. Ibid., 240–41.

74. Dewey, *Logic*, 72.

75. Bentley and Dewey, *Knowing and the Known*, 282.

76. Ibid.

77. Dewey, *Logic*, 76.

78. Dewey, *How We Think*, 189.

79. Dewey's larger point is simply that none of this happens just inside people's heads. It occurs within a larger environment that people experience as genuinely fearful, tragic, uncertain, intimidating, tense, and worrisome—that is to say, problematic—and demands some form of coordinated action to resolve it. As Dewey explains: "It is in the very nature of the indeterminate situation which evokes inquiry to be questionable . . . to be uncertain, unsettled, disturbed. . . . It is the situation that has these traits. We are doubtful because the situation is inherently doubtful. Personal states of doubt that are not evoked by and are not relative to some existential situation are pathological. . . . Consequently, situations that are disturbed and troubled, confused or obscure, cannot be straightened out, cleared up and put in order, by manipulation of our personal states of mind. The attempt to settle them by such manipulations involved what psychiatrists call 'withdrawal from reality.' . . . The habit of disposing of the doubtful as if it belonged only to us rather than to the existential situation in which we are caught and implicated is an inheritance from subjectivistic psychology." It does not take a great leap of imagination to see how the neo-Sophistical argument for "constitutive" rhetoric more often than not ends up championing a kind of rhetorical pathology (Dewey, *Logic*, 109–10).

80. Dewey and Tufts, *Ethics* 5:191.

81. Dewey, "Three Independent Factors in Morals," 280.
82. Dewey, *Logic*, 173.
83. Dewey and Tufts, *Ethics* 7:165.
84. Ibid., 166, 164, 162.
85. Ibid., 165, 162.
86. Plato, *Symposium*, 207e.
87. Dewey, *Experience and Nature*, 303.
88. Ibid., 303; emphasis added.
89. Dewey, *Art as Experience*, 263.
90. Ibid., 263.
91. Dewey, *Experience and Nature*, 285.
92. Ibid., 303.
93. Dewey, *Democracy and Education*, 103–4.
94. Dewey, *Experience and Nature*, 308.
95. Ibid., 187, 170.
96. Dewey, *Art as Experience*, 51.
97. Crick, "Capital and Novel Argument," 337–64.
98. Foucault, *Essential Foucault*, 172.
99. Dewey, *Human Nature and Conduct*, 16.
100. Ibid., 15–16.
101. Burke, *Counter-Statement*, 150–51.
102. Dewey, *Public and Its Problems*, 235.
103. Foucault, *Essential Foucault*, 48.
104. Dewey, *Public and Its Problems*, 235.
105. Dewey, *Human Nature and Conduct*, 49.
106. Dewey, *Democracy and Education*, 33.
107. Dewey, *Human Nature and Conduct*, 54.
108. Dewey, *Public and Its Problems*, 237.
109. Dewey, "Outlawing Peace by Discussing War," 173.
110. Dewey, *Public and Its Problems*, 335.
111. Dewey, *Human Nature and Conduct*, 21.
112. Dewey and Tufts, *Ethics* 7:298–99, 255, 260.
113. Dewey, *Human Nature and Conduct*, 75f, 68, 67.
114. Ibid., 66, 65.
115. Ibid., 75.
116. Dewey, *Experience and Nature*, 235.
117. Burke, *Attitudes Toward History*, 298.
118. Dewey, *Human Nature and Conduct*, 96, 90.
119. Burke, *Permanence and Change*, 69.
120. Dewey, *Experience and Nature*, 292.
121. Dewey, "Appreciation and Cultivation," 113.
122. Dewey, *Human Nature and Conduct*, 54.
123. Dewey, *Art as Experience*, 72.
124. Burke, *Permanence and Change*, 169.
125. Lippmann, *Essential Lippmann*, 86.

126. McGee, "Ideograph," 345.
127. Ellul, *Propaganda*, 90–94.
128. Lippmann, *Essential Lippmann*, 35–36.
129. Dewey, *Individualism Old and New*, 83.
130. Ibid., 83–84.
131. Dewey, *Human Nature and Conduct*, 76, 77.
132. Ellul, *Propaganda*, 169.
133. Smith, "Character Building," 85.
134. Hall, "Introduction," 1.
135. Ibid., 5–6.
136. Bauman, "From Pilgrim to Tourist," 22.
137. Hall, "Introduction," 4.
138. Bauman, "From Pilgrim to Tourist," 24.
139. Ibid., 37; emphasis added.
140. Dewey and Tufts, *Ethics* 7:171.
141. Danisch, "Michel Foucault's Epideictic Rhetoric," 301.
142. Dewey, *Human Nature and Conduct*, 171.
143. Ibid., 256.
144. Dewey, *Democracy and Education*, 120.
145. Farrell, *Norms of Rhetorical Culture*, 1.
146. Dewey and Tufts, *Ethics* 7:167.
147. Wang, *John Dewey in China*.
148. Hauser, *Vernacular Voices*, 32–33, 34.
149. Dewey, *Public and Its Problems*, 27, 16, 17.
150. Westbrook, *John Dewey and American Democracy*, 305.
151. Dewey, *Public and Its Problems*, 320.
152. Asen, "Multiple Mr. Dewey," 177–78.
153. Dewey, *Public and Its Problems*, 129.
154. Ibid., 177.
155. Dewey, "Organization in American Education," 404.
156. Dewey, "Are Sanctions Necessary to International Organization?" 203.
157. Dewey, "Address of Welcome," 263.
158. Dewey, "Organization in American Education," 404.
159. Dewey, *Individualism Old and New*, 62.
160. Dewey, *Liberalism and Social Action*, 79–80.
161. Farrell, *Norms of Rhetorical Culture*, 282.
162. Dewey, *Liberalism and Social Action*, 42.

163. The "classic formulation of the 'rule of public opinion'" is provided by Guizot, whom Habermas cites as providing the three pillars of the public sphere: "It is, moreover, the character of that system, which nowhere admits the legitimacy of absolute power, to compel the whole body of citizens incessantly, and on every occasion, to seek after reason, justice and truth, which should ever regulate actual power. The representative system does this, (1) by discussion, which compels existing powers to seek after truth in common; (2) by publicity, which places these powers when occupied in this

search, under the eyes of the citizens; and (3) by the liberty of the press, which stimulates the citizens themselves to seek after the truth, and to tell it to power." Quoted in Habermas, *Structural Transformation of the Public Sphere*, 101.

164. Dewey, "Basic Values and Loyalties of Democracy," 276.
165. Dewey, *Liberalism and Social Action*, 39, 34, 47, 42, 36, 47.
166. Habermas, *Structural Transformation of the Public Sphere*, 195, 178.
167. Dewey, *Freedom and Culture*, 187.
168. Dewey, *Public and Its Problems*, 365.
169. Charland, "Constitutive Rhetoric," 133.
170. Ibid., 147, 141–42, 139, 140.
171. Ibid., 138.
172. Dewey, *Democracy and Education*, 9.
173. Dewey, *Art as Experience*, 81.
174. Fishman, "Explicating Our Tacit Tradition," 328, 323.
175. Hickman, *John Dewey's Pragmatic Technology*, 70.
176. Dewey, *Public and Its Problems*, 350.
177. Peters, "Public Journalism and Democratic Theory," 104.
178. Latour, *Politics of Nature*, 18.
179. Latour, *Reassembling the Social*, 75.
180. Dewey, *Public and Its Problems*, 216–17.
181. Ibid., 212, 211.
182. Latour, *Reassembling the Social*, 181; emphasis added.
183. Ibid., 176.
184. Dewey, *Public and Its Problems*, 213, 211.
185. Ibid., 215, 216.
186. Ibid., 213, 212.
187. Asen, "Multiple Mr. Dewey," 184.
188. Dewey, *Public and Its Problems*, 213, 211, 213.
189. Ibid., 218–19.
190. Dewey, "Creative Democracy," 227–28.
191. Dewey, *Liberalism and Social Action*, 50.
192. Ibid., 52.
193. Ibid., 51.
194. Dewey, "Organization in American Education," 405.
195. Ibid., 405.
196. Latour, *Reassembling the Social*, 138.
197. Ibid., 261.
198. Latour, *Politics of Nature*, 124.
199. Aristotle, *Rhetoric and the Poetics of Aristotle*, 1357a.
200. Dewey, *Outlines of a Critical Theory of Ethics*, 326.
201. Dewey and Tufts, *Ethics* 7:187.
202. Poulakos, "From the Depths of Rhetoric," 335–52, 337.
203. Crick, "Rhetoric, Philosophy, and the Public Intellectual," 127–39.
204. Burke, *Attitudes Toward History*, introduction; Burke, *Rhetoric of Motives*, 23.

205. Dansich, *Pragmatism and the Necessity of Rhetoric.*
206. Ibid., 191.

CHAPTER 2: *The Rhetoric of Inquiry*

1. Plato, Republic II, 377c.
2. Ziman, *Real Science,* 310.
3. Weaver, *Ethics of Rhetoric,* 86, 109.
4. Poulakos, "Hegel's Reception," 61, 168.
5. Weaver, *Ethics of Rhetoric,* 112.
6. Ibid., 232.
7. Ramus, *Arguments in Rhetoric,* 570.
8. Scott, "On Viewing Rhetoric as Epistemic," 138, 135.
9. Gross, *Rhetoric of Science,* 69.
10. Nelson, Megill, and McCloskey, "Rhetoric of Inquiry," 4.
11. Ziman, *Real Science,* 17.
12. Ibid., 142.
13. Latour, *Science in Action,* 32.
14. Ibid., 61.
15. Dewey, "Logic," 4.
16. Dewey, *Logic,* 57.
17. Ibid., 58.
18. Dewey, *Philosophy and Education,* 32, 35.
19. Dewey, "Logic," 4.
20. Dewey, *Logic,* 58–59.
21. Dewey, *Philosophy and Education,* 32.
22. Aristotle, *Rhetoric,* 1354a5.
23. Ibid.,1354a15.
24. Farrell, *Norms of Rhetorical Culture,* 232.
25. Ibid., 232.
26. Dewey, *Logic,* 1.
27. Ibid., 20.
28. Dewey, *Essays in Experimental Logic,* 82.
29. Zeller, *Outlines of the History,* 19.
30. Kirk, Raven, and Schofield, *Presocratic Philosophers,* 78.
31. Ibid., 79.
32. Aristophanes, *Clouds,* 35.
33. Guthrie, *Sophists,* 186.
34. Habermas, *Between Facts and Norms,* 23.
35. Habermas, *Theory of Communicative Action* 2:124.
36. Ibid. 2:154.
37. Habermas, *Between Facts and Norms,* 360.
38. McGuire and Tuchanska, *Science Unfettered,* 325.
39. Habermas, *Toward a Rational Society,* 103.
40. Ibid., 105.
41. Goodnight, "Personal, Technical, and Public Spheres," 259.

42. Dewey, *Experience and Nature*, 165.
43. Weber, *Protestant Ethic*, 182.
44. Dewey, *Public and Its Problems*, 174–76.
45. Ziman, *Real Science*, 22.
46. Ibid., 79.
47. Dewey, *Experience and Nature*, 165.
48. Ibid., 8–9.
49. Gross, *Rhetoric of Science*, 207, 192.
50. Ceccarelli, *Shaping Science with Rhetoric*, 169.
51. Gross, *Starring the Text*, 21.
52. Ibid., 42–43.
53. Ibid., 153, 157.
54. Condit, *Meanings of the Gene*, 12–13.
55. Dewey, *Experience and Nature*, 104.
56. Dewey, *Logic: The Theory of Inquiry*, 19.
57. Ibid., 27.
58. Ibid., 28.
59. Ibid., 32.
60. Ibid., 43, 46.
61. Ibid., 66.
62. Dewey, *Essays in Experimental Logic*, 441.
63. Ibid., 440–41.
64. Dewey, *Logic*, 61–63.
65. Dewey, *Essays in Experimental Logic*, 76, 440–41.
66. Dewey, *Logic*, 66.
67. Ziman, *Real Science*, 73–74.
68. Ibid., 73–74.
69. Condit, *Meanings of the Gene*, 12.
70. Ziman, *Real Science*, 4.
71. Dewey, *Logic*, 111.
72. Ibid., 114.
73. Ibid., 7.
74. Ibid., 9.
75. McGuire and Tuchanska, *Science Unfettered*, 300, 303.
76. Ibid., 386.
77. Ibid., 263.
78. Shook, "Dewey and Quine on the Logic of What There Is," 113.
79. Dewey, *Logic*, 271.
80. Ibid., 397.
81. Ibid., 418; emphasis added.
82. Ibid., 53.
83. Ibid., 77.
84. Ibid., 77.
85. Dewey, *Public and Its Problems*, 264.
86. Taylor, *Defining Science*, 5.

87. Fuller, *Philosophy, Rhetoric,* xviii.
88. Dewey, *Public and Its Problems,* 169.
89. Ziman, *Real Science,* 180.
90. Dewey, *Public and Its Problems,* 208.
91. Ibid., 213.
92. Feyerabend, "Consolations for the Specialist," 210–13.
93. Ibid., 213–14.
94. Ziman, *Real Science,* 198.
95. I have modified the names for rhetorical purposes. Dewey's original, more unwieldy names are "Indeterminate Situation," "Institution of a Problem," the "Determination of a Problem-Solution," "Reasoning," the "Operational Character of Facts-Meanings," and "Common Sense and Scientific Inquiry."
96. Dewey, *Logic,* 107.
97. Gross, *Starring the Text,* 154.
98. Dewey, *Logic,* 108.
99. Gross, *Starring the Text,* 155.
100. Dewey, *Logic,* 109.
101. Dewey, *Experience and Nature,* 280.
102. Dewey, *Art as Experience,* 121.
103. Dewey and Tufts, *Ethics* 7:186.
104. Condit, *Meanings of the Gene,* 10, 15, 21.
105. Dewey, *Logic,* 111.
106. Ibid., 112.
107. Lessl, "Heresy, Orthodoxy," 18–34, 19.
108. Condit, *Meanings of the Gene,* 33.
109. Dewey, *Logic,* 112–13.
110. Ibid., 113–14.
111. Kuhn, *Structure of Scientific Revolutions,* 148.
112. Ibid., 155–56.
113. Ceccarelli, *Shaping Science with Rhetoric,* 4, 53, 128.
114. Dewey, *Essays in Experimental Logic,* 441, 334, 442.
115. Dewey, *Logic,* 117f.
116. Dewey, "Review of Walter Lippmann's *Public Opinion,*" 343.
117. Dewey, *Public and Its Problems,* 184.
118. Crick, "Conquering Our Imagination," 21–41.
119. Brockman, *Third Culture,* 17.
120. Lyne, "Science Controversy," 38–42, 41.
121. Brockman, *Third Culture,* 76.
122. Lyne, "Science Controversy," 41.
123. Brockman, *Third Culture,* 76.
124. Ibid.
125. Fahnestock, *Rhetorical Figures in Science,* 24.
126. Lyne and Howe, "Rhetoric of Expertise," 148.
127. Ibid., 147.
128. Lyne, "Science Controversy," 40.

129. Dewey, "Democracy and Education in the World of Today," 295.
130. Ibid., 303.
131. Ibid., 297.
132. Dewey, *How We Think*, 27–28.
133. Farrell and Goodnight, "Accidental Rhetoric," 271–300, 297, 296, 299.
134. Ibid., 300.
135. Plato, *Protagoras*, 316d.
136. Latour, *Politics of Nature*, 8, 25, 148.
137. Ziman, *Real Science*, 328.
138. Ibid., 330.
139. Latour, *Politics of Nature*, 129.

CHAPTER 3: *Rhetoric and Aesthetics*

1. Locke, *Essay Concerning Human Understanding*, 3.10.34.
2. Ibid., 3.10.34.
3. Hume, *Enquiry Concerning Human Understanding*, 10.18.
4. Ibid., 12.34.
5. Berkeley, *Treatise*, 1.20.
6. Weaver, *Ethics of Rhetoric*, 15.
7. Plato, *Phaedrus*, 265b.
8. Dewey, *Psychology*, 322–23.
9. Poulakos, "From the Depths of Rhetoric," 336.
10. Emerson, "Eloquence," 89.
11. Dewey, *Psychology*, 322–23, 398, 106.
12. Emerson, "Eloquence," 90.
13. Dewey, *Psychology*, 244.
14. Ibid., 424.
15. Bakhtin, *Dialogical Imagination*, 7, 30.
16. Dewey, *Reconstruction in Philosophy*, 169.
17. Dewey, "Some Stages in Logical Thought," 158.
18. Dewey, *Art as Experience*, 106.
19. Ibid., 3.
20. Ibid., 47.
21. Bakhtin, *Dialogical Imagination*, 255.
22. Dewey, *Art as Experience*, 3.
23. Wichelns, "Literary Criticism of Oratory," 9.
24. Fortunately, however, the "correct" meaning has usually been preserved by an enlightened critic whose words now speak from a nearby plaque on the museum wall.
25. Wichelns, "Literary Criticism of Oratory," 11.
26. Ibid., 22 (emphasis added), 24.
27. Black, "Excerpts from *Rhetorical Criticism*," 47.
28. Ibid., 53.
29. Ironically, in the name of liberating the study of rhetoric, Black destroys the barrier that Wichelns had carefully constructed in order to justify rhetoric as a distinct field of study.

30. Black, "Excerpts from *Rhetorical Criticism*," 56.
31. Quoted in Wichelns, "Literary Criticism of Oratory," 23.
32. Black, "Excerpts from *Rhetorical Criticism*," 56.
33. Ibid., 56.
34. Dewey, *Art as Experience*, 250; emphasis added.
35. Ibid.
36. Ibid., 5.
37. Ibid., 274, 277, 258, 274.
38. Burke, *Language as Symbolic Action*, 296.
39. Ibid.
40. Bakhtin, *Dialogical Imagination*, 324.
41. Ibid., 277, 276.
42. Ibid., 127.
43. Ibid., 110, 113.
44. Ibid., 115.
45. Ibid., 127.
46. Ibid., 46.
47. Ibid., 52–53.
48. Ibid.
49. Ibid., 23.
50. Ibid., 53–54.
51. Ibid., 53.
52. Ibid., 154, 15, 67, 15.
53. Ibid., 15.
54. Ibid., 7.
55. Ibid., 26–27, 9. The mutual attitude of elitism and privilege attached to both arts thus only adds to the public distaste for rhetoric that would condescend to speak the language of common sense. This simply returns us, however, to what Hariman calls the traditional suspicion of *doxa*.
56. Ibid., 15–16.
57. Ibid., 241.
58. Ibid., 108.
59. Ibid., 84.
60. Ibid., 90, 85.
61. Ibid., 136, 14, 107, 109.
62. Ibid., 38, 15, 137.
63. Ibid., 40.
64. Ibid., 278–79.
65. Ibid., 25, 17, 172. Dewey mocks the version of the "tick-tock" theory of rhythm by comparing its even more offensive version, the "tom-tom" theory of rhythm, in which the beating of native drums is held up as the model of rhythm. He says: "Here, too, it is held that a simple, rather monotonous, repetition of beats is the standard, and that it is varied by the addition of other rhythms each of which is itself uniform, while piquancy is introduced by the use of arythmic change. Unfortunately for the supposed objective basis of the theory, tom-tom beats do not occur alone, but as factors in a much

more complex whole of varied singing and dancing. And instead of repetition there is a development, a working to greater pitches of excitement, perhaps a frenzy, that has begun with relative slow and calm movements. What is even more important, the history of music shows that in fact the primitive rhythms, like those of the African negro, are more subtly varied, less uniform, than those of the music of civilized folk, just as those of northern negroes in the United States are usually more conventionalized than those of the south." This observation (which is amusing if one imagines Dewey participating in such musical raptures) is insightful as to why jazz, which originated in the South and was distinct in lacking steady "beats," is often considered the most rhythmic of all music. Dewey, *Art as Experience,* 166.
66. Ibid., 138, 134 (emphasis added).
67. Ibid., 16, 41.
68. Ibid., 77, 177, 64–65.
69. Ibid., 301.
70. Ibid., 29, 39.
71. Dewey, *Art as Experience,* 349, 348.
72. Ibid., 344, 348.
73. Ibid., 345–46.
74. Ibid., 267.
75. Ibid., 242, 268.
76. Ibid., 269.
77. Ibid., 345–46.
78. Ibid., 348.
79. Dewey, "Art as Our Heritage," 256.
80. Dewey, *Art as Experience,* 346.
81. Ibid., 335.
82. Ibid., 238, 239.
83. Ibid., 334–35.
84. Ibid., 334.
85. Booth, *Rhetoric of Fiction,* 385.
86. Dewey, *Art as Experience,* 270.
87. Rorty, *Contingency, Irony, and Solidarity,* 159.
88. Ibid., 141.
89. Dewey, *Art as Experience,* 326.
90. Ibid., 267.
91. Dewey, *Psychology,* 197, 198.
92. Dewey, "Poetry and Philosophy," 123.
93. Dewey, *Art as Experience,* 104.
94. Ibid., 195.
95. Ibid., 329.
96. Ibid., 158, 159.
97. Ibid., 256.
98. Stroud, "John Dewey and the Question," 153–83, 171.
99. Ibid., 209, 210.
100. Ibid., 213.

101. Ibid., 347–49.
102. Ibid., 104.
103. Ibid., 104–5.
104. Ibid., 159.
105. Ibid., 310, 309, 313.

106. This why a term such as "critical rhetoric" is as much a redundancy as a "critical science." Both rhetoric and science, by their very nature, criticize because they engage in analysis, synthesis, and judgment. An uncritical rhetoric would thus be identical to an uncritical science in that they would be nothing more than a recitation of commonplaces.

107. Dewey, *Art as Experience*, 138.

108. As a graduate student I recall being in an elevator with a professor, a true lover of logic, with whom I had taken a course in epistemology. He was an analytic philosopher of the old dualistic school, insisting that a whole was nothing more than the sum of its parts. Hence we had argued after class as to whether Kepler's laws were something "added to" the data set accumulated by observing the location of stars in the sky. He denied that it was. Yet in the elevator I heard him speaking to one of his graduate students, and I heard him ask, with a joyous smile, whether or not the young man ever had those "ah-ha" moments in the shower when some solution to a logical problem suddenly came to him. I left thinking that this man who so vigorously denied the principle of aesthetic experience was, in fact, driven in his work by a desire for those ecstatic moments that arrived in a sudden vision while washing his hair.

109. Dewey, *Art as Experience*, 139.

110. Leff, "Habitation of Rhetoric," 62.

111. Dewey, *Art as Experience*, 198.

112. For example, decorum is falsely aligned with actions consistent with those of Polonius before the king. Although it is true that Hamlet generally lacked a sense of decorum, it is not because he challenged and flabbergasted his audience; Hamlet lacked eloquence because he could never commit his whole self to perform the action that his situation demanded. Hence, to use Dewey's terms, his actions were often "unlovely" because they were done to avoid or to gain something outside of the act, as performing a play primarily to expose the king as a murderer. Similarly, when Hamlet sheathes his sword instead of beheading his father's killer, we feel the disruption of rhythm and continuity that marks his action as unaesthetic. Thus his adherence to a superficial understanding of decorum, defined in this case as obedience to religious doctrines concerning the salvation of the soul, actually inhibits his ability to achieve a richer, if amoral, sense of decorum. In other words, decorum is only possible for Hamlet when he wholeheartedly commits himself to regicide.

113. Dewey, *Art as Experience*, 198.

114. It bears repeating here that "universal" is not the same thing as "transcendental." A universal is a category of logic that means embodying a general process, relationship, or formula capable of being applied to a wide number of particular instances. The statement "If one has a good soul, then one travels to the Isles of the Blessed after death" remains a universal statement even if it lacks the status of factual validity.

115. The fact that the same situation can be approached both decorously and *kairotically* only demonstrates that no situation has an essential nature outside of how it is experienced. A child, for instance, only sees the world through *kairotic* eyes. Every moment seems a crisis because they have such a short sense of time. A centenarian, by contrast, tends to feel at ease even during the biggest crisis, assured that it is simply one more manifestation of the same old story that will resolve itself over time. That is why the young tend to champion *kairos* and the old like to praise decorum, and why the old accuse the young of blowing things out of proportion and the young accuse the old of being stodgy do-nothings. Unfortunately for both parents and children, there is no God's eye view to determine who is right. The only thing they have is the dinner table to work out our differences.

116. Weaver, *Ethics of Rhetoric*, 25.

117. Condit, *Meanings of the Gene*, 23.

Conclusion

1. Dewey, "Art as Our Heritage," 255.
2. Dewey, *Democracy and Education*, 93.
3. Dewey, "Creative Democracy," 229.
4. Ibid., 61.
5. Crick and Poulakos, "Go Tell Alcibiades," 1–22.
6. Dewey, *Common Faith*, 87.
7. Dewey, "Democracy Is Radical," 298–99.
8. Dewey, "Address to the National Association," 224–27.
9. Ibid., 224–30.
10. Arendt, *Human Condition*, 55, 9, 200.
11. Ibid., 241.
12. Peters, *Courting the Abyss*, 265.
13. Dewey, *Freedom and Culture*, 188.

BIBLIOGRAPHY

Alexander, Thomas M. *The Horizons of Feeling: John Dewey's Theory of Art, Experience, and Nature.* Albany: SUNY Press, 1952.

Arendt, Hannah. *The Human Condition.* Chicago: University of Chicago Press, 1998.

Aristophanes. *Clouds.* Translated by William Arrowsmith. In *Aristophanes: Three Comedies,* edited by William Arrowsmith, 1–133. Ann Arbor: University of Michigan Press, 1969.

Aristotle. *The Rhetoric and the Poetics of Aristotle.* Translated by W. Rhys Roberts and edited by Edward P. J. Corbett. New York: Modern Library, 1984.

Asen, Robert. "The Multiple Mr. Dewey: Multiple Publics and Permeable Borders in John Dewey's Theory of the Public Sphere." *Argumentation and Advocacy* 39 (2003): 174–88.

Bakhtin, Mikhail. *The Dialogical Imagination: Four Essays by M. M. Bakhtin.* Austin: University of Texas Press, 1981.

Bauman, Zygmunt. "From Pilgrim to Tourist—or a Short History of Identity." In *Questions of Cultural Identity,* edited by Stuart Hall and Paul du Gay, 18–36. London: Sage Publications, 1996.

Benoit, William L. "The Genesis of Rhetorical Action." *Southern Communication Journal* 59 (1994): 342–55.

Bentley, Arthur F., and John Dewey. *Knowing and the Known.* In *John Dewey: The Later Works,* vol. 16, edited by Jo Ann Boydston, 1–279. 1948. Reprint, Carbondale: Southern Illinois University Press, 1989.

Berkeley, George. *A Treatise Concerning the Principles of Human Knowledge.* In *Berkeley: Essay, Principles, Dialogues with Selections from Other Writings,* edited by Mary Whiton Calkins, 99–216. 1710. Reprint, New York: Charles Scribner's Sons, 1929.

Biesecker, Barbara A. "Rethinking the Rhetorical Situation from Within the Thematic of Difference." *Philosophy and Rhetoric* 22 (1989):110–30.

Bitzer, Lloyd. "Functional Communication: A Situational Perspective." In *Rhetoric in Transition: Studies in the Nature and Uses of Rhetoric,* edited by Eugene E. White, 21–38. University Park: Pennsylvania State University Press, 1980.

———. "The Rhetorical Situation." *Philosophy and Rhetoric* 1 (1969): 1–14.

———. "Rhetoric and Public Knowledge." In *Rhetoric, Philosophy, and Literature: An Exploration,* edited by Don Burks, 67–93. West Lafayette: Purdue University Press, 1978.

Black, Edwin. "Excerpts from *Rhetorical Criticism: A Study in Method.*" In *Readings in Rhetorical Criticism,* edited by Carl R. Burgchardt, 46–57. State College, Pa.: Strata Publishing, 1995.

Booth, Wayne. *The Rhetoric of Fiction.* Chicago: University of Chicago Press, 1983.

Boydston, Jo Ann, ed. *The Poems of John Dewey.* Carbondale: Southern Illinois University Press, 1977.

Brinton, Alan. "Situation in the Theory of Rhetoric." *Philosophy and Rhetoric* 14 (1981): 234–48.

Brockman, John *The Third Culture.* New York: Touchstone, 1995.

Burke, Kenneth. *Attitudes Toward History.* Berkeley and Los Angeles: University of California Press, 1984.

———. *Counter-Statement.* Berkeley and Los Angeles: University of California Press, 1968.

———. *Language as Symbolic Action: Essays on Life, Literature, and Method.* Berkeley and Los Angeles: University of California Press, 1966.

———. *Permanence and Change: An Anatomy of Purpose.* Berkeley and Los Angeles: University of California Press, 1954.

———. *A Rhetoric of Motives.* Berkeley and Los Angeles: University of California Press, 1962.

Burks, Don M. "John Dewey and Rhetorical Theory." *Western Speech* 32 (1968): 118–26.

Ceccarelli, Leah. *Shaping Science with Rhetoric: The Cases of Dobzhansky, Schrodinger, and Wilson.* Chicago: University of Chicago Press, 2001.

Charland, Maurice. "Constitutive Rhetoric: The Case of the Peuple Quebecois." *Quarterly Journal of Speech* 59 (1973): 133–50.

———. "Norms and Laughter in Rhetorical Culture." *Quarterly Journal of Speech* 80 (1994): 339–42.

Cohen, S. Marc, Patricia Curd, and C. D. V. Reeve. *Readings in Ancient Greek Philosophy: From Thales to Aristotle.* Indianapolis: Hackett, 1995.

Condit, Celeste Michelle. *The Meanings of the Gene: Public Debates about Human Heredity.* Madison: University of Wisconsin Press, 1999.

Consigny, Scott. "Rhetoric and Its Situations." *Philosophy and Rhetoric* 7 (1974): 175–86.

Crick, Nathan. "'A Capital and Novel Argument': Charles Darwin's Notebooks and the Productivity of Rhetorical Consciousness." *Quarterly Journal of Speech* 91, no. 4 (2005): 337–64.

———. "Composition as Experience: John Dewey on Creative Expression and the Origins of 'Mind.'" *College Composition and Communication* 55, no. 2 (2003): 254–75.

———. "Conquering our Imagination: Thought Experiments and Enthymemes in Scientific Argument." *Philosophy and Rhetoric* 37, no. 1 (2004): 21–41.

———. "John Dewey's Aesthetics of Communication." *Southern Communication Journal* 69, no. 4 (2004): 303–19.

———. "John Dewey on the Art of Communication." Ph.D. diss., University of Pittsburgh, 2005.

———. "Rhetoric, Philosophy, and the Public Intellectual." *Philosophy and Rhetoric* 39, no. 2 (2006): 127–39.

Crick, Nathan, and John Poulakos. "Go Tell Alcibiades: Comedy, Tragedy, and Rhetoric in Plato's *Symposium.*" *Quarterly Journal of Speech* 94, no. 1 (2008): 1–22.

Danish, Robert. "Power and the Celebration of the Self: Michel Foucault's Epideictic Rhetoric." *Southern Communication Journal* 70, no. 3 (2006): 291–307.

———. *Pragmatism, Democracy, and the Necessity of Rhetoric.* Columbia: University of South Carolina Press, 2007.

Darsey, James. "Joe McCarthy's Fantastic Moment." In *Readings in Rhetorical Criticism,* edited by Carl R. Burgchardt, 428–50. State College, Pa.: Strata Publishing, 1995.

Dewey, John. "Address of Welcome to the League for Industrial Democracy." In *John Dewey: The Later Works,* vol. 14, edited by Jo Ann Boydston, 262–65. 1941. Reprint, Carbondale: Southern Illinois University Press, 1988.

———. "Address to the National Association for the Advancement of Colored People." In *John Dewey: The Later Works,* vol. 6, edited by Jo Ann Boydston, 224–30. 1932. Reprint, Carbondale: Southern Illinois University Press, 1985.

———. "Appreciation and Cultivation." In *John Dewey: The Middle Works,* vol. 6, edited by Jo Ann Boydston, 112–17. 1931. Reprint, Carbondale: Southern Illinois University Press, 1978.

———. "Are Sanctions Necessary to International Organization? No." In *John Dewey: The Later Works,* vol. 6, edited by Jo Ann Boydston, 196–223. 1932. Reprint, Carbondale: Southern Illinois University Press, 1985.

———. *Art as Experience.* New York: Perigree Books, 1934.

———. "Art as Our Heritage." In *John Dewey: The Later Works,* vol. 14, edited by Jo Ann Boydston, 255–57. 1940. Reprint, Carbondale: Southern Illinois University Press, 1988.

———. "The Basic Values and Loyalties of Democracy." In *John Dewey: The Later Works,* vol. 14, edited by Jo Ann Boydston, 275–77. 1941. Reprint, Carbondale: Southern Illinois University Press, 1988.

———. *A Common Faith.* In *John Dewey: The Later Works,* vol. 9, edited by Jo Ann Boydston, 1–60. 1934. Reprint, Carbondale: Southern Illinois University Press, 1986.

———. "Conduct and Experience." In *John Dewey: The Later Works,* vol. 5, edited by Jo Ann Boydston, 218–35. 1930. Reprint, Carbondale: Southern Illinois University Press, 1984.

———. "Context and Thought." In *John Dewey: The Later Works,* vol. 6, edited by Jo Ann Boydston, 3–21. 1931. Reprint, Carbondale: Southern Illinois University Press, 1985.

———. "Creative Democracy—The Task Before Us." In *John Dewey: The Later Works,* vol. 14, edited by Jo Ann Boydston, 224–30. 1941. Reprint, Carbondale: Southern Illinois University Press, 1988.

———. *Democracy and Education.* In *John Dewey: The Middle Works,* vol. 9, edited by Jo Ann Boydston, 1–371. 1916. Reprint, Carbondale: Southern Illinois University Press, 1980.

———. "Democracy and Education in the World of Today." In *John Dewey: The Later Works,* vol. 13, edited by Jo Ann Boydston, 294–303. 1938. Reprint, Carbondale: Southern Illinois University Press, 1988.

———. "Democracy Is Radical." In *John Dewey: The Later Works,* vol. 11, edited by Jo Ann Boydston, 296–302. 1937. Reprint, Carbondale: Southern Illinois University Press, 1987.

———. *Essays in Experimental Logic.* New York: Dover, 1916.

———. "The Ethics of Democracy." In *The Early Works of John Dewey,* vol. 2, edited by Jo Ann Boydston, 227–50. 1888. Reprint, Carbondale: Southern Illinois University Press, 1967.

———. *Experience and Nature*. In *John Dewey: The Later Works*, vol. 1, edited by Jo Ann Boydston, 1–327. 1925. Reprint, Carbondale: Southern Illinois University Press, 1981.

———. "Fred Newton Scott." In *The Early Works of John Dewey*, vol. 4, edited by Jo Ann Boydston, 119–22. 1894. Reprint, Carbondale: Southern Illinois University Press, 1971.

———. "From Absolutism to Experimentalism." In *John Dewey: The Later Works*, vol. 5, edited by Jo Ann Boydston, 147–60. 1930. Reprint, Carbondale: Southern Illinois University Press, 1984.

———. "Half-Hearted Naturalism." In *John Dewey: The Later Works*, vol. 3, edited by Jo Ann Boydston, 73–81. 1927. Reprint, Carbondale: Southern Illinois University Press, 1984.

———. *How We Think*. In *John Dewey: The Middle Works*, vol. 6, edited by Jo Ann Boydston, 105–354. 1910. Reprint, Carbondale: Southern Illinois University Press, 1978.

———. *Human Nature and Conduct*. In *John Dewey: The Middle Works*, vol. 14, edited by Jo Ann Boydston, 1–264. 1922. Reprint, Carbondale: Southern Illinois University Press, 1983.

———. *Individualism Old and New*. In *John Dewey: The Later Works*, vol. 5, edited by Jo Ann Boydston, 41–124. 1930. Reprint, Carbondale: Southern Illinois University Press, 1984.

———. "Logic." In *John Dewey: The Later Works*, vol. 8, edited by Jo Ann Boydston, 3–12. 1933. Reprint, Carbondale: Southern Illinois University Press, 1986.

———. *Logic: The Theory of Inquiry*. New York: Henry Holt, 1938.

———. "Organization in American Education." In *John Dewey: The Middle Works*, vol. 10, edited by Jo Ann Boydston, 397–457. 1917. Reprint, Carbondale: Southern Illinois University Press, 1980.

———. "Outlawing Peace by Discussing War." In *John Dewey: The Later Works*, vol. 3, edited by Jo Ann Boydston, 173–76. 1928. Reprint, Carbondale: Southern Illinois University Press, 1984.

———. *Outlines of a Critical Theory of Ethics*. In *The Early Works of John Dewey*, vol. 3, edited by Jo Ann Boydston, 237–89. 1891. Reprint, Carbondale: Southern Illinois University Press, 1969.

———. *Philosophy and Education in Their Historic Relations*, transcribed from his lectures by Elsie Ridley Clapp and edited by J. J. Chambliss. Boulder, Colo.: Westview Press, 1993.

———. "Poetry and Philosophy." In *The Early Works of John Dewey*, vol. 3, edited by Jo Ann Boydston, 110–24. 1890. Reprint, Carbondale: Southern Illinois University Press, 1969.

———. "The Postulate of Immediate Empiricism." In *John Dewey: The Middle Works*, vol. 3, edited by Jo Ann Boydston, 158–67. 1905. Reprint, Carbondale: Southern Illinois University Press, 1977.

———. *The Public and Its Problems*. Athens: Ohio University Press, 1927.

———. *The Quest for Certainty: A Study of the Relation of Knowledge and Action*. In *John Dewey: The Later Works*, vol. 4, edited by Jo Ann Boydston, 1–251. 1929. Reprint, Carbondale: Southern Illinois University Press, 1984.

———. *Reconstruction in Philosophy.* In *John Dewey: The Middle Works,* vol. 12, edited by Jo Ann Boydston, 77–204. 1920. Reprint, Carbondale: Southern Illinois University Press, 1982.

———. "Review of Walter Lippmann's *Public Opinion.*" In *John Dewey: The Middle Works,* vol. 13, edited by Jo Ann Boydston, 337–44. 1922. Reprint, Carbondale: Southern Illinois University Press, 1983.

———. "Some Stages in Logical Thought." In *John Dewey: The Middle Works,* vol. 1, edited by Jo Ann Boydston, 171–84. 1900. Reprint, Carbondale: Southern Illinois University Press, 1976.

———. "Three Independent Factors in Morals." In *John Dewey: The Later Works,* vol. 5, edited by Jo Ann Boydston, 279–88. 1984. Reprint, Carbondale: Southern Illinois University Press, 1984.

Dewey, John, and James H. Tufts. *Ethics.* In *John Dewey: The Middle Works,* vol. 5, edited by Jo Ann Boydston, 1–463. 1908. Reprint, Carbondale: Southern Illinois University Press, 1978.

———. *Ethics.* In *John Dewey: The Later Works,* vol. 7, edited by Jo Ann Boydston. 1932. Reprint, Carbondale: Southern Illinois University Press, 1985.

Dykhuizen, George. *The Life and Mind of John Dewey.* Carbondale: Southern Illinois University Press, 1973.

Ellul, Jacques. *Propaganda The Formation of Men's Attitudes* (New York: Vintage, 1954).

Emerson, Ralph Waldo. "Eloquence." In *Society and Solitude,* by Ralph Waldo Emerson, 59–100. Boston: Houghton, Mifflin, 1904.

Fahnestock, Jeanne. *Rhetorical Figures in Science.* Oxford: Oxford University Press, 1999.

Farrell, Thomas B. *Norms of Rhetorical Culture.* New Haven: Yale University Press, 1993.

Farrell, Thomas B., and G. Thomas Goodnight. "Accidental Rhetoric: The Root Metaphors of Three Mile Island." *Communication Monographs* 48 (1981): 271–300.

Feyerabend, Paul. "Consolations for the Specialist." In *Criticism and the Growth of Knowledge,* edited by Imre Lakatos and Alan Musgrave (Cambridge: Cambridge University Press, 1965), 210–13.

Fishman, Stephen. "Explicating Our Tacit Tradition: John Dewey and Composition Studies." *CCC* 44 (1993): 315–30.

Foucault, Michel. *The Essential Foucault: Selections from Essential Works of Foucault, 1954–1984,* edited by Paul Rabinow and Nikolas Rose. New York: New Press, 1994.

Fuller, Steve. *Philosophy, Rhetoric, and the End of Knowledge: The Coming of Science and Technology Studies.* Madison: University of Wisconsin Press, 1993.

Garret, Mary, and Xiaosui Xiao. "The Rhetorical Situation Revisited." *Rhetoric Society Quarterly* 23 (1993): 30–40.

Goodnight, Thomas. "The Personal, Technical, and Public Spheres of Argumentation: A Speculative Inquiry in the Art of Public Deliberation." In *Contemporary Rhetorical Theory: A Reader,* edited by John Louis Lucaites, Celeste Michelle Condit, and Sally Caudill, 251–64. New York: Guilford Press, 1999.

Gross, Alan G. *The Rhetoric of Science.* Cambridge: Harvard University Press, 1996.

———. *Starring the Text: The Place of Rhetoric in Science Studies.* Carbondale: Southern Illinois University Press, 2006.

Guthrie, W. K. C *The Sophists.* Cambridge: Cambridge University Press, 1971.

Habermas, Jürgen. *Between Facts and Norms: Contributions to a Discourse Theory of Law.* Translated by William Rehg. Cambridge: MIT Press, 1996.

———. "Questions and Counter-Questions." In *Habermas and Modernity*, edited by Richard J. Bernstein, 192–216. Cambridge: MIT Press, 1985.

———. *The Structural Transformation of the Public Sphere: An Inquiry into a Category of Bourgeois Society.* Translated by Thomas Burger. Cambridge, Mass.: MIT Press, 1989.

———. *Theory of Communicative Action.* Vol. 2, *Lifeworld and System: A Critique of Functionalist Reason.* Boston: Beacon Press, 1987.

———. *Toward a Rational Society: Student Protest, Science, and Politics.* Boston: Beacon Press, 1970.

Hall, Stewart. "Introduction: Who Needs Identity?" In *Questions of Cultural Identity*, edited by Stuart Hall and Paul du Gay. London: Sage Publications, 1996.

Hamilton, Edith. *The Greek Way.* New York: Norton, 1943.

Hauser, Gerard A. "Rhetorical Democracy and Civic Engagement." In *Rhetorical Democracy: Discursive Practices of Civic Engagement*, edited by Gerard A. Hauser and Amy Grim. Mahway, N.J.: Laurence Erlbaum, 2004.

———. *Vernacular Voices: The Rhetoric of Publics and Public Spheres.* Columbia: University of South Carolina Press, 1999.

Havelock, Eric. *The Liberal Temper in Greek Politics.* New Haven: Yale University Press, 1957.

Hickman, Larry A. *John Dewey's Pragmatic Technology.* Indianapolis: Indiana University Press, 1992.

Hume, David. *An Enquiry Concerning Human Understanding.* Edited by Tom L. Beauchamp. 1748. Reprint, Oxford: Oxford University Press, 1999.

Hunsaker, David M., and Craig R. Smith. "The Nature of Issues: A Constructive Approach to Situational Rhetoric." *Western Speech Communication* 40 (1976): 144–56.

Isocrates. *Antidosis.* Translated by George Norlin. In *Isocrates*, vol. 2. Cambridge: Harvard University Press, 1929.

Jaeger, Werner. *Paideia: The Ideals of Greek Culture.* Vol. 1, *Archaic Greece and The Mind of Athens.* Oxford: Basic Blackwell, 1946.

———. *Paideia: The Ideals of Greek Culture.* Vol. 2, *In Search of the Divine Center.* Oxford: Oxford University Press, 1943.

Jamieson, Kathleen Hall. "Generic Constraints and the Rhetorical Situation." *Philosophy and Rhetoric* 6 (1968): 162–70.

Johnstone, Christopher Lyle. "Dewey, Ethics, and Rhetoric: Toward a Contemporary Conception of Practical Wisdom." *Philosophy and Rhetoric* 16 (1983): 185–207.

Kirk, G. S., J. E. Raven, and M. Schofield. *The Presocratic Philosophers.* 2nd ed. Cambridge: Cambridge University Press, 1983.

Kitzhaber, Albert R. *Rhetoric in American Colleges: 1850–1900.* Dallas: Southern Methodist University Press, 1990.

Kuhn, Thomas. *The Structure of Scientific Revolutions.* Chicago: University of Chicago Press, 1996.

Larson, Richard L. "Lloyd Bitzer's 'Rhetorical Situation' and the Classification of Discourse: Problems and Implications." *Philosophy and Rhetoric* 3 (1970): 165–68.

Latour, Bruno. *The Politics of Nature: How to Bring the Sciences into Democracy.* Cambridge: Harvard University Press, 2004.
———. *Reassembling the Social: An Introduction to Actor-Network-Theory.* Oxford: Oxford University Press, 2005.
———. *Science in Action: How to Follow Scientists and Engineers Through Society.* Cambridge: Harvard University Press, 1987.
Leff, Michael. "The Habitation of Rhetoric." In *Contemporary Rhetorical Theory: A Reader,* edited by John Louis Lucaites, Celeste Michelle Condit, and Sally Caudill, 52–64. New York: Guilford Press, 1999.
Lessl, Thomas M. "Heresy, Orthodoxy, and the Politics of Science." *Quarterly Journal of Speech* 74 (1988): 18–34.
Lippmann, Walter. *The Essential Lippmann: A Political Philosophy for Liberal Democracy.* Edited by Clinton Rossiter and James Lare. New York: Random House, 1963.
Locke, John. *An Essay Concerning Human Understanding.* Edited by P. H. Nidditch. 1690. Reprint, London: Oxford University Press, 1975.
Lybarger, Scott, and Craig R. Smith. "Bitzer's Model Reconstructed." *Communication Quarterly* 44 (1996): 197–213.
Lyne, John. "Science Controversy, Common Sense, and the Third Culture." *Argumentation and Advocacy* 42 (2005): 38–42.
Lyne, John, and Henry Howe. "The Rhetoric of Expertise: E. O. Wilson and Sociobiology." *Quarterly Journal of Speech* 76 (1990): 134–51.
Mackin, James A., Jr. "Rhetoric, Pragmatism, and Practical Wisdom." In *Rhetoric and Philosophy,* edited by Richard A. Cherwitz, 275–203. Hillsdale, N.J.: Erlbaum, 1990.
McGee, Michael Calvin. "The Ideograph: A Link between Rhetoric and Ideology." *Quarterly Journal of Speech* 66 (1980): 1–16.
McGuire, J. E., and Barbara Tuchanska. *Science Unfettered: A Philosophical Study in Sociohistorical Ontology* (Athens: Ohio University Press, 2000).
Miller, Carolyn R. "Foreword." In *Rhetoric and Kairos: Essays in History, Theory, and Praxis,* edited by Phillip Sipiora and James S. Baumlin, xi–xii. Albany: SUNY Press, 2002.
Nelson, John S., Allan Megill, and Donald N. McCloskey. "Rhetoric of Inquiry." In *The Rhetoric of the Human Sciences: Language and Argument in Scholarship and Public Affairs,* edited by John S. Nelson, Allan Megill, and Donald N. McCloskey, 3–18. Madison: University of Wisconsin Press, 1987.
Patton, John. "Causation and Creativity in Rhetorical Situations: Distinctions and Implications." *Quarterly Journal of Speech* 65 (1979): 36–55.
Peters, John. *Courting the Abyss: Free Speech and the Liberal Tradition.* Chicago: University of Chicago Press, 2005.
———. "Public Journalism and Democratic Theory: Four Challenges." In *The Idea of Public Journalism,* edited by Theodore L. Glasser, 99–117. New York: Guilford Press, 1999.
Plato. *Statesman,* trans. C. J. Rowe. In *Plato: Complete Works,* edited by John M. Cooper. Indianapolis: Hackett, 1997.
———. *Theaetetus,* trans. M. J. Levett and rev. Myles Burnyeat. In *Plato: Complete Works,* edited by John M. Cooper. Indianapolis: Hackett, 1997.

Poulakos, John. "From the Depths of Rhetoric: The Emergence of Aesthetics as a Discipline." *Philosophy and Rhetoric* 40, no. 4 (2007): 335–52.

———. "Hegel's Reception of the Sophists." In *Western Journal of Speech Communication* 55 (1990): 160–71.

———. "*Kairos* in Gorgias' Rhetorical Compositions." In *Rhetoric and Kairos: Essays in History, Theory, and Praxis,* edited by Phillip Sipiora and James S. Baumlin, 89–96. Albany: SUNY Press, 2002.

———. *Sophistical Rhetoric in Classical Greece.* Columbia: University of South Carolina Press, 1995.

———. "Toward a Sophistic Definition of Rhetoric." *Philosophy and Rhetoric* 16 (1983): 35–48.

Ramus, Peter. Excerpts from *Arguments in Rhetoric against Quintilian.* In *The Rhetorical Tradition: Readings from Classical Times to the Present,* edited by Patricia Bizzell and Bruce Herzberg, 563–83. Boston: Bedford St. Martin's, 1990.

Rorty, Richard. *Consequences of Pragmatism.* Minneapolis: University of Minnesota Press, 1982.

———. *Contingency, Irony, and Solidarity.* Cambridge: Cambridge University Press, 1989.

Schudson, Michael. "Why Conversation Is Not the Soul of Democracy." *Critical Studies in Mass Communication* 14 (1997): 297–309.

Scott, Robert. "On Viewing Rhetoric as Epistemic." In *Contemporary Rhetorical Theory: A Reader,* edited by John Louis Lucaites, Celeste Michelle Condit, and Sally Caudill, 131–39. New York: Guilford Press, 1999.

Shook, John. "Dewey and Quine on the Logic of What There Is." In *Dewey's Logical Theory: New Studies and Interpretations,* edited by F. Thomas Burke, D. Micah Hester, and Robert B. Talisse, 85–91. Nashville: Vanderbilt University Press, 2002.

———. *Dewey's Empirical Theory of Knowledge and Reality.* Nashville: Vanderbilt University Press, 2000.

Smith, Palmer. "Character Building Through Speech Education in High School." *Quarterly Journal of Speech* 9 (1923).

Stewart, Donald C., and Patricia L. Stewart. *The Life and Legacy of Fred Newton Scott.* Pittsburgh: University of Pittsburgh Press, 1997.

Stroud, Scott. "John Dewey and the Question of Artful Communication." *Philosophy and Rhetoric* 41, no. 2 (2008): 153–83.

Taylor, Alan. *Defining Science: A Rhetoric of Demarcation.* Madison: University of Wisconsin Press, 1996.

Vatz, Richard E. "The Myth of the Rhetorical Situation." *Philosophy and Rhetoric* 6 (1973): 154–61.

Wander, Philip. "The Ideological Turn in Modern Criticism." In *Readings in Rhetorical Criticism,* edited by Carl R. Burgchardt, 428–50. State College, Pa.: Strata Publishing, 1995.

Wang, Jessica Ching-Sze. *John Dewey in China: To Teach and To Learn.* New York: State University of New York Press, 2007.

Waterfield, Robin. *The First Philosophers: The Presocratics and the Sophists.* New York: Oxford University Press, 2000.

Weaver, Richard M. *The Ethics of Rhetoric.* Davis, Calif.: Hermagoras Press, 1985.

Weber, Max. *The Protestant Ethic and the Spirit of Capitalism.* Translated by Talcott Parsons. New York: Routledge, 1992.

Westbrook, Robert B. *John Dewey and American Democracy.* Ithaca: Cornell University Press, 1991.

White, Eric C. *Kaironomia: On the Will-to-Invent.* Ithaca: Cornell University Press, 1987.

Wichelns, Herbert A. "The Literary Criticism of Oratory." In *Readings in Rhetorical Criticism,* edited by Carl R. Burgchardt, 26–27. 1925; reprint, State College, Pa.: Strata Publishing, 1995.

Wilkerson, K. E. "On Evaluating Theories of Rhetoric." *Philosophy and Rhetoric* 3 (1970): 82–96.

Zeller, Eduard. *Outlines of the History of Greek Philosophy.* Cleveland: World Publishing, 1955.

Ziman, John. *Real Science: What It Is, and What It Means.* Cambridge: Cambridge University Press, 2000.

INDEX

action, 192
aesthetic: as decorative, 142; as experience, 144; importance of resistance to, 148, 152, 155, 171, 175; in raw, 139–40; and reason, 130; as superficial, 130, 135, 142; versus nonaesthetic, 153
appropriate, 182
Arendt, Hannah, 192
argument, 150, 173, 187
aristocracy, 18
Aristotle, 45, 49, 75, 84, 165, 168, 169, 172
Aristophanes, 90
Arnold, Matthew, 160
art: and civilization, 187; as communication, 136, 161–62; fine and popular, 5; fine and useful, 148–51; as madness, 131; and morality, 157–64; as *techne,* 5, 8, 27, 87, 93, 127–28, 147; as object, 136–37; and science, 148–49, 179; work of, 136, 156
Augustine, Saint, 163

Bakhtin, Mikhail, 134, 136, 141
becoming, ontology of, 8, 15, 22–26, 33, 34, 44, 84, 134, 152, 157; arts of, 22, 35, 79; and democracy, 20, 192; and ethics, 76, 95; and inquiry, 96, 122; and self, 19, 44, 66
Berkeley, Bishop, 130–31
Bitzer, Lloyd, 26–29
Black, Edwin, 137–39, 176
Booth, Wayne, 162, 176
Burke, Kenneth, 48, 52, 53, 78, 140–41, 155, 178, 193

Ceccarelli, Leah, 94, 118–19
Charland, Maurice, 13, 65
character, 56–59
choice, 28–29, 45
Coltrane, John, 155
common sense, 96, 99–103, 105, 107–11, 119–20
communication, 39, 40, 67, 74, 98, 120; face-to-face, 69–72
conceptualism, 104
Condit, Celeste Michelle, 95–96, 102, 114–15, 116, 186
consciousness, 45–47
contextualism, 104–7
continuity, 33–36; and discontinuity, 8
context, 35–36, 48, 66, 104; of discovery and justification, 110
convention, 25, 49, 50
culture, 49

Danisch, Robert, 4, 10, 58
Dawkins, Richard, 120–21
Declaration of Independence, 173–75
decorum, 180–85, 208–9
democracy, 19, 68–73, 135, 164, 177–78, 189; communitarian, 12–13; radical 1, 73, 126, 187; rhetorical versus as unstable, 23–24
Derrida, 27
detachment, 177
Dewey, John: and China, 59; as Christian idealist, 18, 131, 133–34, 168–69; criticism of American politics, 7; explicit writing on rhetoric, 8–10, 133; metaphysics of, 34; as naïve optimist 6–7; on Plato, 24; as poet, 11

discipline, 58
discourse, 47
discussion, 7, 135
doubt, 103
drama, 21–22, 33, 95, 155, 175, 178
dualism, 28, 32, 39, 46, 82, 94, 97, 105, 146, 156

education, 58, 65, 124, 153
Ellul, Jacques, 2, 54–56, 59
eloquence, 168–77, 187
Emerson, Ralph Waldo, 132–34, 144
emotion, 51–53, 147–48, 155–56
end-in-view, 114
enthymeme, 88, 188
epideictic speech, 172–73
ethics, 73–75; circumstantial versus transcendental, 76–77, 81; four dominant democratic virtues, 18; rationalistic versus utilitarian, 16, as situated judgment, 17
ethos, 4
event, 36–41
experience, 31, 35; and nature, 30–33; types of, 164–65

fact, 117–18
Fahnestock, Jeanne, 121
Farrell, Thomas, 3, 4, 13, 59, 64, 88, 125
Feyerabend, Paul, 108–9, 116
figure, 121
form, 142, 144, 151–54, 178; stages of, 154–55; versus formalistic, 152
forum, 123
Foucault, Michel, 2, 4, 8, 20, 47, 48, 57
Fuller, Steve, 107

Gettysburg Address, 175, 184–85
Goodnight, G. Thomas, 91, 125
Gorgias, 44, 74, 183
Great Depression, 190
Gross, Alan, 83, 93–95, 112–13
growth, 19

Habermas, Jürgen, 63–64, 90–91
habit, 48–53, 58, 60, 98, 103
Hall, Stewart, 57
Hamilton, Edith, 24
Hauser, Gerard, 23, 60
Hickman, Larry, 67
Hobbes, Thomas, 24
home, 169–73, 177, 191
Hume, David, 130

idealism, 14, 73–74
ideals, 188
ideographs, 188–89
imagination, 158–60, 176
imitation, 148
impulse, 50, 53
inquiry, 103, 111–23
insincerity, 44
intelligence, 73–75

jazz, 164
Jefferson, Thomas, 173
judgment, 178

kairos, 15, 20–21, 53–54, 75, 88, 104, 135, 181–85, 209
Keats, John, 176
King Jr., Martin Luther, 175, 193
knowing, 34, 107
Kuhn, Thomas, 118

Latour, Bruno, 36, 68–70, 74–75, 84–85, 127–28
Leff, Michael, 180–81
Lessl, Thomas, 116
lifeworld, 90–91, 107
Lippmann, Walter, 54–55, 69
Locke, John, 130
logic, 80, 84, 102, 146, 165; and rhetoric, 87–89; metaphysical, 84, 87; naturalistic, 96–99; origins of, 86–87
Lyne, John, 121, 122

Madison, James, 24
manipulation, 23, 139, 166, 180, 188

mass society, 53–56, 63
materialism, 14
McCarthy, Joseph, 29–30
McGee, Michael Calvin, 54, 60, 198
McGuire, J. E., 91, 103
media, 109, 112, 116, 120–21
Michelangelo, 141–42, 161, 74
Mill, John Stewart, 6, 64
mind, 45–46, 48, 97
music, 160–61, 164

natality, 192
naturalism, 30, 147, 154
nature, 26; Greek understanding of, 22–23
nominalism, 54, 104
novel, 134

object, 36–41
Odysseus, 135
opera, 161
Oppenheimer, Robert, 180

paideia, 3
Parmenides, 23
Paul, Saint, 185
Peirce, Charles Sanders, 103
Peloponnesian War, 24
perception, 28, 30, 41, 146–47
perspective by incongruity, 52
persuasion, 166–67, 173, 187
Peters, John, 7, 10, 68, 193
philosophical fallacy, 35–36, 41, 59, 84
philosophy, 77–78
Plato, 24, 44, 73, 78, 80, 87, 131, 144, 156, 176, 177, 182–83, 185, 188
poetics, 141, 143, 149–51, 156, 175
poiesis, 33, 169, 171
political ecology, 127–78
position, 175
possibility, 158–59
Poulakos, John, 11, 20, 25, 77, 81, 132
power, 192
praxis, 165, 169
Presocratics, 89–90

Prometheus, 5, 14
propaganda, 2, 24, 53–56, 63–64, 143, 164
proposition, 102, 105
prosaic, 149–50
Protagoras, 22, 23, 25–26, 36, 90, 93, 96, 104, 126
public, 54, 59–62, 68, 73
public opinion, 62–65, 72
public sphere, 62–65, 200–201
purpose, 141

Ramus, Peter, 82
rationalism, 24, 81
real, 37
realism, 27, 32, 40, 83, 91, 93, 104, 107
reasoning, 115
recalcitrance, 49, 60, 66
recognition, 144, 145
relativism, 23
religion, 80, 161–62, 170, 180
rhetoric, 21, 22, 26, 28, 47, 112, 122, 141, 166, 167; as academic discipline 9–10, 78, 83; as art 4, 67–68; compared to logic, 87–89; as constitutive, 65–68; critical, 208; as "devices," 83, 85, 111, 121; as epistemic, 82; as good/great, 3, 29, 75, 125, 185; habitation of, 33; and play, 13–14; as radical, 1, 11, 14–16, 85, 126, 187, 192; in raw, 140; of science, 83, 93–96, 126; as type of experience, 185
rhetorical forum, 64
rhetorical situation, 14, 22, 26–30, 41–44, 47, 190, 198; defined, 41, 43
rhythm, 154, 206–7
room, 174
Rorty, Richard, 31, 163

science, 80, 93, 99–102, 105; academic versus industrial, 92–93, 101; components of, 108; postacademic, 101, 128; pure versus applied, 91–92
Scott, Robert, 82–83

self, 49; as becoming, 19; as work of art, 57
situation: moral, 42–43, 89; problematic, 41, 52, 112; technical, 42
Shelley, Percy Bysshe, 176
skepticism, 14, 32, 40, 104
society, 69
sophists, 21, 74, 81, 126, 182–83, 188: attitude of, 10; as experimentalist 5–6; as logicians, 84, 85–87; as rhetoricians, 12, 25; on weaker and stronger arguments, 11–12, 85, 191
spacing, 174
Stroud, Scott, 172
subject, 142–43
substance, 142–43, 152
system, 90–91, 107

Taylor, Charles Alan, 107
technocracy, 91–93
thinking, 41, 47, 190

Thrasymachus, 21
time, 37
Tolstoy, Leo, 177
transaction, 33–36, 67, 96, 106
truth, 37, 39, 103–4
Tuchanska, Barbara, 91, 103

valuation, 26
verification, 106, 116–17
volume, 174

warranted assertions, 100, 103–6, 126
Weaver, Richard, 16, 81–83, 131–32, 185–86
Weber, Max, 92
Wichelns, Herbert, 2–4, 16, 21, 137, 138
Will, 17, 49; as free, 22, 44–47

Ziman, John, 80, 84, 92, 101–2, 108, 110, 128

ABOUT THE AUTHOR

NATHAN CRICK is an assistant professor of communication studies at Louisiana State University. His research has appeared in *College Composition and Communication*, *Philosophy and Rhetoric*, and the *Quarterly Journal of Speech*.